"*The Speed of Trust* is red-hot relevant ... and oversight, it is important to focus on ... asset that can help assure the long-term sustainability or any ... rise. Thanks to Stephen M. R. Covey's new book, you can be well on the way to ... ncing your organization's trust assets for years to come."

—**William G. Parrett**, CEO, Deloitte Touche Tohmatsu;
Senior Partner, Deloitte & Touche USA LLP

"Trust strikes at the heart of our success at JetBlue. Trust is key to the speed of our growth. *The Speed of Trust* articulates better than any book that trust is the one thing that changes everything—in business and in life. With high trust, success comes faster, better, and at lower cost."

—**David Neeleman**, founder and CEO, JetBlue Airways

"Trust reduces transaction costs; it reduces the need for litigation and speeds commerce; it actually lubricates organizations and societies. At last, someone is articulating its true value and presenting it as a core business competency."

—**Marilyn Carlson Nelson**, Chairman and CEO,
Carlson Companies

"Stephen M. R. Covey has done it! He has articulately zeroed in on the leadership challenge of the new millennium—the ability to cultivate and leverage trust. This is a 'must-read' for all aspiring leaders."

—**Douglas R. Conant**, President and CEO,
Campbell Soup Company

"*The Speed of Trust* is a great find. It superbly achieves the goal of providing a road map to peak performance, both for individuals and organizations. But the true genius of the book is its universal relevance, as it combines a highly effective common-sense approach with frank guidance to enhance all relationships in life."

—**J. W. Marriott, Jr.**, Chairman and CEO,
Marriott International, Inc.

"Lack of trust within an organization saps its energy, fosters a climate of suspicion and second-guessing, completely devastates teamwork and replaces it with internal politics. The end result is low morale and the consequent low standards of performance. Stephen M. R. Covey's book is a timely reminder for leaders about what really matters in an organization."

—**Koh Boon Hwee**, Chairman, DBS Bank Ltd.;
former Chairman, Singapore Airlines

"I believe Covey's insights around trust are very revealing to all who think about the practice of leadership. Clearly, without self-trust you can't have organizational trust—and without the latter no real achievement."

—**Michael H. Jordan**, Chairman and CEO, EDS

"In life and business, relationships are important—but they are empty unless they are established and based upon trust. Trust is the fundamental building block for a brand, and it is the glue for any lasting relationship. It is amazing how Stephen M. R. Covey, in *The Speed of Trust*, establishes the essence of what trust is and how it can be established and kept. What a service to the business world and society as a whole!"

—**Horst H. Schulze**, President and CEO, The West Paces Hotel Group; former founding President and COO, The Ritz-Carlton Hotel Company

"*The Speed of Trust* teaches a critical lesson—only organizations with a sterling level of trust garner a culture of true commitment vs. a whirlpool of wishful thinking through forced compliance. Covey powerfully articulates a clear road map for ordinary people like you and me to be capable of extraordinary things!"

—**Pete Beaudrault**, President and CEO, Sbarro; former President and CEO, Hard Rock Café International

"*The Speed of Trust* is a must-read not only for business leaders but for every individual. Mr. Covey defines trust in a most accurate fashion. One can benefit immensely from its contents."

—**Jon M. Huntsman**, founder and Chairman, Huntsman International

"This book is an eye-opener—once you've read it you'll see everything through your 'trust glasses' and understand how and why trust is so important in our professional and personal lives. By demonstrating that trust is tangible, measurable, and, most importantly, something that we can build more easily than we think, Stephen M. R. Covey has written a book that deserves to be read not only by business leaders, but also by everyone interested in improving their relationships with colleagues, friends, and family."

—**Gregory K. Ericksen**, Global Vice-Chair, Strategic Growth Markets, Ernst & Young

"In the 80s, Stephen's father convinced me that trust was the most important leadership attribute to create corporate/organizational success. He was absolutely right . . . over the last two decades Toro flourished because of it. Now, Stephen M. R. Covey convincingly shows why . . . that when the organization trusts its leaders, and everyone becomes trustworthy, then people can operate synergistically and non-defensively, which gets the best results much faster."

—**Ken Melrose**, former Chairman and CEO, The Toro Company; author of *Making the Grass Greener on Your Side*

"Trust me, you can believe Stephen. This is very good stuff. The more people who read this in your circle of influence, the better your life will be, starting with yourself."

—**Blake M. Roney**, Chairman, Nu Skin Enterprises

"*The Speed of Trust* clearly identifies trust as the source of speed in our direct relationships. Covey convincingly validates our experience at Dell—that trust has a bottom-line impact on results and that when trust goes up, speed goes up while costs come down. This principle applies not only in our professional relationships with customers, business partners, and team members but also in our personal relationships, which makes this insightful book all the more valuable."

—**Kevin Rollins**, President and CEO, Dell Inc.

"When I received this book and was asked by Stephen M. R. Covey to read it and offer my comments, my first impulse was, 'I don't have the time.' However, as I read the foreword, then the first few chapters, I could not put it down. It is exactly what business leaders need today. This book gets to the core roots of ethical behavior and integrity and how 'trust' is the most critical factor in effective leaders and organizations. The author discusses with clarity and insight how to develop trust through character and competence and how 'trusted' leaders and organizations do things better, faster, and at lower costs. Everyone should make the time to read this book."

—**Nolan D. Archibald**, Chairman and CEO, Black & Decker Corporation

"Like his father, Stephen M. R. Covey is unafraid of exploring difficult, yet critical topics. His book, *The Speed of Trust*, goes right to the heart of one of the most important issues of our time: the absolute lack of trust. In a world turned upside-down, all who run organizations, all who seek deeper relationships, all who want more meaning in their lives would do well to consider trust as the asset they most desire."

—**David W. Checketts**, Chairman, Sports Capital Partners; former CEO, Madison Square Garden

BUSINESS AUTHORITIES

"This is the book I've waited for! The definitive case that trust literally creates profit, success, and prosperity. With hard-nosed evidence and compelling examples, Stephen M. R. Covey shows us why mastering the value of trust is exactly how the United States and others will compete against the megatrend of globalization. Read this book. Become a 'high trust' leader. Your heart, your company, your stakeholders, and your net worth will thank you very much!"

—**Patricia Aburdene**, author of *Megatrends 2010: The Rise of Conscious Capitalism*

"Trust is the foundation of relationships. *The Speed of Trust* will enable you to build your foundation effectively. I highly recommend this book."

—**John C. Maxwell**, author and speaker;
founder, INJOY Stewardship Services and EQUIP

"Covey convincingly makes his case that trust is the one thing that changes everything. He shows that speed is the currency of success and trust is the source. In an era when so many of our leaders have shown themselves to be strangers to the power of trust, this book is a must-read."

—**Marcus Buckingham**, coauthor of
Now, Discover Your Strengths

"Collaboration is the foundation of the standard of living we enjoy today. Trust is the glue. This is the first book that teaches the 'whats' and the 'hows' of trust. A must-read for leaders at all levels."

—**Ram Charan**, coauthor of the bestseller *Execution*;
author of *Profitable Growth Is Everyone's Business*

"Identifying trust as the critical leadership competency of the new global economy, Stephen M. R. Covey describes how this vital quality can be established, grown, extended, and restored within our society and throughout the world. *The Speed of Trust* is a must-read for all of us."

—**Ken Blanchard**, coauthor of *The One Minute Manager*
and *The Secret*

"*The Speed of Trust* is filled with time-honored wisdom delivered at precisely the right moment. Stephen so persuasively builds the case that trust is the sin qua non of business success that we are left scratching our heads and wondering how something so critical has not been given front row, position one seating in our businesses. A must-read for every leader."

—**Jim Loehr**, Coauthor of *The Power of Full Engagement*;
CEO, The Human Performance Institute

"Well, somebody's got to say it. Like father, like son. A truly wonderful book, Mr. Covey. Congratulations!"

—**Michael Gerber**, founder and Chairman,
E-Myth Worldwide

"Stephen M. R. Covey's book on trust is an exceptional piece of work. He defines and allows us to dig deep and understand trust in ways that have never been exposed. Congratulations."

—**Stedman Graham**, author, speaker, and entrepreneur

"Covey's book underscores the single most important factor—the substrate—that will determine the success (or failure) of any organization in the 21st century: TRUST. This is a powerful read: brave, imaginative, amazingly prescient, and backed up by empirical and analytical heft. A must-read for anyone in a position of responsibility, from a support group to a global corporation."

—**Warren Bennis**, Distinguished Professor of Business Administration; author of *On Becoming a Leader*

"This much-needed book provides many practical examples of how greater trust produces better results, at less cost, sooner—at work and in life. It's invaluable."

—**Spencer Johnson, M.D.**, author of *Who Moved My Cheese?*; coauthor of *The One Minute Manager*

"Stephen Covey's work changed the world. I'd bet the price of this exciting book and more that his son, Stephen M. R. Covey, will have at least as much impact. *The Speed of Trust* is an amazing book starting with its novel and powerful title—my greatest wonder was why it hadn't been written before. From the epigraph—'Speed happens when people truly trust each other'—to the closing bell, this is a book worth savoring—and implementing. Dad Stephen says in the foreword that the book 'strikes at the roots.' And I say to that: Amen!"

—**Tom Peters**, author of *Re-imagine!*; coauthor of *In Search of Excellence*

MARKETING AUTHORITIES

"Why are you reading the blurbs in this book? Simple, because you trust (a few of) us. Trust drives everything in our nonbranded, too-fast world. So trust this: This is an important book. The younger Covey has written a book that matters."

—**Seth Godin**, author of *Small Is the New Big* and *Permission Marketing*

"After you turn off the projector, quit PowerPoint, and end your pitch, most deals come down to a simple question: Do you trust each other? This book is a valuable and timely explanation of how to trust and how to be trusted."

—**Guy Kawasaki**, author of *The Art of the Start*; Managing Director, Garage Technology Ventures

"Consumers are growing ambivalent to boundlessly corrupt political institutions while seizing on social issues those bodies are supposed to address. *The Speed of Trust* provides a path to the kind of transparency people will increasingly demand from brands, corporations, and politicians."

—**Faith Popcorn**, marketing futurist; author of *The Popcorn Report*

"Everything in marketing points to the reality that the profitable companies are those that have earned the confidence of their public. Confidence cannot be overestimated. Stephen M. R. Covey takes this reality one step further by proving not only the value of confidence, but also the way to earn it. *The Speed of Trust* is the ultimate how-to book."

—**Jay Conrad Levinson**, the Father of Guerrilla Marketing;
author of the *Guerrilla Marketing* series

"Good leaders know where they are going. Followers trust it's the right direction. Without trust, you get nowhere."

—**Jack Trout**, author of *Trout on Strategy*; coauthor of *Positioning*

MEDIA AUTHORITIES

"In the world of law and politics, the absence of trust has accomplished everything Stephen describes: promoting divisiveness and disillusionment, exacerbating bureaucratic rule-based relationships, and, ultimately, creating beliefs and behaviors that serve to destroy a free and civil society. Invaluable to every American, *The Speed of Trust* delivers the tools that can restore transparency, honesty, and confidence to a nation in need."

—**Catherine Crier**, former judge; bestselling author;
host of Court TV's *Catherine Crier Live*

"*The Speed of Trust* provides compelling evidence and invaluable information as to how the development of trust—based upon genuine, transparent character and competence—can increase speed and profits. Stephen M. R. Covey shows how the hard, measurable components of trust can also create, cement, and enhance all business and professional relationships. *The Speed of Trust* is a breakthrough work, and should be read by everyone."

—**Ken Lindner**, author of *Crunch Time: 8 Steps to
Making the Right Life Decisions at the Right Times*

"Covey brilliantly focuses on that overlooked bedrock of democratic capitalism—trust. Like the air we breathe, we too often take this critical intangible for granted. As Covey makes clear, we do so at our ultimate competitive peril."

—**Steve Forbes**, President and CEO, Forbes

"This book can change lives when it comes to building trusting personal and professional relationships. Covey helps us understand how to nurture and inspire immediate trust in every encounter, which is the foundation for true and lasting success in life. A very interesting and enlightening read."

—**Larry King**

"Want to be an irresistible positive force? Combine personal responsibility with compassion and respect for others. Want to know how to do this perfectly? Read *The Speed of Trust*."

—**Dr. Laura Schlessinger**, internationally syndicated radio host;
author of *The Proper Care and Feeding of Marriage*

GOVERNMENT, EDUCATION, AND HEALTHCARE AUTHORITIES

"*The Speed of Trust* is absolutely the right book for our times—inspiring, empowering, and immediately useful. People in all walks of life, anywhere in the world, will benefit from its important message: Investing in integrity and reaping the trust dividend can strengthen businesses and enrich lives."

—**Rosabeth Moss Kanter**, Harvard Business School;
author of the bestseller *Confidence: How Winning Streaks
and Losing Streaks Begin and End*

"*The Speed of Trust* comes at a time when 'trust' seems to be speeding toward the endangered species list. That will change as people read Stephen M. R. Covey's insights and guidelines, prohibitions and prescriptions for creating authentic trust in relationships, business, sports, politics, and life. The name 'Covey' has come to represent excellence. This book carries on the tradition."

—**John R. Wooden**, Coach Emeritus, UCLA Basketball;
author of *My Personal Best* and *Wooden on Leadership*

"*The Speed of Trust* is a wonderful book. It is readable, practical, and broadly applicable. Anyone who needs to get crucial things done faster, more effectively, and with less friction ought to read it."

—**Clayton M. Christensen**, Robert & Jane Cizik Professor,
Harvard Business School

"Although it sounds like a cliché, *The Speed of Trust* is a must-read for anyone desiring to lead a nation, a company, a family, or even oneself during these turbulent times. As a student and practitioner of Covey principles for years in military hospitals, medical centers, and staff positions, as well as a CEO of a national medical association, I never was able to distill the essence of leadership as clearly as Stephen M. R. Covey has. This book is critical reading for anyone who desires to lead in a world of polarity, cynicism, and disappointment."

—**Charles H. Roadman II, M.D.**, Lt. General, USAF (Ret.);
Surgeon General, USAF (Ret.)

"Stephen M. R. Covey has written a superior book on the importance of trust. Our principals will greatly benefit from reading this book. It will help them as they create trust with the teachers and the teachers in turn with their students. This book is a must-read."

—**Pedro Garcia, Ed.D.**, Director of Schools,
Metropolitan Nashville Public Schools

"Shortly after becoming Dean of the School of Medicine at UTMB Galveston, I took several of my key leaders to hear Stephen speak on *The Speed of Trust*. It resonated with all of us. Stephen and his team have worked with UTMB's leadership group over the last year and given us both the insight and the ongoing tools to eliminate our 'trust tax' and truly become a productive community. The principles and action plans laid out by Stephen are universal. Anyone who is in a leadership team should read *The Speed of Trust*."

—**Valerie M. Parisi, M.D., M.P.H., M.B.A.**,
Dean of Medicine and Chief Academic Officer,
University of Texas Medical Branch

"Stephen M. R. Covey has researched the concept of trust down to its very core and provided solid, compelling data to prove the breadth of the trust gap, but more importantly, to provide solutions to broken trust. I find daily examples of the speed and alacrity that a trusting relationship yields and Stephen's behavioral principles allow our toughest decisions to be made faster and with far less angst. This book has enormous power to change your life and your organization."

—**Dave Gayler, Ph.D.**, Superintendent of Schools,
Charlotte County, Florida

"In the great tradition of words in the Covey name, *The Speed of Trust* has emphasized and clarified an in-depth understanding of the power of trust. Highly successful performers in business and in sports show a level of trust and understanding that separates them from their competition. Covey has validated this significance in our relationships and in our future successes in *The Speed of Trust*."

—**Pete Carroll**, head Football Coach, National Champion USC Trojans

PERSONAL AND PROFESSIONAL
DEVELOPMENT AUTHORITIES

"Those relationships that will stand the test of time are built upon a foundation of enduring trust. Covey gives us the blueprint for learning how to apply this principle with the important people in our lives."

—**John Gray, Ph.D.**, author of *Men Are from Mars, Women Are from Venus*

POCKET
BOOKS

The
SPEED
of Trust

THE ONE THING THAT CHANGES *EVERYTHING*

STEPHEN M. R. COVEY

with

Rebecca R. Merrill

POCKET
BOOKS

London   New York   Toronto   Sydney

First published in Great Britain by Simon & Schuster UK Ltd, 2006
This edition first published by Pocket Books, 2008
An imprint of Simon & Schuster UK Ltd

Originally published in the US in 2006 by FREE PRESS,
A Division of Simon & Schuster Inc.
1230 Avenue of the Americas
New York, NY 10020

Designed by Nancy Singer Olaguera

3

Simon & Schuster UK Ltd
1st Floor
222 Gray's Inn Road
London WC1X 8HB

www.simonandschuster.co.uk

Simon & Schuster Australia
Sydney

A CIP catalogue record for this book is
available from the British Library

ISBN: 978-1-84739-271-8

Printed and bound in India by
Replika Press Pvt. Ltd.

To my wife, Jeri,
for her constant encouragement,
unbelievable kindness,
and abundant trust

ACKNOWLEDGMENTS

I am deeply grateful to so many who have helped make this book possible. I feel humbled and blessed by others' contributions, and my sentiment is aptly expressed by Albert Einstein, who said: "Every day I remind myself that my inner and outer life are based on the labors of other men, living and dead, and that I must exert myself in order to give in the same measure as I have received and am still receiving." So it is with this book. It could not have been written without the help of many people for whom I am deeply thankful.

Special thanks to the talented Rebecca Merrill for her magnificent assistance in every part of this endeavor, particularly her insights into writing. Without her creative help, we'd still be talking about this book rather than reading it.

Thanks also to:

- Greg Link—the "Link" in CoveyLink, and an amazing and visionary friend and business partner—for his tremendous insight, passion, courage, and influence.
- Barry Rellaford, for his invaluable collaboration, coaching, and encouragement from the beginning.
- Gary Judd, for his remarkable ideas, boldness, and willingness to risk.
- Other members of the extended CoveyLink team for their ongoing support, help, and encouragement, including Ryan Cook, Joshua Covey, Shane Cragun, Chuck Farnsworth, Tami Harmon, Robyn Kaelin, David Kasperson, Suzanne Leonard, Kendall Lyman, Todd King, Craig Pace, Candie Perkins, and Holly Whiting. Thanks also to Han Stice, our researcher, for his hard work and diligence, to Davia King, our intern, for her help in the early stages, and to Mary Wentz for her work on transcription.

- My sister Cynthia Haller, for her many contributions, particularly her stories and ideas that have hopefully helped make this book more interesting.
- My sisters Maria Cole and Catherine Sagers, for their ideas, suggestions, and advice on improving the manuscript.
- Pam Walsh and Kevin Cope, for giving me the courage to take on this project.
- My editor, Dominick Anfuso, for his belief in this book from the outset, and the entire Simon & Schuster team for their valuable contributions.
- Our many clients, who provide an ongoing laboratory to apply and validate the Speed of Trust approach, and for the input and feedback so many have given—particularly for the great insights on "Smart Trust" from a highly synergistic group at Sundance, including Beth DiPaolo, Sandy Staton, and Joan Porraz.
- Many others who read and reviewed various stages of the manuscript, including Bob Allen, Paul Brockbank, Kim Capps, Jean Crowther, Tom Crum, Dave Fairbanks, Dottie Gandy, Joseph Grenny, Bob Guindon, Greg Jewkes, Eric Krueger, Annie Link, Carol Maero-Fetzer, Alex Mandossian, Will Marre, Mette Norgaard, Von Orgill, Tally Payne, Rebecca Saltman, Paul Sanders, Steve Shallenberger, Michael Simpson, James Skinner, Carolyn Strauss, Kylie Turley, Tim Welch, Tessa White, and Lisa Williams. Their feedback was instructive, yet always affirming.

With deep gratitude, I acknowledge my parents, Sandra and Stephen R. Covey, for their profound influence on my life and on my thinking. I also acknowledge many, many other thought leaders, some of whom are referenced throughout the book, for their influence on my thinking and on the development of this book over the past 10 years.

Most importantly, I acknowledge and thank God for the blessings, insights, and support I have felt throughout this project. For me, He is the source of all principles that bring joy and success in life.

CONTENTS

THE THIRD, FOURTH, AND FIFTH WAVES—   233
STAKEHOLDER TRUST

*How to increase speed, lower cost, and maximize the
influence of your organization.*

INSPIRING TRUST   285

*How to extend "Smart Trust," restore trust, and take
the exponential leap of faith that makes all the difference . . .
and why not extending trust is the greatest risk of all.*

NOTES AND REFERENCES   325

INDEX   339

FOREWORD

How can a father "brag" on his son and still be credible—particularly regarding a book on trust?

Consider this. Within three years of entrusting Stephen with the role of CEO in my company, Covey Leadership Center, the company's sales nearly doubled and profit went up over 1,200 percent. During that period, the company branched into 40 different countries and increased in shareholder value from $2.4 million to the $160 million it was worth at the time of the merger he orchestrated with Franklin Quest to form FranklinCovey.

How was this accomplished under Stephen's leadership? In a word—trust. Because of his character and his competence, Stephen was trusted. Also, he extended trust to others. The synergistic effect of being trusted and giving trust unleashed a level of performance we had never experienced before, and almost everyone associated with those events looked on the transformation as the supreme, most exhilarating, and inspiring experience of their business careers.

By the way, Stephen was the "green and clean" seven-year-old son I wrote about in my book *The 7 Habits of Highly Effective People*. You'll be interested (as I was) to read "his side of the story" in this book. From my perspective, Stephen's learning how to keep our yard "green and clean" set a pattern of excellence that has continued throughout his life, and it has manifested itself in the way in which he transformed my company, carried out a number of successful leadership, training, and consulting projects, and produced this book—as well as in everything else he has done.

THREE REASONS WHY I LOVE THIS BOOK

There are three reasons why I believe this book will become a classic. First, it works on the roots. Second, it's deep, practical, and comprehensive. Third, it inspires hope. Let me comment on each in turn.

First, this book *strikes at the roots*. Henry David Thoreau taught that "for every thousand people hacking at the leaves of evil, there is one striking at the roots." You can easily see the importance of "striking at the roots" in other dimensions—for instance, when you compare the impact of focusing on preventing disease instead of merely treating it, or on preventing crime instead of merely enforcing the law. In this book, you begin to see it in business where, instead of compliance, the focus is on optimization through developing an ethical character, transparent motivation, and superb competence in producing sustained, superior results.

It's ironic, but from my experience around the world, Sarbanes-Oxley compliance (or its equivalent) has eclipsed the focus on the mistakenly so-called soft stuff, like trust. CFOs and auditors have replaced people developers and strategic-minded HR practitioners in the throne room. At the same time, one of the hottest topics today is ethics— ethics discussions, ethics curriculum, ethics training, codes of ethics. This book shows that while ethics is fundamentally important and necessary, it is absolutely insufficient. It shows that the so-called soft stuff is hard, measurable, and impacts everything else in relationships, organizations, markets, and societies. Financial success comes from success in the marketplace, and success in the marketplace comes from success in the workplace. The heart and soul of all of this is trust.

This work goes far beyond not only my work, but also beyond anything I have read on the subject of trust. It goes beyond ethical behavior in leadership, beyond mere "compliance." It goes deep into the real "intent" and agenda of a person's heart, and then into the kind of "competence" that merits consistent public confidence. Just think about it— whether you define trust as mutual confidence or loyalty or ethical behavior, or whether you deal with its fruits of empowerment and teamwork and synergy, trust is the ultimate root and source of our influence.

As you read this book, it will inspire you to think like a "social ecologist" so that you see the relationships of all things and how ultimately all things are rooted in trust. It gives an enlarged perspective and a sequential process to transform a culture of low trust into one of high trust.

Second, this book presents a model of trust that is *deep, practical, and comprehensive*. It takes you through an inside-out approach to the 5 Waves of Trust. Like a pebble thrown into a pond, it moves from self to relationships with others to relationships with all stakeholders, including society. Through powerful and practical illustrations, it shows how the principles apply universally, whether it's personally or in a one-on-one relationship, a family, a business, a school, a hospital, a government department, a military unit, or a "not-for-profit."

Third, this book breathes *hope*. As you move sequentially through the chapters, you begin to feel optimistic and inspired that no matter what the situation or how low the trust, you can become an active agent in establishing or restoring trust and in rebuilding relationships, and it doesn't have to take "forever." As Stephen shares his own and others' stories of turning around sour, toxic, costly, sluggish situations, you feel affirmed and empowered. You believe you can do it, and you want to do it, and do it in a way that is sustainable.

THE KEY FACTOR IN A GLOBAL ECONOMY

As we move rapidly into an even more transparent interdependent global reality, trust is more career critical than it has ever been. My interactions with business leaders around the world have made it increasingly evident that "speed to market" is now the ultimate competitive weapon.

Low trust causes friction, whether it is caused by unethical behavior or by ethical but incompetent behavior (because even good intentions can never take the place of bad judgment). Low trust is the greatest cost in life and in organizations, including families. Low trust creates hidden agendas, politics, interpersonal conflict, interdepartmental rivalries, win-lose thinking, defensive and protective communication—all of which reduce the speed of trust. Low trust slows everything—every decision, every communication, and every relationship.

On the other hand, trust produces speed. And, as Stephen points out, the greatest trust-building key is "results." Results build brand loyalty. Results inspire and fire up a winning culture. The consistent production of results not only causes customers to increase their reorders, it also compels them to consistently recommend you to others. Thus, your customers become your key promoters, your key sales and marketing people. In addition, results win the confidence of practical-minded executives and workforces. Consistent results also put suppliers under the main tent as strategic partners, which is so vital in this new world-class, knowledge-worker-based, global economy.

Trust is like the aquifer—the huge water pool under the earth that feeds all of the subsurface wells. In business and in life, these wells are often called innovation, complementary teams, collaboration, empowerment,

Six Sigma, and other expressions of Total Quality Management, brand loyalty, or other strategic initiatives. These wells themselves feed the rivers and streams of human interaction, business commerce, and deal making. They give sustaining quality of life to all relationships, including family relationships, interdepartmental relationships, day-to-day supplier and customer relationships—in fact, any effort to make a sustainable contribution.

A FINAL WORD

This book is a readable, assessable, pragmatic treatment of an extremely timely topic in this new "flat world" we now live in. It comes not just out of anecdotal and personal experiences, but is based on empirical research that demonstrates how the speed of trust can be put into the calculus of all of the important metrics inside organizations and relationships. Measurement is what makes this material so hard-edged and practical and so credible.

Seeing Stephen drill down so much deeper and go beyond my own thinking and adding significant new learning and insight has made me very proud and gratefully humbled at the same time. On the single most important need and subject in life—trust—I believe that Stephen has climbed a new summit, both as a model/practitioner and as a serious and competent thought leader.

I hope you enjoy and benefit from the read. I know I did.

Stephen R. Covey

THE ONE THING THAT CHANGES EVERYTHING

There is one thing that is common to every individual, relationship, team, family, organization, nation, economy, and civilization throughout the world—one thing which, if removed, will destroy the most powerful government, the most successful business, the most thriving economy, the most influential leadership, the greatest friendship, the strongest character, the deepest love.

On the other hand, if developed and leveraged, that one thing has the potential to create unparalleled success and prosperity in every dimension of life. Yet, it is the least understood, most neglected, and most underestimated possibility of our time.

That one thing is trust.

Trust impacts us 24/7, 365 days a year. It undergirds and affects the quality of every relationship, every communication, every work project, every business venture, every effort in which we are engaged. It changes the quality of every present moment and alters the trajectory and outcome of every future moment of our lives—both personally and professionally.

Contrary to what most people believe, trust is not some soft, illusive quality that you either have or you don't; rather, trust is a pragmatic, tangible, actionable asset that you can create—much faster than you probably think possible.

While corporate scandals, terrorist threats, office politics, and broken relationships have created low trust on almost every front, I contend that the ability to establish, grow, extend, and restore trust is not only vital to our personal and interpersonal well-being; it is *the* key leadership competency of the new global economy.

I am also convinced that in every situation, nothing is as fast as the speed of trust. And, contrary to popular belief, trust is something you *can* do something about. In fact, you can get good at creating it!

NOTHING IS AS FAST AS THE SPEED OF TRUST

Speed happens when people . . . truly trust each other.
—EDWARD MARSHALL

If you're not fast, you're dead.
—JACK WELCH

I'll never forget an experience I had several years ago when I worked for a short stint with a major investment banking firm in New York City. We had just come out of a very exhausting meeting, during which it had become evident that there were serious internal trust issues. These issues were slowing things down and negatively affecting execution. The senior leader said to me privately, "These meetings are dysfunctional and a waste of time. I just don't trust 'Mike.' I don't trust 'Ellen.' In fact, I find it hard to trust anyone in this group."

I said, "Well, why don't you work on increasing trust?"

He turned to me and replied seriously, "Look, Stephen, you need to understand something. Either you have trust or you don't. We don't have it, and there's nothing we can do about it."

I strongly disagree. In fact, both my personal life and my work as a business practitioner over the past 20 years have convinced me that there is a *lot* we can do about it. We *can* increase trust—much faster than we might think—and doing so will have a huge impact, both in the quality of our lives and in the results we're able to achieve.

> *You can have all the facts and figures, all the supporting evidence, all the endorsement that you want, but if you don't command trust, you won't get anywhere.*
>
> —NAILL FITZGERALD, FORMER CHAIRMAN, UNILEVER

TRUST ISSUES AFFECT EVERYONE

As I speak to audiences around the world about the Speed of Trust, I repeatedly hear expressions of frustration and discouragement such as these:

I can't stand the politics at work. I feel sabotaged by my peers. It seems like everyone is out for himself and will do anything to get ahead.

I've really been burned in the past. How can I ever trust anyone enough to have a real relationship?

I work in an organization that's bogged down with bureaucracy. It takes forever to get anything done. I have to get authorization to buy a pencil!

The older my children get, the less they listen to me. What can I do?

I feel like my contributions at work are hardly ever recognized or valued.

I foolishly violated the trust of someone who was supremely important to me. If I could hit "rewind" and make the decision differently, I would do it in a heartbeat. But I can't. Will I ever be able to rebuild the relationship?

I have to walk on eggshells at work. If I say what I really think, I'll get fired . . . or at least made irrelevant.

My boss micromanages me and everyone else at work. He treats us all like we can't be trusted.

With all the scandals, corruption, and ethical violations in our society today, I feel like someone has pulled the rug out from under me. I don't know what—or who—to trust anymore.

So what do you do if you're in a situation like one of these—or in any situation where a lack of trust creates politics and bureaucracy, or simply slows things down? Do you merely accept this as the cost of doing business? Or can you do something to counteract or even reverse it?

I affirm that you *can* do something about it. In fact, by learning how to establish, grow, extend, and restore trust, you can positively and significantly alter the trajectory of this and every future moment of your life.

> *Technique and technology are important, but adding trust is the issue of the decade.*
>
> —TOM PETERS, BUSINESS AUTHOR

GETTING A HANDLE ON TRUST

So what is trust? Rather than giving a complex definition, I prefer to use the words of Jack Welch, former CEO of General Electric. He said, "[Y]ou know it when you feel it."

Simply put, trust means *confidence*. The opposite of trust—distrust—is *suspicion*. When you trust people, you have confidence in them—in their integrity and in their abilities. When you distrust people, you are suspicious of them—of their integrity, their agenda, their capabilities, or their track record. It's that simple. We have all had experiences that validate the difference between relationships that are built on trust and those that are not. These experiences clearly tell us the difference is not small; it is dramatic.

Take a minute right now and think of a person with whom you have a high trust relationship—perhaps a boss, coworker, customer, spouse, parent, sibling, child, or friend. Describe this relationship. What's it like? How does it feel? How well do you communicate? How quickly can you get things done? How much do you enjoy this relationship?

Now think of a person with whom you have a low-trust relationship. Again, this person could be anyone at work or at home. Describe this relationship. What's it like? How does it feel? How is the communication? Does it flow quickly and freely . . . or do you feel like you're constantly walking on land mines and being misunderstood? Do you work together to get things done quickly . . . or does it take a disproportionate amount of time and energy to finally reach agreement and execution? Do you enjoy this relationship . . . or do you find it tedious, cumbersome, and draining?

The difference between a high- and low-trust relationship is palpable!

Take communication. In a high-trust relationship, you can say the wrong thing, and people will still get your meaning. In a low-trust relationship, you can be very measured, even precise, and they'll still misinterpret you.

Can you even begin to imagine the difference it would make if you were able to increase the amount of trust in the important personal and professional relationships in your life?

> You can't have success without trust. The word trust embodies almost everything you can strive for that will help you to succeed. You tell me any human relationship that works without trust, whether it is a marriage or a friendship or a social interaction; in the long run, the same thing is true about business, especially businesses that deal with the public.
>
> —JIM BURKE, FORMER CHAIRMAN AND CEO,
> JOHNSON & JOHNSON

THE CRUCIBLE

One of the most formative experiences I've had personally in increasing trust occurred several years ago as a result of the merger between Franklin Quest and Covey Leadership Center to form FranklinCovey Company. As anyone who has ever been through a merger or an acquisition will know, these things are never easy. The merged company had terrific strengths. We had great people, superb content, loyal clients, and productive tools. But the blending of the two cultures was proving to be enormously challenging.

As president of the Training and Education business unit, I had traveled to Washington, D.C., to address about a third of our consultants on the topic of our division's strategy. But a meeting that should have had me looking forward with anticipation literally had my stomach churning.

Several weeks before, the company's new CEO—frustrated (as we all were) with the enormous problems and friction that had beset what had seemed to be a promising merger—had scheduled a meeting of all the consultants in the company. In an effort to "get out" everyone's concerns, he had created a format in which we, as leaders, were to listen, but could not respond, to anything anyone wanted to say. The meeting, scheduled to last four hours, turned into a 10-hour "dump" session. With no one allowed to amend, correct, give context, supply missing information, discuss the other side of the issues, or even show the dilemmas involved, only a small percentage of what was said had real contextual accuracy. Most was misinterpreted, manipulated, or twisted, and some of it was flat-out wrong. There were assumptions, suspicions, accusations, frustrations. And, as leaders, we had reluctantly agreed to a format in which we weren't permitted to say a word.

In the end, we'd had over a dozen such meetings. The whole experience had been brutal, and, with my position of leadership, I had taken it all personally. Having had some experience on Wall Street, I knew mergers were usually hard, but I had thought we could do what needed to be done to make this one work.

The problem was that I had assumed far too much. Mistakenly, I had failed to focus on establishing trust with the newly merged company, believing that my reputation and credibility would already be known. But they weren't, and, as a result, half the people trusted me and the other half didn't. And it was pretty much divided right down Covey or Franklin "party" lines. Those from the Covey side who knew me and had worked with me basically saw my decisions as a sincere effort to use objective, external criteria in every decision and to do what was best for the business—not to try to push a "Covey" agenda . . . in fact, sometimes even bending over backward to avoid it. Those who didn't know me, hadn't worked with me, and didn't trust me interpreted every decision in the exact opposite manner.

In one case, for example, a question had come up concerning the use of the Sundance Resort for one of our leadership development programs. Sundance had been somewhat hard to work with, and some felt we should move the program to another venue. The program director strongly wanted to keep it at Sundance because clients loved the location, and the financial data showed that we were averaging nearly 40 percent more revenue per program held there compared to other venues. I said, "Because the economics are better and the program director strongly recommends that we keep it there, we'll find better ways to work with Sundance." That was an example of a solid business decision I assumed people would understand.

But those who didn't trust me didn't understand. They thought I was trying to push a "Covey" approach. Some even wondered if I was getting some kind of kickback because, as a community leader, I had been asked to serve in an unpaid role on the advisory board for the Sundance Children's Theater. Many suspected my motive. Because there was such low trust, the feeling was, "There's got to be some kind of hidden agenda going on here."

> *The moment there is suspicion about a person's motives,*
> *everything he does becomes tainted.*
>
> —MAHATMA GANDHI

In another situation, I had made the decision to move "Ron," an extremely talented leader who had come from the Covey side into a different position because, like many of us, he had gotten caught in merger politics and had polarized the two camps. I had decided to go outside the organization for Ron's replacement so that there would be no perception that the new manager was a "Covey" person or a "Franklin" person.

When I made this announcement, I thought people would be excited by my attempt to bring in new talent. But among those who didn't trust me, no one even heard the part about bringing in someone from the outside to replace Ron as manager; all they heard was that he was still in the company, and they wanted him gone.

Time after time, my actions had been misinterpreted and my motives questioned, even though I had involved both Covey and Franklin camps in making decisions. As you might imagine, some who had no idea of my track record and results had assumed that the only reason I was in my position of leadership was simply that I was Stephen R. Covey's son and that I had no credibility on my own.

As a result of all this, I'd had to make decisions much more slowly. I tried to project how every decision would be interpreted by each of the cultures. I began to worry about baggage and risk. I started playing a political game that I'd never played before—one that I never *had* to play before, because it had never been part of who I was.

As I thought about everything that had transpired, I came to the realization that if I didn't take the tough issues head-on, the current situation would simply perpetuate itself—probably even get worse. My every decision would be second-guessed and politicized. Getting anything done would be like trying to move through molasses. We were facing increasing bureaucracy, politics, and disengagement. This was wasting enormous amounts of time, energy, and money. The cost was significant.

Besides, I thought, given how badly things were going, what did I have to lose?

So when I walked into the consultant meeting that day in Washington, D.C., I basically said, "Look, we're at this meeting to talk about strategy. And if that's what you want to talk about, that's what we'll talk about. But if you would rather talk about the merger issues that are really on your minds, we'll talk about those. We'll talk about any of the tough questions you have: Who's staying and who's going? Who's making what decisions? What criteria are being used? Why aren't we more informed? What if we don't trust those making the decisions? What if we don't trust you, Stephen, to make some of these decisions?"

At first, people were stunned that I would bring up these difficult issues, including their perception of me. Many were also wondering what my real agenda was. But they soon realized that I wasn't hiding anything. I was being transparent and candid. They could tell I genuinely wanted to open things up. As the meeting progressed, they could see that I wasn't operating from any hidden agenda; I was sincerely trying to do what was right for the business.

As it turned out, the scheduled one-hour strategy meeting turned into a full day's discussion of their concerns: Whose buildings were we going to use? Which compensation plan would we adapt? Whose sales model would we use? Are you, Stephen, really competent to make these decisions? What is your track record? What are your criteria?

I openly acknowledged that these were challenging issues. I candidly shared the thinking and rationale behind the decisions and the process by which they were made, or were being made. I shared all the data I could share, and if I couldn't share it, I explained why. I listened and sought to understand their concerns. Based on their recommendations, I made several commitments around improvements.

At the end of the day, there was a renewed feeling of hope and excitement. One participant told me that I had established more trust in one day than I had in the prior several months. More than anything else, I realized, it was a starting place, an acknowledgment of the value of our transparent communication. I also realized that the real test, however, would be on how I followed through. At least now, people could see my behavior through new eyes, not tainted by the lens of low trust.

Word from this meeting spread, and within the next few months, I was able to meet with the other consultants and go through the same process with the same results. I followed a similar course with other groups and divisions. In a very short period of time, we were able to establish trust with our entire business unit. As far as my unit was concerned, this increased trust dramatically changed everything. We were able to increase speed, lower cost, and improve results in all areas.

Though I eventually left FranklinCovey to start my own company and write this book, I am happy to report that they have weathered the storms created by the merger and are now doing very well. On a personal basis, the whole experience helped me to understand trust far more clearly than in premerger times when trust was high and things were good.

First, I learned that I had assumed way too much. I assumed I had trust with people, when in fact I didn't. I assumed that people were aware of my track record and Covey Leadership Center's track record, which they were not. I assumed that because I was teeing up the tough issues in my private meetings and making decisions based on objective business criteria, this was being reported down line, but it was not.

I also learned that I had been politically naïve. Yes, I made mistakes. But I didn't make the mistakes I was being accused of making. The most significant mistake I made was in not being more proactive in establishing and increasing trust. As a result, I experienced firsthand both the social and the hard, bottom-line economic consequences of low trust.

In addition, I learned that trust truly does change everything. Once you create trust—genuine character- and competence-based trust—almost everything else falls into place.

A CRISIS OF TRUST

You don't need to look far to realize that, as a global society, we have a crisis of trust on our hands. Consider recent newspaper headlines:

- "Employees' New Motto: Trust No One"
- "Companies Urged to Rebuild Trust"
- "Both Sides Betray the Other's Trust"
- "20 NYSE Traders Indicted"
- "Ethics Must Be Strengthened to Rebuild People's Trust"
- "Relationships Fall Apart as Trust Dwindles"
- "Now Who Do You Trust?"

News headlines reveal the symptoms of the compelling truth: Low trust is everywhere. It permeates our global society, our marketplace, our organizations, our relationships, our personal lives. It breeds suspicion and cynicism, which become self-perpetuating, resulting in a costly, downward cycle.

Consider our society at large. Trust in almost every societal institution (government, media, business, health care, churches, political parties, etc.) is significantly lower than a generation ago, and in many cases, sits at historic lows. In the United States, for example, a 2005 Harris poll revealed that only 22% of those surveyed tend to trust the media, only 8% trust political parties, only 27% trust the government, and only 12% trust big companies.

Perhaps even more telling is the loss of trust with regard to people trusting other people. A recent survey conducted by British sociologist David Halpern reveals that only 34% of Americans believe that other people can be trusted. In Latin America, the number is only 23%, and in Africa, the figure is 18%. Halpern's research also shows that four decades ago in Great Britain, 60% of the population believed other people could be trusted; today, it's down to 29%.

The "good" news of this study—relatively speaking—is that 68% of Scandinavians (Denmark, Sweden, and Norway) and 60% of the people in the Netherlands believe others can be trusted, indicating that there are some higher-trust societies. And Mexico's figure—though a low 31%—is up from 1983's 19%, which indicates that it is possible to increase societal trust.

> *Whether you're on a sports team, in an office or a member of a family, if you can't trust one another there's going to be trouble.*
>
> —JOE PATERNO, HEAD FOOTBALL COACH, PENN STATE UNIVERSITY

On the organizational level, trust within companies has also sharply declined. Just look at what the research shows:

- Only 51% of employees have trust and confidence in senior management.
- Only 36% of employees believe their leaders act with honesty and integrity.
- Over the past 12 months, 76% of employees have observed illegal or unethical conduct on the job—conduct which, if exposed, would seriously violate the public trust.

What about trust at the personal relationship level? While this naturally varies with regard to particular relationships, trust is a major issue for most people in at least some relationships (and too often with their most significant relationships, such as with a boss or coworker or a spouse or child at home).

Consider the following:

• The number one reason people leave their jobs is a bad relationship with their boss.
• One out of every two marriages ends in divorce.

Relationships of all kinds are built on and sustained by trust. They can also be broken and destroyed by lack of trust. Try to imagine any meaningful relationship without trust. In fact, low trust is the very definition of a bad relationship.

What about trust at the individual level? Consider the percentage of students who acknowledged that they cheated in order to improve their odds of getting into graduate school.

• Liberal arts students—43%
• Education students—52%
• Medical students—63%
• Law students—63%
• Business students—75%

How does it make you feel to know that there's more than a 50% chance that the doctor who's going to perform surgery on you cheated in school? Or a 75% chance that the company you're going to work for is being led by someone who didn't consider honesty important?

Recently, when I presented this data to a group of attorneys, they were thrilled to find out that they were not in last place! And they chided me because—with my MBA—I was! (It didn't help when I further pointed out that 76% of MBAs were willing to understate expenses that cut into their profits, and that convicts in minimum-security prisons scored as high as MBA students on their ethical dilemma exams.)

Talk about a crisis of trust!

Society, organizations, and relationships aside, there's an even more fundamental and powerful dimension to self trust. Often, we make commitments to ourselves—such as setting goals or making New Year's resolutions—that we fail to fulfill. As a result, we come to feel that we can't even fully trust ourselves. If we can't trust ourselves, we'll have a hard time trusting others. This personal incongruence is often the source of our suspicions of others. As my father has often said, we judge ourselves by our intentions and others by their behavior. This is why, as we'll discuss later, one of the fastest ways to restore trust is to make and keep commitments—even very small commitments—to ourselves and to others.

Truly, we are in a crisis of trust. It affects us on all levels—societal, institutional, organizational, relational, and personal—and it has a perpetuating effect. While many of us may be fairly resilient, with each new violation of trust or corporate scandal, we tend to recover a little more slowly. We wonder what else is out there. We become increasingly suspicious of other people. We begin to project the behavior of the few upon the many, and we are paying for it dearly.

> *Every time one of these high-level and deep-seated incidents [scandals] is uncovered, the American public trusts a little bit less. We just don't bounce back as fast.*
>
> —ROBERT ECKERT, CEO, MATTEL

THE ECONOMICS OF TRUST

A cynic might ask, "So what? Is trust really more than a nice-to-have social virtue, a so-called hygiene factor? Can you measurably illustrate that trust is a hard-edged economic driver?" I intend to answer these questions emphatically in this book by clearly demonstrating the strong business case for trust.

Here's a simple formula that will enable you to take trust from an intangible and unquantifiable variable to an indispensable factor that is both tangible and quantifiable. The formula is based on this critical insight: Trust always affects two outcomes—speed and cost. When trust goes down, speed will also go down and costs will go up.

$$\downarrow \text{Trust} = \downarrow \text{Speed} \uparrow \text{Cost}$$

When trust goes up, speed will also go up and costs will go down.

$$\uparrow \text{Trust} = \uparrow \text{Speed} \downarrow \text{Cost}$$

It's that simple, that real, that predictable. Let me share a couple of examples.

Immediately following the 9/11 terrorist attacks, our trust in flying in the U.S. went down dramatically. We recognized that there were terrorists bent on harming us, and that our system of ensuring passenger safety was not as strong as it needed to be.

Prior to 9/11, I used to arrive at my home airport approximately half an hour before takeoff, and I was quickly able to go through security. But after 9/11, more robust procedures and systems were put in place to increase safety and trust in flying. While these procedures have had their desired effect, now it takes me longer and costs me more to travel. I generally arrive an hour and a half before a domestic flight and two to three hours before an international flight to make sure I have enough time to clear security. I also pay a new 9/11 security tax with every ticket I buy. So, as trust went down, speed also went down and cost went up.

Recently, I flew out of a major city in a high-risk area in the Middle East. For geopolitical reasons, the trust in that region was extremely low. I had to arrive at the airport four hours before my flight. I went through several screenings, and my bag was unpacked and searched multiple times by multiple people. And every other passenger was treated the same.

Clearly, extra security measures were necessary, and in this instance I was grateful for them, but the point remains the same: Because trust was low, speed went down and cost went up.

> *Our distrust is very expensive.*
>
> —RALPH WALDO EMERSON

Consider another example. The Sarbanes-Oxley Act was passed in the U.S. in response to the Enron, WorldCom, and other corporate scandals. While it appears that Sarbanes-Oxley may be having a positive effect in improving or at least sustaining trust in the public markets, it is also clear that this has come at a substantial price. Ask any CEO, CFO, or financial person in a company subject to Sarbanes-Oxley rules about the amount of time it takes to follow its regulations, as well as the added cost of doing so. It's enormous on both fronts. In fact, a recent study pegged the costs of implementing one section alone at $35 billion—exceeding the original SEC estimate by 28 times! Compliance regulations have become a prosthesis for the lack of trust—and a slow-moving and costly prosthesis at that. Again, we come back to the key learning: When trust is low, speed goes down and cost goes up.

> *When you break the big laws, you do not get liberty; you
> do not even get anarchy. You get the small laws.*
>
> —G. K. Chesterton, British author

On the other hand, when trust is high, speed goes up and cost goes down. Consider the example of Warren Buffett—CEO of Berkshire Hathaway (and generally considered one of the most trusted leaders in the world)—who recently completed a major acquisition of McLane Distribution (a $23 billion company) from Wal-Mart. As public companies, both Berkshire Hathaway and Wal-Mart are subject to all kinds of market and regulatory scrutiny. Typically, a merger of this size would take several months to complete and cost several million dollars to pay for accountants, auditors, and attorneys to verify and validate all kinds of information. But in this instance, because both parties operated with high trust, the deal was made with one two-hour meeting and a handshake. In less than a month, it was completed.

In a management letter that accompanied his 2004 annual report, Warren Buffett wrote: "We did no 'due diligence.' We knew everything would be exactly as Wal-Mart said it would be—and it was." Imagine—less than one month (instead of six months or longer), and no "due diligence" costs (instead of the millions typically spent)! High trust, high speed, low cost.

> *The world is changing very fast. Big will not beat small
> anymore. It will be the fast beating the slow.*
>
> —Rupert Murdoch, Chairman and CEO,
> News Corporation

Consider the example of another legendary leader, Herb Kelleher, chairman and former CEO of Southwest Airlines. In Robert K. Cooper and Ayman Sawaf's book, *Executive EQ*, the authors share a remarkable story. Walking down the hall one day, Gary Barron—then executive vice president of the $700 million maintenance organization for all Southwest—presented a three-page summary memo to Kelleher outlining a proposal for a massive reorganization. On the spot, Kelleher read the memo. He asked one question, to which Baron responded that he shared the concern and was dealing with it. Kelleher then replied, "Then it's fine by me. Go ahead." The whole interaction took about four minutes.

Not only was Kelleher a trusted leader, he also extended trust to others. He trusted Barron's character and his competence. And because he trusted that Barron knew what he was doing, the company could move with incredible speed.

Here's another example on a much smaller scale. "Jim," a vendor in New York City, set up shop and sold donuts and coffee to passersby as they went in and out of their office buildings. During the breakfast and lunch hours, Jim always had long lines of customers waiting. He noticed that the wait time discouraged many customers who left and went elsewhere. He also noticed that, as he was a one-man show, the biggest bottleneck preventing him from selling more donuts and coffee was the disproportionate amount of time it took to make change for his customers.

Finally, Jim simply put a small basket on the side of his stand filled with dollar bills and coins, trusting his customers to make their own change. Now you might think that customers would accidentally count wrong or intentionally take extra quarters from the basket, but what Jim found was the opposite: Most customers responded by being completely honest, often leaving him larger-than-normal tips. Also, he was able to move customers through at twice the pace because he didn't have to make change. In addition, he found that his customers liked being trusted and kept coming back. By extending trust in this way, Jim was able to double his revenues without adding any new cost.

Again, when trust is low, speed goes down and cost goes up. When trust is high, speed goes up and cost goes down.

> *Transcendent values like trust and integrity literally translate into revenue, profits and prosperity.*
>
> —PATRICIA ABURDENE, AUTHOR OF *MEGATRENDS 2010*

Recently, as I was teaching this concept, a CFO—who deals with numbers all the time—came up to me and said, "This is fascinating! I've always seen trust as a nice thing to have, but I never, ever, thought of it in terms of its impact on economics and speed. Now that you've pointed it out, I can see it everywhere I turn.

"For example, we have one supplier in whom we have complete trust. Everything happens fast with this group, and the relationship hardly costs us anything to maintain. But with another supplier, we have very little trust. It takes forever to get anything done, and it costs us a lot of time and effort to support the relationship. And that's costing us money—too much money!"

This CFO was amazed when everything suddenly fell into place in his mind. Even though he was a "numbers" guy, he had not connected the dots with regard to trust. Once he saw it, everything suddenly made sense. He could immediately see how trust was affecting everything in the organization, and how robust and powerful the idea of the relationship between trust, speed, and cost was for analyzing what was happening in his business and for taking steps to significantly increase profitable growth.

I know of leading organizations who ask their employees directly the following simple question in formal, 360-degree feedback processes: *"Do you trust your boss?"* These companies have learned that the answer to this one question is more predictive of team and organizational performance than any other question they might ask.

Once you really understand the hard, measurable economics of trust, it's like putting on a new pair of glasses. Everywhere you look, you can see the impact—at work, at home, in every relationship, in every effort. You can begin to see the incredible difference high-trust relationships can make in every dimension of life.

THE TRUST TAX

The serious practical impact of the economics of trust is that in many relationships, in many interactions, we are paying a hidden low-trust tax right off the top—and we don't even know it!

Three summers ago, when my son Stephen turned 16, he got his first job. He was very excited. He was going to be a manager of a shop that sold snow cones.

His first couple of weeks went really well, and he was thrilled when he received his first paycheck. He tore open the envelope and looked expectantly at the check. Suddenly, a frown covered his face. "Dad," he exclaimed, "this is not right!" He thrust the paper at me. "Look," he said. "They've done the math all wrong."

"What do you mean?" I asked as my eyes went over the paper.

"Look right here," he said, pointing. "I'm supposed to be making eight dollars an hour. I worked for 40 hours. That should come to $320. Right?"

I looked at the paper, and, sure enough, he'd worked for 40 hours and the check was only for about $260.

I said, "That's right, Stephen. But look a little higher—there on the paycheck stub. See these words—'federal income tax'?"

"What?" he responded incredulously. "You mean I'm paying *taxes*?"

"Yes, you are," I replied. "And there's more. See, here's 'state income tax,' 'Social Security tax,' 'Medicare tax' . . ."

"But, Dad," he practically wailed, "I don't even need Medicare!"

"No, son, you don't," I replied, "but your grandfather does! Welcome to the real world."

Probably no one really likes to pay taxes. But we do so because they serve a greater societal cause (and also because it's the law). But what if you didn't even know you were paying taxes? What if they were hidden—being taken right off the top without your even being aware? And what if they were completely wasted taxes—if they were going right down the drain and doing absolutely no good to anyone anywhere?

Unfortunately, low-trust taxes don't conveniently show up on your income statement as a "cost of low trust." But just because they're hidden doesn't mean they're not there. Once you know where and what to look for, you can see these taxes show up everywhere—in organizations and in relationships. They're quantifiable. And they're often extremely high.

> *Mistrust doubles the cost of doing business.*
>
> —PROFESSOR JOHN WHITNEY,
> COLUMBIA BUSINESS SCHOOL

You've undoubtedly seen this tax in action many times—perhaps in a conversation where you can tell that your boss, your teenager, or someone else is automatically discounting everything you say by 20 percent, 30 percent, or even more. This is what I was experiencing firsthand in the difficult days of the FranklinCovey merger. If you think about it, you've probably been the one taxing some of those interactions yourself, discounting what you're hearing from others because you don't trust them.

In some situations, you may even have had to pay an "inheritance tax" when you've stepped into a role that was occupied by someone who created distrust before you. When you move into a new personal or work relationship, or if you step in as the new leader in a low-trust culture, it's possible that you're being taxed 30, 40, 50 percent, or more for something you didn't even do! I recently consulted with one executive who lamented that the manager she replaced had destroyed trust with the organization so dramatically that the culture was taxing her for all of his behavior, even though she was new to the organization.

As bestselling author Francis Fukuyama has said: "Widespread distrust in a society . . . imposes a kind of tax on all forms of economic activity, a tax that high-trust societies do not have to pay." I contend that this low-trust tax is not only on economic activity, but on all activity—in every relationship, in every interaction, in every communication, in every decision, in every dimension of life.

THE TRUST DIVIDEND

I also suggest that, just as the tax created by low trust is real, measurable, and extremely high, so the *dividends* of high trust are also real, quantifiable, and incredibly high. Consider the speed with which Warren Buffett completed the McLane acquisition and how quickly Gary Barron's massive reorganization proposal was approved. Consider the doubling of revenues for Jim the donut and coffee vendor. Consider the speed with which you can communicate in your own relationships of high trust—both personal and professional.

When trust is high, the dividend you receive is like a performance multiplier, elevating and improving every dimension of your organization and your life. High trust is like the leaven in bread, which lifts everything around it. In a company, high trust materially improves communication, collaboration, execution, innovation, strategy, engagement, partnering, and relationships with all stakeholders. In your personal life, high trust significantly improves your excitement, energy, passion, creativity, and joy in your relationships with family, friends, and community. Obviously, the dividends are not just in increased speed and improved economics; they are also in greater enjoyment and better quality of life.

THE HIDDEN VARIABLE

One time I hired a guide to take me fly fishing in Montana. As I looked out over the river, he said, "Tell me what you see." Basically I told him I saw a beautiful river with the sun reflecting off the surface of the water. He asked, "Do you see any fish?" I replied that I did not. Then my guide handed me a pair of polarized sunglasses. "Put these on," he said. Suddenly everything looked dramatically different. As I looked at the river, I discovered I could see *through* the water. And I could see fish—a lot of fish! My excitement shot up. Suddenly I could sense enormous possibility that I hadn't seen before. In reality, those fish were there all along, but until I put on the glasses, they were hidden from my view.

In the same way, for most people, trust is hidden from view. They have no idea how present and pervasive the impact of trust is in every relationship, in every organization, in every interaction, in every moment of life. But once they put on "trust glasses" and see what's going on under the surface, it immediately impacts their ability to increase their effectiveness in every dimension of life.

Whether it's high or low, trust is the "hidden variable" in the formula for organizational success. The traditional business formula says that strategy times execution equals results:

$$S \times E = R$$

(Strategy times Execution equals Results)

But there is a hidden variable to this formula: trust—either the low-trust tax, which discounts the output, or the high-trust dividend which multiplies it:

$$(S \times E)T = R$$

([Strategy times Execution] multiplied by Trust equals Results)

You could have good strategy and good execution (10 on a 1 to 10 scale), but still get derailed by low trust. Or high trust could serve as a performance multiplier, creating synergy where the whole is more than the sum of its parts. Just look at the math:

Strategy	x	Execution	=	Result	Tax or dividend	=	Net Result
10	x	10	=	100	Less 40% tax	=	60
10	x	10	=	100	Less 10% tax	=	90
10	x	10	=	100	Plus 20% dividend	=	120

A company can have an excellent strategy and a strong ability to execute, but the net result can be either torpedoed by a low-trust tax or multiplied by a high-trust dividend. As one eminent consultant on this topic, Robert Shaw, has said, "Above all, success in business requires two things: a winning competitive strategy, and superb organizational execution. Distrust is the enemy of both." I submit that while high trust won't necessarily rescue a poor strategy, low trust will almost always derail a good one.

Perhaps more than anything else, the impact of this "hidden variable" makes a powerful business case for trust. According to a study by Warwick Business School in the UK, outsourcing contracts that are managed based on trust rather than on stringent agreements and penalties are more likely to lead to trust dividends for both parties—as much as 40 percent of the total value of a contract. A 2002 study by Watson Wyatt shows that total return to shareholders in high-trust organizations is almost three times higher than the return in low-trust organizations. That's a difference of nearly 300 percent! An education study by Stanford professor Tony Bryk shows that schools with high trust had more than a three times higher chance of improving test scores than schools with low trust. On a personal level, high-trust individuals are more likely to be promoted, make more money, receive the best opportunities, and have more fulfilling and joyful relationships.

One of the reasons why the hidden variable of trust is so significant and compelling in today's world is that we have entered into a global, knowledge worker economy. As *New York Times* columnist Thomas Friedman observes in *The World Is Flat*, this new "flat" economy revolves around partnering and relationships. And partnering and relationships thrive or die based on trust. As Friedman says:

> *Without trust, there is no open society, because there are not enough police to patrol every opening in an open society. Without trust, there can also be no flat world, because it is trust that allows us to take down walls, remove barriers, and eliminate friction at borders. Trust is essential for a flat world. . . .*

This is why I again affirm: *The ability to establish, grow, extend, and restore trust with all stakeholders—customers, business partners, investors, and coworkers—is the key leadership competency of the new global economy.*

Below, I've summarized the impact of trust taxes and dividends in both organizations and personal relationships. As you look at this summary, I suggest you ask yourself: Is my organization paying taxes or receiving dividends? And what about me—am I a walking tax or a walking dividend?

Also, think about your relationships both in and out of work. Ask yourself: Where in this summary do these relationships fit? And where can I focus my effort to make the greatest difference in my life?

A SUMMARY OF TAXES AND DIVIDENDS

The 80% Tax (Nonexistent Trust)

In the organization . . .	In personal relationships . . .
• Dysfunctional environment and toxic culture (open warfare, sabotage, grievances, lawsuits, criminal behavior) • Militant stakeholders • Intense micromanagement • Redundant hierarchy • Punishing systems and structures	• Dysfunctional relationships • Hot, angry confrontations or cold, bitter withdrawal • Defensive posturing and legal positioning ("I'll see you in court!") • Labeling of others as enemies or allies • Verbal, emotional, and/or physical abuse

The 60% Tax (Very Low Trust)

In the organization . . .	In personal relationships . . .
• Unhealthy working environment • Unhappy employees and stakeholders • Intense political atmosphere with clear camps and parties • Excessive time wasted defending positions and decisions • Painful micromanagement and bureaucracy	• Hostile behaviors (yelling, blaming, accusing, name-calling) followed by periods of brief contrition • Guarded communication • Constant worrying and suspicion • Mistakes remembered and used as weapons • Real issues not surfaced or dealt with effectively

The 40% Tax (Low Trust)

In the organization . . .	In personal relationships . . .
• Common "CYA" behavior • Hidden agendas • Militant stakeholders • Political camps with allies and enemies • Many dissatisfied employees and stakeholders • Bureaucracy and redundancy in systems and structures	• Energy draining and joyless interactions • Evidence gathering of other party's weaknesses and mistakes • Doubt about others' reliability or commitment • Hidden agendas • Guarded (often grudging) dispersing of information

The 20% Tax (Trust Issues)

In the organization . . .	In personal relationships . . .
• Some bureaucratic rules and procedures • Unnecessary hierarchy • Slow approvals • Misaligned systems and structures • Some dissatisfied employees and stakeholders	• Regular misunderstandings • Concerns about intent and motive • Interactions characterized by tension • Communications colored by fear, uncertainty, doubt, and worry • Energy spent in maintaining (instead of growing) relationships

No Tax/No Dividend (Trust Is Not an Issue)

In the organization . . .	In personal relationships . . .
• Healthy workplace • Good communication • Aligned systems and structures • Few office politics	• Polite, cordial, healthy communications • A focus on working together smoothly and efficiently • Mutual tolerance and acceptance • No worries

The 20% Dividend (Trust Is a Visible Asset)

In the organization . . .	In personal relationships . . .
• The focus is on work • Effective collaboration and execution • Positive partnering relationships with employees and stakeholders • Helpful systems and structures • Strong creativity and innovation	• Cooperative, close, vibrant relationships • A focus on looking for and leveraging one another's strengths • Uplifting and positive communication • Mistakes seen as learning opportunities and quickly forgiven • Positive energy and positive people

The 40% Dividend (World-class Trust)

In the organization . . .	In personal relationships . . .
• High collaboration and partnering	• True joy in family and friendships, characterized by caring and love
• Effortless communication	• Free, effortless communication
• Positive, transparent relationships with employees and all stakeholders	• Inspiring work done together and characterized by purpose, creativity, and excitement
• Fully aligned systems and structures	• Completely open, transparent relationships
• Strong innovation, engagement, confidence, and loyalty	• Amazing energy created by relationships

Now I suggest you take any mission-critical project you need to work on and look at it in terms of this summary. Say you need to pull people together to have a project completed within six weeks. Ask yourself: What's the level of trust in the culture? Am I paying a tax or getting a dividend? If so, what percent? What impact is that going to have on speed and cost and on my ability to execute this project effectively?

Now consider what would happen if you were able to change that percentage. What if you were able to move from a 20 percent tax to a 20 percent dividend? What difference would that make in your ability to execute your project?

Think about what's happening in your personal relationships or in your family. Ask yourself: What's the level of trust? What impact is that having on quality of life for me and for the people I care about? What if I could move from a tax to a dividend? What difference would it make?

TRUST MYTHS

Examples such as the McLane acquisition, the Kelleher reorganization approval, and others I've shared in this chapter go a long way toward dispelling some of the debilitating myths that keep us from enjoying the dividends of high trust.

One myth, for example, is that trust is "soft"—it's something that's nice to have, but you really can't define it, quantify it, measure it. As I hope you can tell by now, the exact opposite is true. Trust is hard. It's real. It's quantifiable. It's measurable. In every instance, it affects both speed and cost, and speed and cost can be measured and quantified. To change the level of trust in a relationship, on a team, or in an organization is to dramatically impact both time and money—and quality and value, as well. Another myth is that trust is slow. While restoring trust may take time, both establishing and extending trust can be done quite fast, and, once established, trust makes the playing field exceptionally quick. You don't have to look far beyond these examples I've given or even the speed with which you communicate and get things done in your own relationships to see the reality that truly, nothing is as fast as the speed of trust.

Below is a chart listing these and some of the other myths that get in the way of understanding and acting effectively on trust issues, along with their contrasting realities.

MYTH	REALITY
Trust is soft.	Trust is hard, real, and quantifiable. It measurably affects both speed and cost.
Trust is slow.	Nothing is as fast as the speed of trust.
Trust is built solely on integrity.	Trust is a function of both character (which includes integrity) and competence.
You either have trust or you don't.	Trust can be both created and destroyed.
Once lost, trust cannot be restored.	Though difficult, in most cases lost trust can be restored.
You can't teach trust.	Trust can be effectively taught and learned, and it can become a leverageable, strategic advantage.
Trusting people is too risky.	Not trusting people is a greater risk.
Trust is established one person at a time.	Establishing trust with the one establishes trust with the many.

Probably the most insidious myth of all is the one expressed by the senior leader of that investment bank I worked for briefly in New York City: "You either have trust or you don't, and there's nothing you can do about it."

You *can* do something about trust! For 20 years, I've been a business practitioner. I've been responsible for building and running organizations, for developing teams, for reporting to boards, getting results, and having to "hit the numbers." During many of those years, I've also done consulting work with dozens of well-known companies—many of which had good strategies and good execution abilities, but fell short of being able to accomplish what they wanted to without being able to explain why. I have been a husband, a father, a member of a large extended family with many multifaceted relationships. I have served in community situations in which I have counseled individuals and families dealing with complex trust issues. And in all of my experience, I have never seen an exception to the basic premise of this book: Trust is something you *can* do something about—and probably *much* faster than you think!

Once again, I affirm that nothing is as fast as the speed of trust. Nothing is as fulfilling as a relationship of trust. Nothing is as inspiring as an offering of trust. Nothing is as profitable as the economics of trust. Nothing has more influence than a reputation of trust.

Trust truly is the one thing that changes everything. And there has never been a more vital time for people to establish, restore, and extend trust at all levels than in today's new global society.

Whether you approach the opportunity and challenge of increasing trust in relation to your personal life, your professional life, or both, I can promise you, it *will* make an enormous difference in every dimension of your life.

YOU CAN DO SOMETHING ABOUT THIS!

As you go to work, your top responsibility should be to build trust.

—ROBERT ECKERT, CEO, MATTEL

If you are familiar with my father, Dr. Stephen R. Covey, and his book *The 7 Habits of Highly Effective People*, you may remember the story he tells about trying to teach his son how to take care of the yard. He labeled the story "Green and Clean." My father uses the story as an example of teaching principles of stewardship and responsibility to a young child.

Well, I'm the son in that story, and I'd like to tell you my side of it! It's true that I did learn about stewardship and responsibility from that experience, but I also learned something I have come to believe is even more important—something that has had a profound effect on me my entire life.

I was seven years old and my father wanted me to take care of the yard. He said, "Son, here's the yard and here's your job: It's 'green' and 'clean.' Now, here's what I mean by that." He walked over to our neighbor's yard, pointed to the grass, and said, "That's green." (He couldn't use our own yard as an example because under his stewardship it was rather yellow at the time.) He said, "Now, how you get our yard green is up to you. You're free to do it any way you want except paint it. You can turn on the sprinklers. You can carry the water in buckets. You can even spit on it if you want. It makes no difference to me. All I care about is that the color is green."

Then he said, "And this is what I mean by clean." He got two sacks and together we cleared the papers, sticks, and other debris off half the lawn so that I could see the difference. Again, he explained to me that how I accomplished the goal was up to me—the important thing was that the lawn was "clean."

Then my father said something very profound. He said, "Now you need to know that when you take this job, I don't do it anymore. It's your job. It's called a stewardship. Stewardship means 'a job with a trust.' I trust you to do the job, to get it done." He set up a system for accountability. He said we would walk around the yard twice a week so that I could tell him how things were going. He assured me that he would be around to help me when I asked, but he made it clear to me that the job was truly mine—that I would be my own boss and that I alone would be the judge of how well I was doing.

So the job was mine. Apparently, for four or five days, I did nothing. It was during the heat of the summer, and the grass was dying fast. Remnants of a neighborhood barbecue we'd had a few days ago were all over the lawn. It was messy and unkempt. My father wanted to take over the responsibility or scold me, but he didn't want to violate the agreement we'd established.

So when the time came for an accounting, he said, "Son, how's it going in the yard?" I said, "Just fine, Dad." Then he asked, "Is there anything I can do to help?" I said, "No, everything's just fine." So he said, "Okay, let's take that walk we agreed to take."

As we walked around the yard, I suddenly began to realize that it was neither "green" nor "clean." It was yellow and it was a mess. According to my father, my chin began to quiver and I broke down into tears and wailed, "But, Dad, it's just so hard."

He said, "What's so hard? You haven't done one thing." After a moment of silence, he asked, "Would you like me to give you some help?"

Remembering that his offer of help had been part of our agreement and sensing a glimmer of hope, I quickly replied, "I would."

He said, 'What would you like me to do?"

I looked around. "Could you help me pick up that garbage over there?" He said he would. So I went inside and got two sacks, and he helped me pick up the garbage just as I had asked him to do.

From that day forward, I took responsibility for the yard . . . and I kept it "green" and "clean."

As I've said, my father uses this story as an example of stewardship delegation or win-win agreements. But, as a seven-year-old, I was too young to understand what all those big words even meant. What I remember most about this experience was simply this: *I felt trusted!* I was too young to care about money or status. Those things didn't motivate me. What motivated me was my father's trust. I didn't want to let him down. I wanted to show him that I was capable and responsible. My father had extended trust to me, and that inspired me and created a sense of responsibility and integrity that has stayed with me throughout my life.

> *Few things can help an individual more than to place responsibility on him, and to let him know that you trust him.*
>
> —BOOKER T. WASHINGTON

HOW TRUST WORKS

As I learned that day with my father (and have relearned on almost every level since), trust is one of the most powerful forms of motivation and inspiration. People want to be trusted. They respond to trust. They thrive on trust. Whatever our situation, we need to get good at establishing, extending, and restoring trust—not as a manipulative technique, but as the most effective way of relating to and working with others, and the most effective way of getting results.

In order to do that, we first need to understand how trust works.

In my presentations I often ask audiences to consider the question, Who do you trust? Think about your own experience with regard to this question. Who do *you* trust? A friend? A work associate? Your boss? Your spouse? A parent? A child? Why do you trust this person? What is it that inspires confidence in this particular relationship?

Now consider an even more provocative question: Who trusts you? People at home? At work? Someone you've just met? Someone who has known you for a long time? What is it in you that inspires the trust of others?*

Most of us tend to think about trust in terms of character—of being a good or sincere person or of having ethics or integrity. And character is absolutely foundational and essential. But as I suggested in the previous chapter, to think that trust is based on *character only* is a myth.

---

* For a free online survey to assess the level of trust colleagues, friends, and others have in you, visit www.speedoftrust.com.

Trust is a function of two things: character and *competence*. Character includes your integrity, your motive, your intent with people. Competence includes your capabilities, your skills, your results, your track record. And both are vital.

With the increasing focus on ethics in our society, the character side of trust is fast becoming the price of entry in the new global economy. However, the differentiating and often ignored side of trust—competence—is equally essential. You might think a person is sincere, even honest, but you won't trust that person fully if he or she doesn't get results. And the opposite is true. A person might have great skills and talents and a good track record, but if he or she is not honest, you're not going to trust that person either. For example, I might trust someone's character implicitly, even enough to leave him in charge of my children when I'm out of town. But I might not trust that same person in a business situation because he doesn't have the competence to handle it. On the other hand, I might trust someone in a business deal whom I would never leave with my children—not necessarily because he wasn't honest or capable, but because he wasn't the kind of caring person I would want for my children.

While it may come more naturally for us to think of trust in terms of character, it's equally important that we also learn to think in terms of competence. Think about it—people trust people who make things happen. They give the new curriculum to their most competent instructors. They give the promising projects or sales leads to those who have delivered in the past. Recognizing the role of competence helps us identify and give language to underlying trust issues we otherwise can't put a finger on. From a line leader's perspective, the competence dimension rounds out and helps give trust its harder, more pragmatic edge.

Here's another way to look at it: The increasing concern about ethics has been good for our society. Ethics (which is part of character) is foundational to trust, but by itself is insufficient. You can't have trust without ethics, but you can have ethics without trust. Trust, which encompasses ethics, is the bigger idea.

After I presented the Speed of Trust at a recent conference, the head of sales of a major pharmaceutical company came up to me and said, "*Thank you* for reinforcing what I've been telling our group—that results are vital to establishing trust and that we have to hit our numbers every month. When we achieve them, the organization trusts us more, our leaders trust us more, our peers trust us more . . . everyone trusts us more. When we don't, we lose trust and budgetary support. It's that simple."

Again, character and competence are both necessary. Character is a constant; it's necessary for trust in any circumstance. Competence is situational; it depends on what the circumstance requires. My wife, Jeri, recently had to have some surgery. We have a great relationship—she trusts me and I trust her. But when it came time to perform the surgery, she didn't ask me to do it. I'm not a doctor. I don't have the skills or the competence to do it. Even though she trusts me in most arenas, she knows I don't have the skills to perform surgery.

Once you become aware that both character and competence are vital to trust, you can see how the combination of these two dimensions is reflected in the approach of effective leaders and observers everywhere. People might use different words to express the idea, but if you reduce the words to their essence, what emerges is a balancing of character and competence.

Consider the following:

- Jack Welch—former CEO of GE—talks about managers being judged on their performance in two dimensions: "Live the values" (character) and "Deliver results" (competence).
- Jim Collins—author of *Good to Great*—talks about a Level 5 leader having "extreme personal humility" (character) and "intense professional will" (competence). In *Built to Last*, he speaks of the need to "preserve the core" (character) and "stimulate progress" (competence).
- Warren Buffett—CEO of Berkshire Hathaway—prioritizes "integrity" (character) and "intelligence" (competence) as the qualities he looks for in people.
- Ram Charan—author of numerous books and consultant to several Fortune 500 CEOs—emphasizes the need to be a "leader of the people" (character) and a "leader of the business" (competence).
- Saj-Nicole Joni—noted expert on trust—writes of the importance of "personal trust" (character) and "expertise trust" (competence).
- Leadership theory deals with what a leader is (character) and what a leader does (competence).
- Performance modeling considers the primary outputs as "attributes" (character) and "competencies" (competence).
- Ethics theory says, "Do the right thing" (character) and "Get the right thing done" (competence).
- Decision-making approaches focus on balancing the "heart" (character) with the "head" (competence).

The list could go on and on, consistently emphasizing the importance of both character and competence as vital to sustained success and leadership. On a personal note, you might find it helpful to reinforce these two dimensions in your mind by employing a fun little mnemonic device we have used in our family. We have two family values that are very important to us, two things we keep coming back to time and time again. To help my younger children remember these values, I decided to tell them, "Just think of the sound made by two bongo drums: *Boom—boom! Boom—boom!*" As I would "hit" the imaginary bongo drums, I would repeat the two values over and over.

Sometime later, we had to deal with a very tough family issue. We were all gathered together struggling with how we should handle it. I began asking each of the children, "What do you think we should do?"

Suddenly, my six-year-old looked at me and he started beating "bongo drums" on the living room table. He said essentially, "This is what you taught us, Dad; let's go back to our values. These are what will help us solve this problem." And they did.

Since I have been working on trust, other words to those bongo drum beats keep ringing in my ears: "Character—competence. Character—competence." The bongo drum idea helps me remember that it's not just a function of character, though that is clearly the foundation. Trust is equal parts character and competence. Both are absolutely necessary. From the family room to the boardroom, you can look at any leadership failure, and it's always a failure of one or the other.

THE 5 WAVES OF TRUST

Several years ago, some of my associates and I were working with a small group of people from a major multinational corporation. Their initial response was, "We *love* this leadership content! It's right on. But our division leaders don't understand this. They are the ones who really need to hear it."

A short time later, we presented the content to their division leaders. Their response was, "We are in full agreement with everything you're saying. This approach is great! The problem is that the people who really need it are our bosses."

When we presented it to their bosses, they said, "We are enthusiastic about this content! It's very insightful and helpful. But our counterparts in the five divisions don't understand this. They are the ones who need to hear it."

Their counterparts said the problem was the executive team who supervised and managed the divisions. The executive team said the problem was the CEO. When we finally reached the CEO, he said, "This content is great, but I'm powerless. I can do nothing. It's all in the hands of the board." I am certain that, had we gone to the board, they would have said the problem was Wall Street!

As my father has taught so eloquently, "If you think the problem is *out there*, that very thought *is* the problem."

As we eventually taught the people on each level of this major corporation, your boss, your division leader, your CEO, your board, your spouse, your children, your friends, your associates may *all* have problems as far as trust (or anything else) is concerned. *But that does not mean that you are powerless!* In fact, you probably have no idea how powerful you can be in changing the level of trust in any relationship if you know how to work "from the inside out."

The key is in understanding and learning how to navigate in what I've come to call the "5 Waves of Trust." This model derives from the "ripple effect" metaphor that graphically illustrates the interdependent nature of trust and how it flows from the inside out. It defines the five levels, or contexts, in which we establish trust. It also forms the structure for understanding and making trust actionable as we go through the next three sections of this book.

Although we will be discussing each wave in depth, I'd like to give you a quick overview of the 5 Waves now so that you will have the context to better understand each wave as you go along.

THE FIRST WAVE: SELF TRUST

The first wave, Self Trust, deals with the confidence we have in our-selves—in our ability to set and achieve goals, to keep commitments, to walk our talk—and also with our ability to inspire trust in others. The whole idea is to become, both to ourselves and to others, a person who is worthy of trust. The key principle underlying this wave is *credibility*, which comes from the Latin root *credere*, meaning "to believe." In this first wave, we will explore the "4 Cores of Credibility," where we will discuss ways to increase our credibility in order to firmly establish trust with ourselves and with others. The end result of high character and high competence is credibility, judgment, and influence.

THE SECOND WAVE: RELATIONSHIP TRUST

The second wave, Relationship Trust, is about how to establish and increase the "trust accounts" we have with others. The key principle underlying this wave is *consistent behavior*, and in this section, we will discuss 13 key behaviors common to high-trust leaders around the world. These behaviors are based on the principles that govern trust in relationships. They are practitioner-based and validated by research. Most exciting is the fact that these 13 behaviors can be learned and applied by any individual at any level within any organization, includ-ing the family. The net result is a significantly increased ability to gen-erate trust with all involved in order to enhance relationships and achieve better results.

THE THIRD WAVE: ORGANIZATIONAL TRUST

The third wave, Organizational Trust, deals with how leaders can gen-erate trust in all kinds of organizations, including businesses, not-for-profit organizations, government entities, educational institutions, and families, as well as in teams and other microunits within organizations. If you've ever worked with people you trusted—but in an organization you didn't—or in a situation where the organization's systems and structures promoted distrust, you will easily recognize the critical na-ture of the third wave. The key principle underlying this wave, *align-ment*, helps leaders create structures, systems, and symbols of organizational trust that decrease or eliminate seven of the most insidi-ous and costly organizational trust taxes, and create seven huge organi-zational trust dividends.

THE FOURTH WAVE: MARKET TRUST

The fourth wave, Market Trust, is the level at which almost everyone clearly understands the impact of trust. The underlying principle behind this wave is *reputation*. It's about your company brand (as well as your personal brand), which reflects the trust customers, investors, and others in the marketplace have in you. Everyone knows that brands powerfully affect customer behavior and loyalty. When there is a high-trust brand, customers buy more, refer more, give the benefit of the doubt, and stay with you longer. This material will help you not only improve your own brand and reputation as an individual, it will also help you improve your organization's brand and reputation in the marketplace.

THE FIFTH WAVE: SOCIETAL TRUST

The fifth wave, Societal Trust, is about creating value for others and for society at large. The principle underlying this wave is *contribution*. By contributing or "giving back," we counteract the suspicion, cynicism, and low-trust inheritance taxes within our society. We also inspire others to create value and contribute, as well.

Depending on our roles and responsibilities, we may have more or less influence as we move out through each successive wave. However, we all have extraordinary influence on the first two waves, and this is where we need to begin. As we move through the book, it will become clear that even trust at the societal level (the fifth wave) can specifically be traced back to issues at the individual level (the first wave), and that individual trust issues actually become geometrically multiplied as we move outward through the waves. For example, trust issues at the individual level with certain Enron leaders initially rippled throughout their relationships and organization, and eventually into the marketplace and society at large. And the ripple effect was magnified the farther out it went, ultimately becoming one of the primary triggers that brought about significant reform (the Sarbanes-Oxley Act). This puts a premium on always starting at the first wave with ourselves.

The final section deals with Inspiring Trust. This includes learning how to extend "Smart Trust"—how to avoid gullibility (blind trust) on one hand and suspicion (distrust) on the other and how to find that "sweet spot" where extending trust creates big dividends for everyone. It also involves restoring trust and increasing your propensity to trust. While there is risk in trusting other people, there's far greater risk in not trusting them. The ability to know when and how to extend Smart Trust will enable you to move the fulcrum over and create incredible leverage, so that you get things done with greater speed and lower cost. Perhaps even more importantly, it will inspire and release those to whom you extend trust.

RESTORING TRUST

Before we move into our discussion of the 5 Waves, I want to take a moment to reaffirm that it is possible not only to build trust, but also to restore it. Obviously, there are some circumstances in which trust has truly been damaged beyond repair or where others may not give us a chance to restore it. But I am convinced that for most of us, these circumstances are few, and that our ability to restore trust is much, much greater than we think.

> *The best time to plant a tree is twenty years ago.*
> *The second best time is today.*
>
> —CHINESE PROVERB

Consider the experience of "Tom," who had been with a large real-estate development company for many years, ultimately becoming a partner in the firm. At one point, the real-estate market turned upside down and the company began to split apart. A lot of infighting ensued, and Tom left the company. A lawsuit was filed. A countersuit was filed. As a major partner, Tom had an economic interest in dozens of buildings. Incredibly, after several years, the discovery and due diligence of the litigation process were still going on.

Finally, Tom decided there must be a better way. He called "Chris," the partner who was then in charge of the business, and said, "Let's talk—just the two of us without our attorneys." Tom and Chris had been partners for several years, but in the midst of everything that had been going on, the trust had fallen apart. However, Chris agreed to the meeting.

Tom went in with the intent to genuinely seek to understand Chris' point of view. He listened. He verbally reflected back his understanding of what Chris was saying. Once Chris felt understood, he was willing to listen to Tom.

As they interacted, a measure of the trust these former business partners had once shared was quickly rekindled. Even though circumstances split them apart, they still felt the connection, and in that very meeting, they were able to agree on a handshake deal to resolve the dispute.

Through a process of listening and restoring a portion of the trust that had once been there, these two men created a solution they could implement in thirty days, and they ended the rancor, the pain, the time drain, and the money drain that had been part of an ongoing legal battle for the past several years.

> *While corporate leadership still has a long way to go in restoring trust, the research makes one thing crystal clear: Americans expect CEOs to take the lead, make a meaningful commitment to trust-building, be accountable—and deliver on the promise of trust through corporate behavior.*
>
> —RICH JERNSTEDT, CEO OF GOLIN/HARRIS

For another example, consider the relationship between former U.S. presidents John Adams and Thomas Jefferson. These two men were "the voice" and "the pen," respectively, of the Declaration of Independence, and labored tirelessly for America's independence from Great Britain. Brought together as ambassadors in Paris between the American and French Revolutions—neither of them knowing what was in store for the United States or France, or for each other—they grew exceptionally close. Jefferson became like a father to Adams' son, John Quincy, and was ardently admired by Adams' wife, Abigail, who referred to him as "one of the choice ones of the earth."

On returning to the United States, however, these two men espoused different political views, which put a strain on their friendship. In accordance with the law at the time, when Adams—a Federalist—was elected as second president of the United States, Jefferson—a Republican—became vice president by default, having received the second-greatest number of votes.

Adams expected the same kind of support and friendship from his vice president that Adams had shown George Washington when he served in that position. Instead, it seemed to Adams that Jefferson was disloyal, extremely partisan, and politically ambitious. By the end of Adams' presidency, their relationship was filled with rancor and bitterness.

Years later, their mutual friend Dr. Benjamin Rush (who was also a signer of the Declaration of Independence) encouraged Adams to extend an "olive branch" to Jefferson. Adams did so, sending a "Happy New Year's" note wishing Jefferson good health and happiness. Jefferson immediately responded, delighted at the prospect of a renewed friendship. He wrote: "A letter from you calls up recollections very dear to my mind. It carried me back to the times when, beset with difficulties and dangers, we were fellow laborers in the same cause, struggling for what is most valuable to man, his right of self-government."

Adams wrote to their mutual friend Rush, declaring: "Your dream is out . . . you have wrought wonders! You have made peace between powers that never were at war." Later, when Adams brought a letter to read from Thomas Jefferson at a family gathering, he was asked how he could be on such good terms with a man from whom he had suffered so much abuse. He replied:

> *I do not believe that Mr. Jefferson ever hated me. On the contrary, I believe he always liked me. . . . Then he wished to be President of the United States, and I stood in his way. So he did everything that he could to pull me down. But if I should quarrel with him for that, I might quarrel with every man I have had anything to do with in life. This is human nature. . . . I forgive all my enemies and hope they may find mercy in Heaven. Mr. Jefferson and I have grown old and retired from public life. So we are upon our ancient terms of goodwill.*

Adams and Jefferson enjoyed a rich and satisfying friendship and correspondence for fourteen years before they both passed away, amazingly, on the same day: the Fourth of July, 1826, the fiftieth anniversary of the American Declaration of Independence. Among Adams' most memorable words to Jefferson were these: "While I breathe, I shall be your friend."

SEE/SPEAK/BEHAVE

The purpose of this book is to enable you to *see*, *speak*, and *behave* in ways that establish trust, and all three dimensions are vital.

Remember the story I shared in the previous chapter of the Montana fishing guide who gave me glasses to see the fish beneath the river's surface? This book will give you a pair of "trust glasses" so that you'll be able to *see* trust in an entirely different and exciting way—a way that will open your eyes to the possibilities and enable you to increase trust and the dividends of trust on every level.

It will also give you a language to *speak* about trust. Sometimes you know that you don't trust someone or that someone doesn't trust you, but you can't explain why and don't know how to improve the situation. This book will enable you to name the underlying issues involved, and it will give you the language to describe those issues and to talk about and resolve them.

Finally, this book will help you develop the *behaviors* that establish and grow trust—particularly, the 13 Behaviors of high-trust people and leaders worldwide. As you learn about these behaviors and recognize the impact when people practice them—and when they don't—you will understand how you can behave in ways that quickly build enduring trust.

Much has been said about the importance of changing paradigms in changing behavior—in other words, changing the way you *see* will automatically change what you do and the results you get. And I agree that a new way of seeing, a paradigm shift, has an enormous impact on doing and on results.

However, from a pragmatic standpoint, I am equally convinced that speaking and behaving differently can also have an enormous impact on the way you see and the results you get. The very act of serving someone, for example, can quickly cause you to see that person differently—even to feel love and compassion which you have not felt before. I call this a *behavior shift*—a shift in which our behaviors ultimately bring about a shift in the way we see the world. I am also convinced of the power of a *language shift*. The way we talk about things can create a shift in how we see and how we behave, as well as in how others see us.

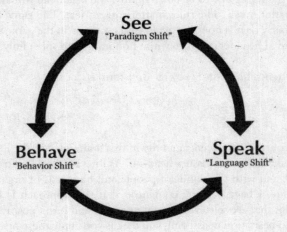

See
"Paradigm Shift"

Behave
"Behavior Shift"

Speak
"Language Shift"

Clearly, these three dimensions are interdependent, and whenever you effect a change in one dimension, you effect a change in all three. For this reason, this book will focus on *see*, *speak*, and *behave* so that you will have not only the paradigms, but also the language and the behaviors needed to establish and grow trust.

MAKING IT HAPPEN

With an understanding of the Speed of Trust, some of the issues around trust at every level, and how trust works, we're now ready to move into the actionable steps that make establishing, restoring, and extending trust possible. As you go through the remaining sections in this book, keep in mind that whatever your role at work or at home, you are an influencer. You are a leader, even if only of yourself.

Over time, I have come to this simple definition of leadership: *Leadership is getting results in a way that inspires trust.* It's maximizing both your current contribution and your ability to contribute in the future by establishing the trust that makes it possible.

The means are as important as the ends. How you go about achieving results is as important as the results themselves, because when you establish trust, you increase your ability to get results the next time. And there's always a next time. To get things done in ways that destroy trust is not only shortsighted and counterproductive; it is ultimately unsustainable. As the courageous explorer Sir Ernest Shackleton put it: "Life to me is the greatest of all games. The danger lies in treating it as a trivial game, a game to be taken lightly, and a game in which the rules don't matter much. The rules matter a great deal. The game has to be played fairly or it is no game at all. And even to win the game is not the chief end. The chief end is to win it honorably and splendidly."

> *Trust is absolutely key to long-term success.*
>
> —JIM BURKE, FORMER CHAIRMAN AND CEO,
> JOHNSON & JOHNSON

I encourage you to engage fully in this material. Ask the hard questions. Take the jugular issues head-on. As I have focused on trust in my own life and with thousands of people and hundreds of organizations worldwide, I have become convinced that this approach is based on principles that are self-evident and universal and bring positive results. I have no hesitation in assuring you that as you apply these principles in your own life, you will see immediate benefits. You will build long-term capacity. You will build stronger, more sustainable relationships. You will get better outcomes. You will have more opportunities, more influence, and more fun. You will learn how to establish, grow, restore, and extend the one thing that dramatically impacts everything else in your life—trust.

THE FIRST WAVE— SELF TRUST

The Principle of Credibility

The 5 Waves of Trust model serves as a metaphor for how trust operates in our lives. It begins with each of us personally, continues into our relationships, expands into our organizations, extends into our marketplace relationships, and encompasses our global society at large. This reflects the strength of the "inside-out" approach: to build trust with others, we must first start with ourselves.

The First Wave—Self Trust—is where we learn the foundational principle that enables us to establish and sustain trust at all levels. That principle is *credibility*, or believability. This is where we ask ourselves, Am I credible? Am I believable? Am I someone people (including myself) can trust?

The good news is that we can increase our credibility, and we can increase it fast, particularly if we understand the four key elements, or four "cores," that are fundamental. Two of these cores deal with character; two with competence. What gives trust its harder, more pragmatic edge is recognizing that competence is as vital to trust as character, and that both character and competence are within our ability to create or to change.

As we develop these four cores, we increase our personal credibility. We then have the foundation from which we can establish and sustain trust in all relationships in life.

THE 4 CORES
OF CREDIBILITY

*Leadership may have to come in a different package.
It's got to be credible. . . . Overall, it's about credibility,
walking the talk.*

—Anne Mulcahy, Chairman and CEO, Xerox

Imagine that you are in a court of law. You've been called as an expert witness, and the lawyer for the prosecution is attempting to convince the jury that you are a credible witness. What will he try to prove?

First, that you are a person of integrity—that you are honest and congruent, that you have a reputation for being truthful, and that you would not lie.

Second, that you have good intent—that you're not trying to deceive or protect anyone, that you don't have any hidden motive or agenda that would color your testimony.

Third, that your credentials are excellent, that you do, indeed, have expertise, knowledge, skill, and capability in the area in which you are called to testify.

And fourth, that you have a good track record, that you have demonstrated your capabilities effectively in other situations in the past, that you produce results, and that there is good reason to believe that you will do so now.

Now the lawyer for the defense gets up, and he's going to attempt to convince the jury that you're *not* credible. What will he try to prove? The exact opposite.

Perhaps that you lack integrity—that you are dishonest or have lied in the past, or that you're "flaky" or have some character flaw that would discredit your testimony. Or that you have some hidden agenda or some motive to "spin" your testimony in the prosecutor's behalf. Or that your credentials are lacking and you are not qualified to testify in the area of your supposed expertise. Or that your track record is tarnished or lacking—that you haven't produced good results or demonstrated the ability to accurately discern the facts.

As my lawyer friends affirm, it basically boils down to these four issues: your integrity, your intent, your capabilities, and your results. Your credibility—as an expert witness, as a person, as a leader, as a family, as an organization—depends on these four factors. And that credibility would be vital to the case, particularly if there were no irrefutable physical evidence, thus implying that the verdict would really come down to the credibility of people's testimonies. In such cases, it is the credibility of the witnesses that's really on trial.

In a recent case that relied on testimony rather than tangible evidence, the defense attorney asked the judge to hold a pretrial hearing to "determine if the complaining witness is even credible enough to provide reliable testimony." As a *USA Today* headline read in the midst of the Enron trial, "Verdict Could Hinge Solely on [Skilling's] Credibility on Stand." Following a "guilty" verdict, the new headline read, "Jurors: Ex-Enron Execs Not Credible."

In court or in life, a lot can depend on whether you are believable—or not. For example, during the 2005 governmental investigation of the AIG insurance transaction with General Re (owned by a subsidiary of Warren Buffett's company, Berkshire Hathaway), Warren Buffett's reputation for ethics and integrity clearly gave him the benefit of the doubt even before any details of the transaction concerns were known. An ethics professor at Wharton Business School said, "Given his track record, I'd be inclined to give him the benefit of the doubt." Another CEO said, "Here's somebody who is wealthy and visible enough that everything has been scrutinized. He has not just a reputation, but a track record." Buffett, of course, was cleared of any wrongdoing, but he never even suffered any taint for being "in the area" because of his unquestioned credibility.

> *I have never had anyone refuse to deal with me for lack of trust.*
>
> —JON HUNTSMAN, CHAIRMAN OF
> HUNTSMAN CORPORATION

BEING CREDIBLE—TO YOURSELF AND TO OTHERS

The First Wave of Trust—Self Trust—is all about credibility. It's about developing the integrity, intent, capabilities, and results that make you believable, both to yourself and to others. And it all boils down to two simple questions: 1) Do I trust myself? and 2) Am I someone others can trust?

With regard to having trust in self, it often begins with the little things. I remember one extremely busy time in my life where for about a five-month period I was staying up until 2:00 or 3:00 A.M. every night to finish a project. I'd wake up to my alarm clock in the morning (which I had set quite early so I could exercise) only to reach over, turn it off, and go back to sleep. Since I was getting so little sleep at the time, I'd justify what I was doing by telling myself that I needed the sleep more than the exercise.

After I had done this for a time, I started thinking, Why am I setting this alarm so early? I know I'm not going to get up to exercise when it goes off. Why am I even doing this? Not only had this repeated behavior weakened my self-confidence, it had become a self-fulfilling prophecy. When I set the alarm, I didn't believe I was going to get up; instead, I believed I was going to rationalize why I shouldn't. Setting the alarm had become a joke.

Finally, I decided to change my approach. I determined that instead of using the ringing alarm each morning as a decision point, I would make a decision the night before and set my alarm when I really intended to get up. From that time forward, if I set it early, I would get up and follow through on my commitment to exercise, regardless of how little sleep I'd had. But sometimes I would set it to go off later because I genuinely felt I needed the sleep. Whatever decision I made when I set the alarm, I wanted my commitment to be clear and to act with integrity. Otherwise, I would continue to lose trust in my ability to do what I had made a personal commitment to do. While this may seem like a somewhat trivial example, it turned out to be very meaningful to me in terms of building self trust.

Research shows that many of us don't follow through on the goals we set or don't keep the promises and commitments we make to ourselves. For example, while almost half of Americans set New Year's resolutions, research shows that only 8 percent actually keep them.

What happens when we do this time after time? What's the net result of repeated failure to make and keep commitments to ourselves? It hacks away at our self-confidence. Not only do we lose trust in our ability to make and keep commitments, we fail to project the personal strength of character that inspires trust. We may try to borrow strength from position or association. But it's not real. It's not ours . . . and people know it. And whether we realize it or not, that impacts the bottom line.

Though we all know it intuitively, research also validates that a person's self-confidence affects his or her performance. This is one reason why Jack Welch of GE always felt so strongly that "building self-confidence in others is a huge part of leadership."

The lack of self trust also undermines our ability to trust others. In the words of Cardinal de Retz, "A man who doesn't trust himself can never really trust anyone else."

The good news in all of this is that every time we do make and keep a commitment to ourselves or set and achieve a meaningful goal, we become more credible. The more we do it, the more confidence we have that we *can* do it, that we *will* do it. The more we trust ourselves.

> Self-trust is the first secret of success . . . the essence of heroism.
>
> —RALPH WALDO EMERSON

With regard to being someone others can trust, I'd like to share an experience my father had a few years ago in a men's clothing store in Canada. He was being helped by the manager of the store and a newly hired trainee. As he was considering the cost of purchasing a fairly expensive coat, he mentioned that he would have to add to the cost a duty tax that would be imposed on it when he came back into the United States.

"Don't worry about the duty," the store manager said with a quick smile. "Just wear it!"

"What?" my father said.

"Just wear the coat!" the manager repeated. "Then you won't have to pay the tax."

"But I have to sign a form," my father exclaimed. "I have to declare the things I've bought and am bringing into the country."

"Don't declare it; just wear it," the manager said once again. "Don't worry about the tax."

My father was silent for a moment, and then he said, "Look, frankly I'm not as worried about having to pay the tax as I am about this new salesman you're training. He's watching you. He's learning from you. What is he going to think when you sign his commission? What kind of trust is he going to have in you in managing his career?"

Can you see why employees don't trust their managers? Most of the time, it's not the huge, visible withdrawals like Enron and WorldCom ethics violations that wipe out organizational trust. It's the little things—a day at a time, a weak or dishonest act at a time—that gradually weaken and corrode credibility.

> Little things count. Like when someone calls in to talk to a manager and his assistant says he is in a meeting when he is not. It's the little things that your employees notice.
>
> —FRANK VANDERSLOOT, PRESIDENT AND
> CEO OF MELALEUCA

What kind of impact do these constant withdrawals have on the effectiveness of the organization? On job satisfaction? On employee retention? On the bottom line? What kind of tax is the organization paying as a result? And what is the impact on the speed with which things are done?

On the other hand, what happens when you *do* give people someone credible whom they can trust? Let me share with you the story of Wally Thiim. Shortly before the Desert Storm campaign to liberate Kuwait in 1990, Thiim was made battalion commander of a cavalry unit of 2,000 men in Ft. Hood, Texas—by reputation, the worst unit there. But within a short time under his command, the unit made amazing progress, passing the other units to score so high on ARTEPS (army proficiency tests) that then Colonel Tommy Franks, division chief of staff, commended them for top performance.

When Thiim's unit was deployed to Saudi Arabia, before they went into battle, Thiim asked his men to spontaneously point to those they would trust to lead them in a life-and-death situation. They unanimously pointed to the officers who had led them from worst to best unit at Ft. Hood. Their credibility had been proven; they were clearly worthy of trust.

> You cannot prevent a major catastrophe, but you can build an organization that is battle-ready, that has high morale, that knows how to behave, that trusts itself, and where people trust one another. In military training, the first rule is to instill soldiers with trust in their officers, because without trust they won't fight.
>
> —PETER DRUCKER

A friend of mine recently shared an example of how the idea of giving people someone they can trust has impacted her on the family level. She said:

> *Years ago as a young mother, I read an article entitled "Can Your Child Trust You?" The author pointed out how, as parents, we will often tell a young child "no!" over and over instead of following through in meaningful ways to ensure that he obeys the first time. As a result, children learn that if they keep at something long enough, they can usually wear a parent out and eventually get their way. They don't develop trust that adults mean what they say when they say "no."*
>
> *This author then suggested effective ways to follow up and to build trust. For example, if you've said "no" to a toddler and he doesn't obey, then you immediately go pick him up and move him away from whatever he was doing.*
>
> *This one idea has had a profound positive impact on the way I have interacted with my children over the years. It takes time and effort up front. It takes deep commitment and follow-through. But it pays incredible dividends. Instead of wasting time having to repeat yourself over and over, you answer once. Your child learns to trust that you mean what you say.*

You see the opposite of this in homes everywhere. You see parents who give their children instructions, and then fail to follow through when those instructions are ignored. You see children "get by" with things because their parents are so caught up in their own projects or in conversation with other adults that they simply don't pay attention. And you see the results in teenagers who consistently push against the limits and ignore what their parents say. Granted, teenagers come with their own set of problems and are highly influenced by their peers. But I'm confident that building a high-trust relationship has a significant impact on the satisfaction of both parents and teens during those challenging years and also on the character those children develop and on the kind of parents, employees, and citizens they become.

One study by a leading consulting firm showed that building personal credibility was the second-most-identified behavior of leaders. Interestingly, Harvard Business School asks for input in three fundamental areas from those who write letters of recommendation for prospective students. One of the three is the following:

The Harvard Business School is committed to developing outstanding leaders who can <u>inspire trust and confidence</u> in others. Please comment on the applicant's behavior (e.g., respect for others, honesty, integrity, accountability for personal behavior) within your organization in the community [emphasis added].

> The only way to build trust professionally or personally is by being trustworthy.
>
> —GERARD ARPEY, CEO, AMERICAN AIRLINES

Keep in mind, credibility is something we *can* do something about. We can choose to increase the self trust that flows from the inside out and affects every dimension of our lives—and the lives of others, as well.

HOW CREDIBLE ARE YOU?

In our on-site client programs, we often do a one-on-one, prework exercise with individual participants where we give them picture cards of the people they work with and ask them to quickly sort them into two stacks: "I tend to trust this person" or "I tend to not trust this person." If someone has very recently come into the organization, we allow a third possibility: "I don't know this person well enough yet to determine whether or not I trust him or her."

It's always interesting to see how fast people can make these decisions. As they see each picture, most people have an immediate feeling of trust or distrust that is easy to discern. It's also interesting that in most cases, the same people tend to be trusted or not trusted by all.

Think about the people you know, one by one. Which stack would you immediately put their pictures in? Why?

Now for the tougher questions: If your picture were included in a group of picture cards handed to the people who know you, which stack would they put your picture in? And why?

As I said in the beginning of this chapter, there are four factors that create credibility. Before proceeding further, you might be interested in taking the following self-analysis questionnaire that will help you evaluate where you think you are in each of these areas.

I'll warn you in advance that these questions are challenging. They require sincere soul-searching and deep evaluation. But I encourage you to take the questionnaire and to be completely honest with yourself. It will help you understand the basic elements of personal credibility, evaluate where you may be lacking, and focus your efforts where they will bring the greatest results. The very act of truthfully answering these questions will help you increase Self Trust.

As you read each set of statements in each part of the questionnaire, circle the number that best describes where you feel you are on the continuum: 1 means you identify with the statement on the left; 5 means you feel best described by the statement on the right. 2, 3, or 4 mark various positions in between.*

PART ONE

I sometimes justify telling "white lies," misrepresent people or situations, or "spin" the truth to get the results I want.	1 2 3 4 5	At every level, I am thoroughly honest in my interactions with others.
At times, there's a mismatch between what I think and what I say, or between my actions and my values.	1 2 3 4 5	What I say and do is what I really think and feel; I consistently "walk" my "talk."
I am not fully clear on my values. It's difficult for me to stand up for something when others disagree.	1 2 3 4 5	I am clear on my values and courageous in standing up for them.

---

* For automatic scoring, take this questionnaire online at www.speedoftrust.com and receive a complimentary analysis and specific tips to increase your personal credibility.

PART ONE (continued)

It's hard for me to acknowledge that someone else may be right, or that there is additional information out there that may cause me to change my mind.	1	2	3	4	5	I am genuinely open to the possibility of learning new ideas that may cause me to rethink issues or even redefine values.
I have a difficult time setting and achieving personal goals or commitments.	1	2	3	4	5	I am able to consistently make and keep commitments to myself and to others.

TOTAL PART ONE SCORE _____ **(Possible 25)**

PART TWO

I don't really care that much about people, except those closest to me. It's hard for me to think about concerns outside of my own challenges in life.	1	2	3	4	5	I genuinely care about other people and am deeply concerned about the well-being of others.
I don't think a lot about *why* I do what I do. I've rarely (if ever) tried to do deep interior work to improve my motives.	1	2	3	4	5	I am consciously aware of my motives and I refine them to make sure that I'm doing the right things for the right reasons.
In my dealings with others, I usually focus on getting what I want.	1	2	3	4	5	I actively seek solutions that provide a "win" for everyone involved.

PART TWO (continued)

	1 2 3 4 5	
Based on my behavior, most people wouldn't necessarily think I had their best interests in mind.	1 2 3 4 5	Other people can clearly tell by the things I do that I really do have their best interests in mind.
Deep down, I believe that if someone else gets something (resources, opportunities, credit), that means I don't.	1 2 3 4 5	I sincerely believe that there is more than enough of everything to go around.

TOTAL PART TWO SCORE _____ (Possible 25)

PART THREE

I feel like I'm not really utilizing my talents in my current job.	1 2 3 4 5	There is a high match between my talents and my opportunities in the work I'm doing.
I have not gained the knowledge or fully developed the skills I need to really be effective at work.	1 2 3 4 5	I have acquired the knowledge and mastered the skills required for my job.
I seldom take time to improve my knowledge and skills at work or in any other area in my life.	1 2 3 4 5	I relentlessly upgrade and increase my knowledge and skills in all the important areas of my life.
I'm not really sure what my strengths are; I'm more focused on trying to improve in my areas of weakness.	1 2 3 4 5	I've identified my strengths, and my greatest focus is on using them effectively.

PART THREE (continued)

	1 2 3 4 5	
At this point, I really don't know much about how to build trust.	1 2 3 4 5	I know how to effectively establish, grow, extend, and restore trust, and I consciously work to make it happen.

TOTAL PART THREE SCORE _____ **(Possible 25)**

PART FOUR

	1 2 3 4 5	
I don't have a very good track record. My résumé certainly won't knock anyone's socks off.	1 2 3 4 5	My track record clearly gives others the confidence that I will achieve desired results.
I focus my efforts on doing what I've been told to do.	1 2 3 4 5	I focus my efforts on delivering results, not activities.
When it comes to communicating my track record, either I don't say anything (I don't want to come across as bragging), or I say too much and turn people off.	1 2 3 4 5	I appropriately communicate my track record to others in a way that inspires confidence.
I often fail to finish what I start.	1 2 3 4 5	With rare exception, if I start something, I finish it.
I don't worry as much about *how* I get the results—just that I get them.	1 2 3 4 5	I consistently get results in ways that inspire trust.

TOTAL PART FOUR SCORE _____ **(Possible 25)**

TOTAL QUESTIONNAIRE SCORE _____ **(Possible 100)**

Now take a look at your scores. If your total score is between 90 and 100, you have high personal credibility. You demonstrate both character and competence. Likely, you know what's important to you and you translate it into action in your daily life. You care about people. You are aware of your own capabilities and you develop and use them effectively to produce positive outcomes. As a result, you feel confident and people tend to trust you.

If your score is between 70 and 90, you may have a bit of a credibility gap, which will manifest itself either in lower self trust or in some degree of failure to inspire the trust of others.

If you scored 70 or below, you likely have a more serious credibility problem. You may want to do some careful analysis of the specific areas in which you gave yourself lower marks. As we go through this chapter, you will be able to focus on specific ways to improve in those areas.

THE 4 CORES

Each part in the questionnaire corresponds to one of the "4 Cores of Credibility." These are the foundational elements that make you believable, both to yourself and to others. You will recognize them as the same elements that would prove or destroy your credibility as an expert witness in a court of law.

The first two cores deal with character; the second two with competence. And all four are necessary to self trust.

Core 1: Integrity

The first core deals with issues of *integrity*. This is what most people think about when they think of trust. To many, "integrity" basically means "honesty." While integrity includes honesty, it's much more. It's integratedness. It's walking your talk. It's being congruent, inside and out. It's having the courage to act in accordance with your values and beliefs. Interestingly, most massive violations of trust are violations of integrity.

Core 2: Intent

The second core deals with issues of *intent*. This has to do with our motives, our agendas, and our resulting behavior. Trust grows when our motives are straightforward and based on mutual benefit—in other words, when we genuinely care not only for ourselves, but also for the people we interact with, lead, or serve. When we suspect a hidden agenda from someone or we don't believe they are acting in our best interests, we are suspicious about everything they say and do.

Both integrity and intent are matters of *character.*

> There are no moral shortcuts in the game of business—or life. There are, basically, three kinds of people: the unsuccessful, the temporarily successful, and those who become and remain successful. The difference is character.
>
> —JON HUNTSMAN, CHAIRMAN, HUNTSMAN CHEMICAL

Core 3: Capabilities

The third core deals with issues of *capabilities.* These are the abilities we have that inspire confidence—our talents, attitudes, skills, knowledge, and style. They are the means we use to produce results. A family doctor might have integrity and his motives might be good, but unless he's trained and skilled to perform the task at hand (brain surgery, for example) he'll be lacking in credibility in that area. Capabilities also deal with our ability to establish, grow, extend, and restore trust.

Core 4: Results

The fourth core deals with issues around *results.* This refers to our track record, our performance, our getting the right things done. If we don't accomplish what we are expected to do, it diminishes our credibility. On the other hand, when we achieve the results we promised, we establish a positive reputation of performing, of being a producer . . . and our reputation precedes us.

Both capabilities and results are matters of *competence.*

> A good leader is probably no different in any culture in the sense that a good leader must have credibility. That is something one establishes . . . based on the way one handles himself and by his established track record.
>
> —DR. VICTOR K. FUNG, GROUP CHAIRMAN, LI & FUNG

As I've said, each of these cores is vital to credibility not only in a court of law, but in any situation. For example, you may have a person who has great integrity, good intent, and a marvelous track record. But if he/she doesn't have the capabilities necessary for a particular job, you won't trust that person to do that job. Or you may have a person who has great integrity, is extremely capable, and has produced excellent results. But if you sense that he/she doesn't really care about you or about your "win" in a particular negotiation, you won't fully trust that person in that situation. In the following chapters, as we look at each core in depth, we will consider the impact of not having that particular core. We will also consider the impact of having that core, but not the other three.

Many of the people you interact with at this point will not recognize these vital 4 Cores of Credibility as parts of the greater whole. They won't realize that your credibility has four dimensions and that you can rate high in some and low in others. They will only see the whole—either you have credibility or you don't.

That's one reason why it's so important for you to understand these 4 Cores. They will help you understand your own credibility and focus on areas where you need to improve. They will give you the wisdom to know how to behave to establish trust. And, as we'll discuss later, they will also give you the judgment to learn how to extend "Smart Trust" to others.

> *Ask yourself . . . mercilessly: Do I exude trust? E-x-u-d-e. Big word. Do I smack of "trust"? Think about it. Carefully.*
>
> —Tom Peters

One way to visualize the importance of all 4 Cores of Credibility is through the metaphor of a tree. *Integrity* is essentially below the surface. It is the root system out of which everything else grows. *Intent* becomes somewhat more visible. It is the trunk that emerges from beneath the surface out into the open. *Capabilities* are the branches. They are the capacities that enable us to produce. *Results* are the fruits—the visible, tangible, measurable outcomes that are most easily seen and evaluated by others.

To look at the 4 Cores of Credibility in this way will enable you to see the interrelatedness of all four and the vital importance of each. It will also help you see credibility as a living, growing thing that can be nurtured. As we go through each of the cores, we will come back to this metaphor of the tree to look more specifically at why each is important and how it relates to the other three.

CHARTING YOUR COURSE

With an understanding of the 4 Cores of Credibility, I'd like you to now go back to the questionnaire results on pages 51 to 53 and reconsider your scores.

Part	Core	Score
1	Integrity	
2	Intent	
3	Capabilites	
4	Results	
Total		

What are your strengths? Which areas need the most improvement?

Whatever your current level of credibility, I am convinced this material will help. At the very least, it will give you language to understand and talk about credibility and trust issues and make them actionable. One of my associates who has taught the Speed of Trust content for several years now recently said, "It's not that I was not credible to begin with. But simply becoming more aware of these things, having a language to talk about them, and behaving in ways that inspire trust has dramatically increased my credibility and my ability to influence others."

As you read the following chapters, be aware that these 4 Cores of Credibility apply not only individually, but also organizationally. A vice president of marketing in a large company recently told me that these 4 Cores would become their marketing blueprint. He said, "We need to be credible as an organization. We need to ensure that customers understand our reputation around integrity. We need to declare our intent to help them win. We need to show them our capabilities to add value to their organizations. We need to demonstrate our results and track record to them so that they will stay with us. The net result of all of this will be credibility, and with that credibility we'll be able to establish and sustain long-term relationships of trust. Our business has already demonstrated that long-term trust relationships are the key to profitable growth."

Our purpose in the next four chapters is to explore each of the 4 Cores in depth—to understand more about what they are, why they are vital to credibility and trust, and how we can improve them in a way that increases trust on every level from the inside out. At the end of each chapter, I've zeroed in on the three top "accelerators," or focused things you can do to make the greatest difference. I suggest you read each of the chapters for understanding and context, then go back and start with the one or two action steps you feel will make the greatest difference for you.

CORE 1—INTEGRITY
ARE YOU CONGRUENT?

I look for three things in hiring people. The first is personal integrity, the second is intelligence, and the third is a high energy level. But, if you don't have the first, the other two will kill you.

—WARREN BUFFETT, CEO, BERKSHIRE HATHAWAY

In the third round of the 2005 Italia Masters tournament in Rome, tennis champion Andy Roddick was paired against Fernando Verdasco from Spain. It was match point in favor of Roddick. When Verdasco hit his second serve, the line judge called the ball "out," and the crowd began to cheer for Roddick. Verdasco moved toward the net to shake hands, as if the match were over.

But Andy Roddick didn't accept the point. Instead, he said that the ball was "in" and called the umpire's attention to a slight indentation on the clay court which showed that the ball had landed *on*—not *beyond*—the line. Surprised, the umpire allowed Roddick to overrule him and the point was awarded to Verdasco.

Everyone was amazed. In a game not typically played on the honor system—but on the umpire's calls—Roddick had made a call against himself and went on to lose the match.

Though Andy Roddick lost the match that day, he gained something far greater. He gained credibility. He gained trust. How did this display of integrity give him credibility? Look at it this way: How are the umpires going to respond the next time Andy Roddick challenges a call? Most likely, they will treat his challenge with the utmost respect. His reputation is known; his credibility will precede him.

Also, how do you think Andy Roddick felt about himself? How *might* he have felt if he chose to accept the win, knowing all along that the ball really wasn't out?

Andy Roddick's behavior on the court that day has become a symbol to me of what I now call "the Roddick Choice"—demonstrating integrity even when it is costly. It illustrates the clear connection between integrity, credibility, and trust—both with others and with ourselves.

> To me, integrity, the root word, really has to do with the whole man, with character, with completeness and goodness. I think of a man or woman of integrity as someone who is balanced and complete, with high character. A person of principle.
>
> —HANK PAULSON, CHAIRMAN AND CEO, GOLDMAN SACHS

To use the metaphor of the tree, integrity is the root. Even though it's underground and not even visible most of the time, it is absolutely vital to the nourishment, strength, stability, and growth of the entire tree. We've all seen people with enormous capability, strong results, even sometimes good intent who unfortunately go about what they're doing in a dishonest or unprincipled way. It's "the ends justify the means" mentality. It leads to manipulation, deceit, fraud, extortion, and scandal—to the Enrons, the WorldComs, the betrayals that destroy marriages and relationships of every kind. Going back to the metaphor of the expert witness, there's no way a person would be considered credible if the other side could prove that she lacked integrity.

On the other hand, to have integrity only—and not the other three cores—is to be a "nice guy," maybe even a thoroughly honest person, who is basically useless. In our tree metaphor, he's like a stump—not good for much. You might trust him to keep a confidence, but there's no way you would trust him to get anything done. He is honest—but irrelevant.

Again, all four cores are vital to credibility and trust.

THE PROBLEM WITH THE RENAISSANCE OF "ETHICS"

So what is integrity? In today's world, many people equate integrity with "ethics." Perhaps at least one good outcome of the recent increase in corporate and other scandals is that it has incited a virtual renaissance of ethics. And most people recognize that the lack of ethics in today's world promotes distrust.

> [O]ut of the ashes of crisis, corruption, and public distrust, a grassroots movement to revitalize the ethics and spirit of free enterprise is gaining momentum and attracting millions.
>
> —PATRICIA ABURDENE, AUTHOR OF *MEGATRENDS 2010*

The problem in organizations, however, is that many "ethics" solutions focus on *compliance*. The compliance definition of "ethics" is not one of integrity or integratedness; it is a watered-down, devalued definition that essentially means "follow the rules." Ethics training, therefore, is often focused exclusively on conformity to Sarbanes-Oxley and other regulatory and rules-based legislation—and not on clarifying values and fostering integrity to those values and to enduring principles.

As a result, companies have huge, complex policy manuals. In addition, people can be duplicitous or even brutal in how they treat others, but unless they're caught fudging on an expense account or violating some other measurable rule, as long as they're getting results, most companies typically won't do anything about it.

> Rules cannot take the place of character.
>
> —ALAN GREENSPAN, FORMER CHAIRMAN,
> U.S. FEDERAL RESERVE

As we'll talk about later in the Third Wave—Organizational Trust—ultimately the problems we're facing in organizations today cannot be solved with this kind of "follow the rules," outside-in compliance approach. As Chris Bauer, a psychologist and corporate ethics trainer, has observed:

> *What we're really talking about here isn't a law enforcement or regulatory issue. It's a psychological issue—an absence of core values, confusion about what is the right thing to do. I see a lot of companies saying that they're going to tighten their rules. I don't see a lot of them saying that they're going to work to be extremely clear about what their values are, and give people training on how those values translate into actual behavior.*

Only as corporations focus on trust and integrity—on congruence rather than compliance—will they really be able to promote true organizational credibility and trust. As Albert Camus said, "Integrity has no need of rules."

DEFINING INTEGRITY

To most people, integrity means honesty. Though some don't consciously realize it, honesty includes not only telling the truth, but also leaving the right impression. It's possible to tell the truth, but leave the wrong impression. And that's not being honest.

> *Whoever is careless with the truth in small matters cannot be trusted with important matters.*
>
> —ALBERT EINSTEIN

Most managers would describe themselves as honest, and yet research shows that most employees don't believe management is honest or communicates honestly. The English writer Maria Louise Ramé said, "I have known a thousand scamps; but I never met one who considered himself so." Her point is humorously dramatized by Captain Jack Sparrow in the movie *Pirates of the Caribbean*, when he says: "I'm dishonest, and a dishonest man you can always trust to be dishonest . . . honestly. It's the honest ones you want to watch out for, because you can never predict when they're going to do something incredibly . . . stupid."

Certainly integrity includes honesty—telling the truth and leaving the right impression. But there are at least three additional qualities that are equally vital.

Congruence. "Integrity" comes from the same Latin root as the words "integrated" and "integer." A person has integrity when there is no gap between intent and behavior . . . when he or she is whole, seamless, the same—inside and out. I call this "congruence." And it is congruence—not compliance—that will ultimately create credibility and trust.

People who are congruent act in harmony with their deepest values and beliefs. They walk their talk. When they feel they ought to do something, they do it. They're not driven by extrinsic forces, including the opinions of others or the expediency of the moment. The voice they listen and respond to is the quiet voice of conscience.

A great example of congruence is Mahatma Gandhi. At one point in his life, he was invited to speak before the House of Commons in England. Using no notes, he spoke for two hours and brought an essentially hostile audience to a rousing standing ovation. Following his speech, some reporters approached his secretary, Mahadev Desai, incredulous that Gandhi could mesmerize his audience for such a long time with no notes. Desai responded:

> *What Gandhi thinks, what he feels, what he says, and what he does are all the same. He does not need notes. . . . You and I, we think one thing, feel another, say a third, and do a fourth, so we need notes and files to keep track.*

Gandhi was not only congruent within himself, he was also congruent with the principles he stood for. Not only did he have roots, he had a taproot that plunged deep into the reservoir of timeless principles that govern in life.

> My life is an indivisible whole, and all my activities run into one another. . . . My life is my message.
>
> —MAHATMA GANDHI

By drawing on the power of such principles and living in a way that was totally congruent to them, Gandhi was able to produce amazing positive results in India and throughout the world—despite the fact that he never held public office or any formal leadership position.

When you consistently demonstrate inner congruence to your belief system and to principles, you inspire trust in both professional and personal relationships. People feel you are strong, solid, and dependable, and that you are committed to live in ways that are certain to bring positive results and validate their confidence in you.

Humility. Integrity also includes humility. In doing the research for *Good to Great*, renowned business expert Jim Collins examined good companies that were transformed into great companies to discover the reason for their extraordinary success. Two things he found surprised him.

The first was that, despite his desire to "ignore the executives" in his research, the data strongly demonstrated that leadership mattered a great deal. As Collins observed, "All the good-to-great companies had Level 5 leadership at the time of transition."

The second was what characterized this "Level 5" leadership. Collins said:

> *We were surprised, shocked really, to discover the type of leadership required for turning a good company into a great one. Compared to high-profile leaders with big personalities who make headlines and become celebrities, the good-to-great leaders seem to have come from Mars. Self-effacing, quiet, reserved, even shy—<u>these leaders are a paradoxical blend of personal humility and professional will</u>. They are more like Lincoln and Socrates than Patton or Caesar* [emphasis added].

So how does humility manifest itself in leadership and in life? A humble person is more concerned about *what* is right than about *being* right, about *acting* on good ideas than *having* the ideas, about *embracing* new truth than *defending* outdated position, about *building the team* than *exalting self*, about *recognizing contribution* than *being recognized* for making it.

Being humble does not mean being weak, reticent, or self-effacing. It means recognizing principle and putting it ahead of self. It means standing firmly for principle, even in the face of opposition. Humble people can negotiate intensely. They can drive hard bargains. They can express themselves firmly and clearly in intense situations in close personal relationships. But they do not get caught up in arrogance, bravado, manipulation, or win-lose power plays. They recognize that there are timeless principles that govern in organizations and relationships, and they try to act in alignment with those principles. They do not seek to become a law unto themselves.

Humble people also realize clearly that they do not stand alone, but rather on the shoulders of those who have gone before, and that they move upward only with the help of others. As Alcoholics Anonymous and other recovery programs are quick to point out, the foundation of dealing with some of our most difficult life challenges is the wisdom and humility to accept the fact that there are some things we simply cannot do without help beyond ourselves.

The opposite of humility is arrogance and pride. It's putting ego first—above principles, above others.

Courage. Integrity also includes the courage to do the right thing—even when it's hard. This is the kind of courage demonstrated by people like Andy Roddick at the Italia Masters, or by Sherron Watkins,

Cynthia Cooper, and Coleen Rowley, three courageous whistle-blowers at Enron, WorldCom, and the FBI respectively, who were honored as *Time* magazine's 2002 Persons of the Year.

To see this kind of courage in the lives of those around us inspires us all to be more courageous. I recently came across a story of courage related by the wife of a man who was in medical school some years ago. She said:

> *Getting into medical school is pretty competitive, and the desire to do well and be successful puts a great deal of pressure on the new incoming freshmen. My husband had worked hard on his studies and went to attend his first examination. The honor system was expected behavior at the medical school. The professor passed out the examination and left the room. Within a short time, students started to pull little cheat papers out from under their papers or from their pockets. My husband recalled his heart beginning to pound as he realized it is pretty hard to compete against cheaters. About that time a tall, lanky student stood up in the back of the room and stated: "I left my hometown and put my wife and three little babies in an upstairs apartment and worked very hard to get into medical school. And I'll turn in the first one of you who cheats, and you better believe it!" They believed it. There were many sheepish expressions, and those cheat papers started to disappear as fast as they had appeared. He set a standard for the class which eventually graduated the largest group in the school's history.*

The man who stood up in the classroom that day later became a respected physician. Certainly what he did was neither comfortable nor easy. But it demonstrated the kind of courage required by integrity—the kind of courage that affirmed timeless principles, lifted others, and made life better for all of us who depend on a physician's knowledge and skill when our health and our lives are at stake.

> Courage is the first of the human qualities because it is a quality which guarantees all the others.
>
> —WINSTON CHURCHILL

As you consider people you believe have integrity, can you see these qualities playing out in their lives? Undoubtedly, they are honest. But are they also congruent, humble, and courageous? What effect do you think their integrity has on the way they feel about themselves? What effect does this have on the way you feel about them? Are they credible in your eyes? Do you trust them?

To one degree or another, we can probably all improve in each of these areas. By doing so, we can also improve our own credibility and ultimately increase the speed and lower the cost of everything we do.

HOW TO INCREASE YOUR INTEGRITY

So how do we go about increasing our integrity?

First, we need to consider what degree of integrity we currently have. At this point, you might find it helpful to review the following questions based on the self-assessment questionnaire.

- Do I genuinely try to be honest in all my interactions with others?
- Do I typically "walk my talk"?
- Am I clear on my values? Do I feel comfortable in standing up for them?
- Am I open to the possibility of learning new truths that may cause me to rethink issues or even redefine my values?
- Am I able to consistently make and keep commitments to myself?

I urge you to really think about these questions and answer them candidly. You may also want to do what we do in our Speed of Trust workshops—get feedback from your boss, peers, direct reports, customers, friends, or family members concerning their perception of you in each of these areas. Because we all have "blind spots," we sometimes tend to overestimate or underestimate our own level of strength.

In addition, I'd like to suggest three high-leveraged "accelerators" that make a powerful difference in increasing integrity.

1. Make and Keep Commitments to Yourself

There is absolutely nothing you can do that will increase integrity faster than learning how to make and keep commitments to yourself. In the Second Wave—Relationship Trust, we'll talk about the power of making and keeping commitments to others. But there's no way you will be able to do that effectively if you haven't first learned to make and keep commitments to yourself.

Part of my family heritage is the story of how my great-grandfather Stephen Mack Covey started the Little America hotel chain. While working as a sheepherder in the 1890s, he got caught in a blizzard one winter night in the middle of Wyoming. As the storm raged, the effects of the 50-mile-per-hour winds and below-zero temperatures became so intense that he genuinely thought he wasn't going to survive. As he hunkered down, he made a commitment to himself and to God that if he made it through the night, he would build a shelter for others right there in that obscure, unpopulated location as a symbol of his gratitude.

Well, he did make it through the night, and although it took some time, he eventually built that "shelter" out there in the middle of nowhere. Today, there's only a gas station and the sprawling Little America Motel. But the town of Little America, Wyoming, now has its own place on the map, and it has become a popular tourist stop. It also became the foundation of an extraordinary business career. Before he died, my great-grandfather had established several strong regional businesses, including hotels, apartments, petroleum interests, and financial services.

Now, I'm sure it would have been easy for someone in my great-grandfather's situation to say, "It would be ridiculous to build a motel out here in the middle of nowhere!" Nobody knew about that commitment except my great-grandfather and God. But Stephen Mack Covey had made a serious commitment to himself, and he kept it. And the power of his keeping that commitment has had a profound impact on all of his descendants, including me.

The more experience I've had, both personally and professionally, the more convinced I have become of the importance of making and keeping commitments to ourselves. These can be big commitments, like my great-grandfather's, or they can be small commitments, even very small commitments, such as getting up when the alarm clock goes off, not overeating, or speaking respectfully to others, even when provoked to do otherwise. Every time we make and keep a commitment to ourselves—large or small—we increase our self-confidence. We build our reserves. We enlarge our capacity to make and keep greater commitments, both to ourselves and to others.

As you consider how you might step up your ability to make and keep commitments to yourself, let me suggest a few important things to keep in mind:

First, don't make too many commitments. If you do, you're setting yourself up for failure. Differentiate between a goal, a direction, a focus, and an actual commitment. When you make a commitment to yourself, do so with the clear understanding that you're pledging your integrity.

Second, treat a commitment you make to yourself with as much respect as you do the commitments you make to others. Whether it's a commitment of time (an appointment with yourself to exercise or read or sleep) or a commitment to prioritize your energy and focus, treat it—and yourself—with respect.

Third, don't make commitments impulsively. I learned this lesson the hard way one time when we were having a family discussion about health. It was around New Year's, and as we were talking, we decided that we all needed to drink more water instead of soda pop. I started to really get caught up in the spirit of improvement, and—filled with bravado (but no humility)—I said, "I'll tell you what I am going to do. I am going to make a commitment to myself to drink nothing but water for this entire year! No soda, no juices—nothing but water!" Well, that was foolish and I lived to regret it. I kept the commitment, but it was hard. Out of the experience, I learned to be careful about making commitments and to make sure they were made out of humility, and not pride.

Finally, understand that when keeping your commitment becomes hard, you have two choices: You can change your behavior to match your commitment, or you can lower your values to match your behavior. One choice will strengthen your integrity; the other will diminish it and erode your confidence in your ability to make and keep commitments in the future. In addition, that shift in direction with regard to values—even if it's slight—will create a change in trajectory that will create a far more significant difference in destination down the road.

So I encourage you to learn to make and keep commitments to yourself with wisdom. There is no faster way to build self trust.

2. Stand for Something

> *Be valued and principle based. Know what you stand for, and live by those standards.*
>
> —GEORGE FISCHER, CHAIRMAN, EASTMAN KODAK

The chairman and CEO of American Express, Ken Chenault, has created a book for all employees called *Next Chapter (A Guide to the New American Express)*. This book provides an outline of where the company is going in the future and how it plans to get there. One of the key tenets reads as follows:

Stand for Something. *Some value(s) can't be quantified. Success at any cost isn't the point. It's winning the right way that matters. . . . We also must consistently prove through our actions that we stand for the right things—customer commitment, quality, integrity, teamwork, respect for people, good citizenship, a will to win, personal accountability and so much more.*

If you're going to have integrity—or integratedness—you have to have a core, something to which you must be true. You can't work from the inside out if you don't even know what's inside. So you need to have a center. You need to have identified values. You need to know what you stand for and you need to stand for it, so that others know, too.

> To believe in something, and not to live it, is dishonest.
>
> —Mahatma Gandhi

A great example of integrity, both in keeping a commitment and in standing for something, is Jon Huntsman, chairman of Huntsman Chemical. As he relates in his book, *Winners Never Cheat*, following lengthy negotiations, Huntsman agreed to sell 40 percent of a division of his company to Great Lakes Chemical. A simple handshake with Emerson Kampen, chairman and CEO of Great Lakes, sealed the $54 million deal.

However, Great Lakes dragged their feet in preparing the written agreement. In the six and a half months it took them to get the deal down on paper, the price of raw materials had decreased substantially, Huntsman profits had tripled, and Huntsman margins had reached an all-time high. Forty percent of the division had increased in value from $54 million to $250 million.

With the deal not yet signed, Kampen called Huntsman and said that while he didn't feel he should pay the full difference in value, he thought it was only fair that he should pay half. So he offered to split the difference. But Huntsman said no; they had shaken hands and agreed on $54 million and he would stick to that price.

Kampen said, "But that's not fair to you!"

Huntsman's response was, "You negotiate for your company, Emerson, and let me negotiate for mine."

Kampen was so impressed with this display of integrity that, even though he and Huntsman were never personally close, he prearranged for Huntsman to be one of two people to speak at his funeral.

Obviously, Jon Huntsman stood for something. As he said in writing about this experience, "Even though I could have forced Great Lakes to pay an extra $200 million for that 40 percent ownership stake in my company, I never had to wrestle with my conscience or to look over my shoulder. My word was my bond."

Jon Huntsman knew what was important to him. His values were clear. He didn't have to struggle when circumstances challenged those values. And clearly, standing for his values inspired trust.

> It's not hard to make decisions when you know what your values are.
>
> —ROY DISNEY, FORMER VICE CHAIRMAN,
> WALT DISNEY COMPANY

An excellent way to identify the values you want to stand for is to go through some kind of purpose- or values-clarification process. I have found nothing more valuable than the creation of a mission statement or credo, whether it be personal, family, or organizational. Creating an expression of what you stand for—and living by it—will pay great dividends in helping you become credible and trusted.

> Who you are, what your values are, what you stand for . . .
> They are your anchor, your north star. You won't find them
> in a book. You'll find them in your soul.
>
> —ANNE MULCAHY, CHAIRMAN AND CEO, XEROX

3. Be Open

You've probably been around people you consider close-minded or arrogant—people who don't really listen to you because they think there's nothing you could say they don't already know; people who refuse to consider new ways of looking at things because they are convinced that theirs is the only accurate way of thinking; people who will stare truth in the face and reject it because they're not willing to accept the possibility that there is some reality, some principle out there, they weren't even aware of. How does that ego-invested attitude affect your ability to relate to these people? How does it affect your perception of their credibility? How does it affect your willingness to extend trust?

Openness is vital to integrity. It takes both humility and courage—humility to acknowledge that there are principles out there you may not currently be aware of, and courage to follow them once you discover them. Throughout history, most paradigm shifts in science have been shifts from traditional thinking—shifts that took this kind of humility and courage.

A good way to increase integrity, then, is to work on being open. Consider Anwar Sadat, who served as the third president of Egypt from 1970 until his assassination in 1981. Raised in a culture and leading the government of one nation among many that were strongly anti-Israeli, Sadat nevertheless demonstrated openness when the voice of conscience urged him to pursue peace. Despite the outrage of his Arab neighbors, he drew upon a lesson he had learned earlier in life as he sat in a cell in the Cairo Central Prison: "[H]e who cannot change the very fabric of his thought will never be able to change reality, and will never, therefore, make any progress." He traveled to Israel, met with Israeli Prime Minister Menachem Begin, and spoke to the Knesset. He subsequently traveled to the United States and met with Begin and then U.S. President Jimmy Carter. Their discussions led to the Camp David Accords, for which both Begin and Sadat received the Nobel Peace Prize.

A few years ago, both my father and I had the privilege of having lunch with Sadat's widow, Jehan, and then hearing her speak. What I remember best about her description of her husband's experience was his willingness to be open and to relearn what he thought he had already known.

People like Anwar Sadat or South Africa's Nelson Mandela or Mikhail Gorbachev of the former Soviet Union play out on the main stage of human drama the same theme we see repeated in our own interactions with coworkers, family members, and friends. To be open inspires credibility and trust; to be closed fosters suspicion and mistrust.

As you evaluate your own openness, you might ask yourself:

- Do I believe that the way I see the world is totally accurate and complete—or am I honestly willing to listen to and consider new viewpoints and ideas?
- Do I seriously consider differing points of view (from a boss, direct report, team member, spouse, or child), and am I willing to be influenced by them?

- Do I believe there may be principles that I have not yet discovered? Am I determined to live in harmony with them, even if it means developing new thinking patterns and habits?
- Do I value—and am I involved in—continual learning?

To the degree to which you remain open to new ideas, possibilities, and growth, you create a trust dividend; to the degree you do not, you create a trust tax that impacts both your current and future performance.

THE IMPACT ON SPEED AND COST

> *Greed destroys wealth. Trust and integrity, by contrast, foster prosperity.*
>
> —PATRICIA ABURDENE, AUTHOR OF *MEGATRENDS 2010*

These three "accelerators"—make and keep commitments to yourself, stand for something, and be open—will help you increase your integrity. They will also increase the speed and decrease the cost with which you do the important things in your life—every time!

The greater your integrity—the more honest, congruent, humble, and courageous you are—the more credibility you will have and the more trust you will inspire. The more you will be able to transform trust taxes into trust dividends in every dimension of your life.

CORE 2—INTENT
WHAT'S YOUR AGENDA?

> *In law, a man is guilty when he violates the rights of another. In ethics, he is guilty if he only thinks of doing so.*
>
> —IMMANUEL KANT

I hope my parents will forgive me for sharing a rather funny story about them, but it really does help me make the point.

One day this past winter, my dad and mom (whom I'll refer to by name—Stephen and Sandra) were returning from their cabin in Montana. They were extremely tired, as they had spent the morning snowmobiling with young family members. Stephen felt he was too tired to drive, so Sandra took the wheel while he lay down in the backseat of the car and instantly fell asleep.

After a couple of hours, Sandra could barely keep her eyes open, so she pulled to the side of the freeway and woke Stephen, saying she couldn't wait to crawl into the backseat and have her turn to sleep. They opened the car doors and got out to make the switch. Stephen slipped into the driver's seat, and as Sandra was about to shut his door and go to the back, she suddenly remembered that their new car had a special feature that allowed people to raise or lower the chassis for convenience. Because of her bad knee, she said to Stephen, "Please lower the car so I can get in easier," and she slammed the doors so he could do it.

Almost immediately, Sandra was surprised to see the car begin to quickly move forward. Thinking Stephen was pretending to leave her (which was a logical conclusion, given his sense of humor), she started chasing after the car. Suddenly, the car sped up, and she was left standing on the side of the freeway all alone.

As it was winter and she didn't have a coat on and was in her stocking feet, Sandra thought this was not the right time for a joke, and Stephen was really going to get it when he came back! But after ten minutes of standing alone on the freeway freezing, she finally came to the conclusion that Stephen must have thought she had gotten into the car and was asleep in the backseat!

Apparently, Stephen never heard Sandra ask for the car to be lowered, and when he heard the back door slam, he assumed she was in. Knowing how exhausted she was, he thought that she had instantly fallen asleep among the cozy blankets and pillows. Since Sandra liked to make a lot of stops for restroom breaks and snacks, Stephen thought if he remained really quiet, she might just sleep the whole way and he could make good time getting home.

As luck would have it, a man in another car had seen Stephen drive off and leave Sandra, and he saw her chase the car down the freeway. Doing what he thought was his civic duty, he called the highway patrol and reported that he had just seen a man abandon a woman on the side of the road.

Soon, a patrol car pulled up to Sandra, and the patrolman asked Sandra what had happened.

"My husband left me here, but I don't think he knows," she said.

Suspecting potential domestic abuse, he asked, "Did you have a fight, ma'am? Why would he leave you and drive off?"

"I'm sure he thinks I'm in the backseat asleep."

"He thinks you're in the backseat of his car? Don't you think it's strange that he wouldn't notice you weren't there?"

"No, I'm sure he thinks I'm sound asleep."

"What's your name?"

"Sandra Covey."

There was a long pause. "Are you any relation to Stephen Covey, the author? I had a class from him once!"

"He's the one who left me!"

As Sandra and the patrolman continued to talk, Sandra remembered Stephen had a cell phone with him, so they called him.

"Mr. Covey, this is the highway patrol. You need to pull over immediately, and I need to know your exact location."

Confused as to how the highway patrol had his cell phone number, and wondering if he was speeding, he said, "All right, officer. I think

I'm somewhere by Idaho Falls, but I don't know exactly because I've been asleep. My wife has been driving up until about 10 or 15 minutes ago. I'll ask her where we are."

Then he yelled toward the backseat, "Sandra! Sandra! Wake up! There's a highway patrolman on the phone and he wants to know our exact location."

"Mr. Covey! Mr. Covey!" the patrolman said loudly into the phone. "Your wife isn't there."

"She's just asleep in the backseat," Stephen replied impatiently. "Wait! I'll pull over and wake her up." So Stephen pulled over and looked in the backseat. Then he began frantically searching through the blankets and pillows. Sandra wasn't there!

"My wife is missing!" he exclaimed.

"She's in the car with me!" the patrolman replied.

"With you? Well, how did she get there?"

"You left her on the side of the road a while ago."

"What?" he said incredulously. "You mean she didn't get in? Oh, I can't believe it! I wondered why she was so quiet!"

Well, the patrol car finally found Stephen and they all had a good laugh as they pieced together what happened . Stephen said, "My kids just won't believe this one."

The patrolman said, "That's nothing! Wait until I tell the guys down at the department. It's a classic!"

THE IMPORTANCE OF INTENT

Now here's a question for you: If you'd seen all this going on, what would you have thought was Stephen's *intent*?

At first, Sandra assumed his intent was to play a joke by pretending to leave her. Why? Because he has quite a sense of humor and he's done many things like that before. Once she realized what had happened, however, she assumed Stephen had not known she was not in the car, and that his intent in not trying to interact with her was to let her sleep. Why? Because she knew his character. She knew he cared about her, would want her to rest, and would never consciously leave her in that situation.

The man who phoned the highway patrol, on the other hand, didn't know Stephen's character, and he evidently assumed Stephen's intent was to abandon Sandra. Why? Who knows? Maybe he'd had experience with abandonment in his own life. Or maybe he had been sensitized to the possibility (as most of us have) by our social culture of increasing abandonment and abuse.

The highway patrolman also didn't know Stephen's character, and at first, he assumed there was some kind of bad intent involved. Why? Likely because he had seen a lot of domestic abuse in his profession, and his experience created the lens through which he initially viewed the events.

What was Stephen's real intent? Obviously, there was *no* intent to leave Sandra freezing at the side of the road. I'd like to say that his whole intent in not trying to talk to her was to give her the chance to get a good rest. But, as he himself admitted, he also really wanted to get home as quickly as possible, and he knew she would want to stop along the way if she were awake.

This whole experience brings up some of the important issues we're dealing with when we talk about intent:

- Intent matters.
- It grows out of character.
- While we tend to judge ourselves by our intent, we tend to judge others by their behavior.
- We also tend to judge others' intent based on our own paradigms and experience.
- Our perception of intent has a huge impact on trust.
- People often distrust us because of the conclusions they draw about what we do.
- It is important for us to actively influence the conclusions others draw by "declaring our intent."

THE IMPACT OF INTENT ON TRUST

The World Economic Forum does an annual worldwide study comparing the amount of trust people have in various institutions, including national governments, global companies, and large local companies. Can you guess who has come out on top every year since the survey began? It's the NGOs—those private national and international not-for-profit "Non-Governmental Organizations" involved in addressing societal issues such as health, human rights, poverty, and the environment.

In surveys comparing trust levels in various professions, can you guess who consistently comes out dead last? It's the politicians.

So what's the difference? Why is our trust in NGOs so high and our trust in politicians so low? Think about the 4 Cores of Credibility. For the most part, both NGOs and politicians have strong capabilities. Both have established track records of results. To some extent, integrity may be more of an issue for politicians (or political opponents or the media may try to ascribe problems to integrity issues).

I contend that, by far, the primary differentiator between our perceptions of NGOs and politicians is a matter of *intent*—either the real intent or the assumed or ascribed intent of those involved. What is their motive or agenda? Do they really care about what's best for everyone involved? Or are they primarily interested in political power, party politics, their own ego, or in what they can get out of it for themselves?

With NGOs, the motives are generally honorable and clear; the agenda is to add value to a specific, beneficial purpose or mission. With politicians, however, intent is often seen as doing what is best for the politician or for the party, but not necessarily for the whole.

The impact of intent issues on trust is dramatic. Some time ago, a translator for CNN mistranslated one word in a speech given by President Mahmoud Ahmadinejad of Iran. Instead of developing "nuclear *technology*," President Ahmadinejad was reported to have talked about developing "nuclear *weapons*." In the already highly charged political environment surrounding Iran's nuclear interests, CNN was immediately thrown out of Iran. Hossein Shariatmadari, chief editor of the *Kayhan* newspaper, said, "*The distortion was deliberate* with the aim of preventing the impact of the president's comments on the public opinion."

Notice the immediate focus on and ascription of motive or intent . . . and the result. Following a public apology, CNN was allowed back into Iran. But in this instance—and in dozens of interactions each day, if we have eyes to see—the dramatic impact of intent issues becomes blazingly apparent.

Going back to our "expert witness" metaphor, one of the focal efforts of the opposition would be to discredit a witness based on intent: Why would this person be giving this testimony? What is she going to get out of it? Is there a conflict of interest? Is she getting paid by the company she's testifying for? If the opposition can give any cause to suspect intent, the witness's testimony will be tainted.

The intent focus becomes an even more important issue—in fact, a pivotal issue—for the person who is on trial. "What motive might this person have for committing this crime?" In most trials, intent, or motive, is a major determining factor.

As illustrated in the tree metaphor, intent is represented by the trunk—partly unseen underground, partly visible above. While our motives and agendas are deep inside in our own hearts and minds, they become visible to others through our behaviors and as we share them with others.

Like each of the other cores, intent is vital to trust. A person with integrity, capability, and results—but poor intent—would be someone who is honest and has capabilities and results, but whose motive is suspect. Maybe he/she wants to win, even at the expense of others. And others can sense that, and thus feel that they can't fully extend trust. On the other hand, a person of good intent without the other three cores (integrity, capability, and results) would be a caring person who is dishonest or cowardly with no developed talents or skills and no track record. Again, all 4 Cores are vital.

As we prepare to explore the issue of intent, you may want to ask yourself questions such as the following:

- How often do I discount (or "tax") what someone says because I am suspicious about that person's intent?
- What kind of tax is my organization paying because employees don't trust management's intent? What is the impact on speed and cost?
- What kind of tax are we paying as a team because we are suspicious of one another's motives?
- What kind of tax am I paying because people question my own intent?
- What can I do to improve and better communicate my intent?

Questions such as these will help you prepare your mind and heart as we look at what constitutes intent and how we can improve it.

WHAT IS "INTENT"?

In the dictionary, intent is defined as "plan" or "purpose." I am convinced that no discussion of intent would be complete without talking about three things: motive, agenda, and behavior.

Motive. Motive is your reason for doing something. It's the "why" that motivates the "what."

The motive that inspires the greatest trust is genuine caring—caring about people, caring about purposes, caring about the quality of what you do, caring about society as a whole. Think about it: Are you going to trust someone who could really care less about you . . . or about work . . . or about principles, or values, or anyone or anything else?

People just want to know that somebody knows, and cares.

—DENNIS P. LESTRANGE, FORMER SENIOR VICE PRESIDENT,
IKON OFFICE SOLUTIONS

The trust we have in people and in organizations comes, in part, from believing that they do care. I remember as a child when my parents had to discipline me for one infraction or another, they always did it with love. I didn't like the discipline. Often I resented it. But there was never a question in my mind or heart that my parents were doing it because they cared. I always knew that I could trust their love for me.

Companies worldwide recognize the importance of caring. How many advertisements do you see that communicate—either in words or through visual image association—messages such as these: "We care about you." "We care about quality." "We care about the environment." "We care about our communities and making a positive difference." Companies hope that by communicating this image of caring, you will have trust in and buy their services and products.

Much has been written recently about how caring actually leads to better performance. Works such as *The Art of Caring Leadership* and *Contented Cows Give Better Milk* clearly validate the strong connection between concern for others and performance. Yahoo executive Tim Sanders writes about the impact of caring in very practical terms in *Love Is the Killer App*, in which he shows how caring and compassion for others can be translated into specific behaviors that constitute a better way of doing business for all. I maintain that this undeniable connection between caring and performance exists because caring and concern engender trust.

Clearly, motive matters, and the motive of caring will do more than anything else to build credibility and trust. But what if you genuinely don't care? What if your real motive is profit or accumulation or recognition—period? What if you really don't care about customers or employees? Should you try to convince them that you do?

If you really don't care—and you don't want to care—that's fine. But you need to understand that *you will pay a tax because of it!* Whatever you say or do will take more time and it will cost more because you will not gain the credibility and trust that come from caring. You may think you're already getting good results, but you need to ask yourself a bigger question: What am I leaving on the table?

You also need to understand that if you act like you care when you really don't, ultimately—if not immediately—you will have a "comeuppance" and the tax will be even greater. In fact, there are few trust taxes that are higher than those attached to duplicity, particularly regarding motive.

> The only thing worse than a coach or CEO who doesn't care about his people is one who pretends to care. People can spot a phony every time. They know he doesn't care about them, and worse, his act insults their intelligence.
>
> —JIMMY JOHNSON, FORMER COACH,
> DALLAS COWBOYS AND MIAMI DOLPHINS

So if you really don't care—and you have no intent to change— you're generally much better off being transparent about it and simply recognizing that you're paying a tax because of it. However, if you don't care now, but *you sincerely desire to care*, there are definitely things you can do to elevate your motive, to improve your intent. I will address this issue in the last part of this chapter.

Agenda. Agenda grows out of motive. It's what you intend to do or promote because of your motive.

The agenda that generally inspires the greatest trust is seeking mutual benefit— genuinely wanting what's best for everyone involved. It's not just that you care about others; you also genuinely want them to win. Yes, you're seeking a win for yourself; that's natural, desirable, and to be expected. But you're also seeking a win for all others involved. You recognize that life is interdependent, so you seek out solutions that build trust and benefit all.

> Having spent many years trying to define the essentials of trust, I arrived at the position that if two people could say two things to each other and mean them, then there was the basis for real trust. The two things were "I mean you no harm" and "I seek your greatest good."
>
> —JIM MEEHAN, BRITISH PSYCHOLOGIST AND POET

The opposite of a mutual benefit agenda is a self-serving agenda: "I want to win—period." If that's your agenda, you might get results. But you need to ask yourself: Are these the best possible results I could be getting? And: Are these results sustainable over time? The answer to both of these questions is "no." Sooner or later, you will pay a huge tax. And your approach will not be sustainable. Instead of building bridges of credibility and trust, you're creating roadblocks of suspicion and distrust.

Let me share with you the experience of Shea Homes—an outstanding example of the dividends that come from a genuine mutual benefit agenda. In the construction industry, which is typically very "win/lose" and adversarial between contractors and subcontractors, Shea Homes decided to create a different model. Among the many steps they took, they renamed their subs as "trade partners" and opened their financials to them on shared projects. They were transparent. Their operating premise was, "We want to win, but we want you to win, too. And together, we can better help our customers win. So how can we make this work?"

The difference between this and the traditional adversarial approach was like night and day. And the results they achieved reflected an enormous trust dividend on nearly every measure: the number of days it took them to build homes went down, costs went down, quality errors decreased, customer satisfaction increased, and referrals from customers increased. They made more money. Their partners made more money. Their customers were happier. Everybody won.

The Shea Homes example clearly shows the impact of a mutual benefit agenda on trust. It also shows the power of having an agenda that is *open* as opposed to *hidden* or *closed*. You've probably been in dozens, if not hundreds, of meetings or interactions where you felt that people were not being up-front with you about what they really wanted or were trying to accomplish—in other words, they were operating with hidden agendas. Most likely, these agendas were recognizable to you to one degree or another, and they made you feel suspicious, wary, guarded, and uncomfortable. Think about the tax that was being paid as a result. Think about the impact on speed and cost. Think about the dividend everyone could have enjoyed instead had there been no concern about veiled motives or disguised intent—if all agendas had been out in the open, and particularly if the main agenda had been to do what was genuinely best for all involved.

Behavior. Typically, behavior is the manifestation of motive and agenda. *The behavior that best creates credibility and inspires trust is acting in the best interest of others.* When we do so, we clearly demonstrate the intent of caring and the agenda of seeking mutual benefit. And this is where the rubber meets the road. It's easy to say "I care" and "I want you to win," but it is our actual behavior that demonstrates whether or not we mean it.

> *I feel that you have to be with your employees through all their difficulties, that you have to be interested in them personally. I want them to know that Southwest will always be there for them.*
>
> —HERB KELLEHER, CHAIRMAN, SOUTHWEST AIRLINES

An excellent example of behaving in a way that demonstrates caring and inspires trust is Howard Shultz, founder and chairman of Starbucks. In 1997, three Starbucks employees were murdered during a robbery attempt at one of the Starbucks stores in Washington, D.C. On hearing about it, Howard Shultz immediately chartered a plane to D.C. He spent an entire week there, working with the police, consoling the victims' families, and meeting with employees. He attended the funerals. But then he went well beyond what might be expected by announcing that he was going to devote all future profits from the store to "organizations working for victims' rights and violence prevention."

By demonstrating such deep caring and concern for these three employees and their families, Howard Shultz demonstrated care and concern for the thousands of Starbucks employees and their families. And they felt it. There was no doubt in anybody's mind that he cared. They thought, "Wow, if he would do this for these people and their families, he would do that for me. I'm proud to work for this company."

Putting a positive twist on the mafia creed—"Punish one, teach a hundred"—Shultz demonstrated that in showing profound concern for the few, you teach an entire company. And those who worked for the company extended the caring they felt to the way in which they treated their customers, resulting in what Schultz has called "a higher-quality employee, an employee that cares more." This is one of the reasons why Starbucks has such a great culture, performs well, and has been named as one of the 100 Best Companies to Work for in America.

Unfortunately, this outstanding example is not the norm. In many organizations, the message communicated by behavior is not "We care"; it's "You're expendable, replaceable. What we care about is profit." In fact, research shows that:

- Only 29% of employees believe that management cares about them developing their skills.
- Only 42% believe that management cares about them at all.

What kind of impact is that having on trust and on the speed and cost required in these organizations to get things done?

Acting in the best interest of others is a behavior that typically flows out of a caring motive and an agenda of mutual benefit. However, there are times when observable behavior that communicates one message is, in reality, an act of duplicity or deceit. It's the "I care about you" show of an "I really could care less about you, but I want to project the image of caring" person. Don't forget that *the real behavior here is deceit*, and this is what will almost always come across in the end. The show is not sustainable, and the resulting devastation to one's credibility—and ultimately to trust—is immense.

THE TRUSTEE STANDARD

When we believe people truly are acting in our best interest, we tend to trust them. When we believe that they are not acting in our best interest, we do not trust them.

It's that simple.

Think about the word "trustee." A "trustee" is someone who is given legal authority to manage money or property on behalf of someone else. The fiduciary standard is that a trustee will act in the "best interest" of the person he/she represents. The very word "trustee" communicates the idea that this person is "entrusted" to do so. This is what I call the "trustee standard": acting in the best interest of others.

Think about the whole issue of unionism. Unions are a reality in much of organizational life worldwide and aren't necessarily bad. They represent good people and are often found in great companies such as Southwest, Toyota, and Saturn.

But the fundamental reason most unions are formed (particularly in the U.S.) is that employee groups do *not* trust that management will act in their best interests. In other words, employees feel they need to organize to act in their own best interests because management will not. Thus, unionism itself is typically a fruit of distrust, coming from a perceived violation of the trustee standard.

> I think every good company has got to have . . . a partnership relationship, really, with their employees. You have got to work in their best interest . . . and eventually it will come back to the company.
>
> —SAM WALTON, FOUNDER, WAL-MART AND SAM'S CLUB

BAD EXECUTION OF GOOD INTENT

It's important to keep in mind that sometimes, unfortunately, poor behavior turns out to be bad execution of good intent. That certainly was the case when my father left my mother stranded alone on the highway! His intent was good, but his execution was poor.

It's also good to keep in mind that people typically judge us—and we judge them—based on observable behavior. Thus, we need to do all we can to ensure that our behavior accurately reflects our true motives and agendas.

Also, we need to be careful how we judge others. I have a friend who constantly ascribes negative motives to drivers who exhibit what he considers inappropriate behavior (such as cutting him off) when he's on the road. His wife always comes up with other possibilities: "Well, maybe he has to get to the hospital" or "Maybe he's late to pick up his little daughter" or "Maybe his dog died." As Scottish author J. M. Barrie said, "Never ascribe to an opponent [or I would say to anyone] motives meaner than your own."

I would also say to be careful to not interpret the intent of others by projecting your own intent onto their behavior—and also to realize that often others may be interpreting your intent in this way. As your experience will undoubtedly tell you (and as I discovered deeply and personally through the FranklinCovey merger experience a few years ago), none of us likes to have bad motives unfairly attributed to our behavior. Again, we tend to judge others based on their behavior, and ourselves based on our intent. In almost all situations, we would do well to recognize the possibility—even probability—of good intent in others . . . sometimes despite their observable behavior.

In choosing to look beyond the behavior of others (especially teenage children or troubled coworkers) and affirming our belief in them and in their positive intent, we lift them. Our own behavior in doing so gives expression to our higher motives and caring intent.

HOW TO IMPROVE INTENT

Fundamentally, intent is a matter of the heart. It's something you can't fake—at least not for long. But it is something you can definitely work on and improve.

Some people genuinely have poor intent. Though they may not be aware of it or even admit it, deep inside they seek their own profit, position, or possessions above people, above principle, above everything else.

Others have good intent—they sincerely want to do what's right and seek the welfare of others—but their expression or execution of intent is poor.

Though we may not realize it, most of us deal with at least some degree of challenge in both of these areas. If we're really honest, we have to admit that sometimes our motives are not completely pure. Sometimes we approach situations with hidden agendas—even tiny ones—that keep us from being appropriately transparent with others. Sometimes we manifest behaviors that don't demonstrate caring, openness, and concern. To whatever degree these challenges are part of our lives, we are being taxed, both personally and professionally.

The challenge, then, is to improve intent. So here are the top three accelerators I recommend to help you do it.

1. Examine and Refine Your Motives

It's human tendency to assume we have good—or at least, justifiable—intent. At times, our intent genuinely is good; at other times, we rationalize (tell ourselves "rational lies") in order to justify our intent to ourselves and to others. So how do we get down to the deepest level to really examine our motives, discover why we really do what we do, and change what needs to be changed?

One good way is to regularly ask soul-searching questions, such as the following:

- *In an interaction with a child:* Are my actions motivated by genuine caring and love? Am I really seeking the best interests of this child? Am I humble enough to admit it if I am wrong? Or am I really trying to impose my will on this child?
- *In an interaction with a spouse:* Am I sincerely listening to what my spouse has to say? Am I genuinely open to his/her influence? Do I understand where he/she is coming from? Or am I focused on explaining my point of view, being right, or getting my way?
- *In an interaction with a work team:* Am I quick to see and acknowledge the contribution of every team member? Am I focused on a "win" for the entire team? Or am I primarily focused on my own "win"—on being the "hero," on being recognized for my own ideas?
- *In a business deal:* Do I genuinely want what's best for us both? Do I really understand what constitutes a "win" for the other party? Have I clearly thought through and can I express what constitutes a "win" for me? Am I open to synergy and third alter-

natives? Or do I really want to 'win," regardless of what happens to the other party?

In my own life, the more I have interacted with others on every level of life—in my family, friendships, work, church, and community associations—the more I have come to realize the importance of regularly examining my motives. As I have had occasion to speak to groups in my church, for example, I have come to realize the value of constantly asking myself this question: Am I seeking to bless, or to impress? This helps me keep my purpose in mind and to speak with greater openness and integrity.

Another good way to examine your motives is to use an adaptation of the "five whys"—a simple problem-solving technique made popular in the 1970s by the Toyota Production System. Toyota's idea was to start with the end problem and work backward through a series of "whys" until you get to the root cause. We have found this process works very well with self and others to discover real intent.

For example, suppose you're feeling undervalued, unappreciated, and generally upset about your current situation at work, and you set up a meeting with your boss to discuss it. Going through the "five whys" with yourself in advance could have a significant effect on the content of the meeting and on the outcome.

1. Why am I feeling unappreciated and undervalued? *Because I don't think the people around here see the good work I do.*
2. Why do I think they don't see the good work I do? *Because they seem to be totally focused on the new blood—the "rising stars."*
3. What makes me think they're focused on the rising stars? *The fact that Sarah got promoted last week—and it should have been me!*
4. Why do I think Sarah got promoted instead of me? *I don't know. Maybe that's what I really want to talk to my boss about.*
5. Why do I want to talk to the boss about it? *Well, I suppose my original intent was to vent and complain about Sarah's promotion. But I guess what I really want to understand is what I can do to add more value to the company so that I will be considered more seriously when future promotions come around.*

Generally, after "five whys," you're either down to the real intent or very close to it. Once you discover the real "why," you can decide whether you're satisfied with your intent or you want to change it. The key is simple: If your intent is based on principles (caring, contributing, seeking mutual benefit, acting in the best interest of others), it will bring you trust dividends; if it's not, you're going to be paying a tax.

So if you need to refine or elevate your intent, I suggest a few ideas:

First, make sure you have identified the principles that will bring the results you want.

Second, recognize that you may need help to create this deep inner change—and seek it. For some, this will involve searching out role models, reading biographies of caring people, or creating a mental/spiritual daily diet of the uplifting, caring thoughts expressed in the wisdom literature throughout the ages. It might include seeking help from caring mentors or through meditation and prayer. At the very least—and foundational to all other help—rescripting will require the constant assistance of our own conscience. Listening and responding to that deep inner voice will lead us to higher motives and clearer intent.

Third, behave your way into the person you want to be. Behavior is not only the outgrowth of motive and agenda; it is also an important tool in improving intent. For example, if you're not now a person who cares much about others—but you have the desire to be—then act on that desire. Behave in caring ways. Do caring things. In the doing—with desire—we are re-created better than we were.

2. Declare Your Intent

Recently a man asked me how he could properly communicate his company's strengths and results to prospective clients without coming across as being arrogant and bragging and turning them off in the process (which had been a problem). I told him, "Declare your intent. Let your clients know why you're sharing your strengths and results—that it's not to build yourself up; it's to gain their confidence that you have the abilities and track record to serve them well."

Declaring your intent and expressing your agenda and motives can be very powerful, particularly if your behavior is being misinterpreted or misconstrued by others. It's also valuable as a means of establishing trust in new relationships.

Doug Conant, CEO of Campbell Soup Company, recently told me that within the first hour of working with new coworkers or other business partners, he lets them know how he operates so that people can know what to expect. He tells them explicitly that his agenda includes building trust with them, and that he wants them to gain trust in him as they see him do what he says he will do. Additionally, Doug finds that declaring his intent not only builds trust, it also puts more accountability on him to be true to what he's said.

The main reason why declaring intent increases trust is that it "signals your behavior"—it lets people know what to look for so that they can recognize, understand, and acknowledge it when they see it. Their response, then, is much like what happens when someone buys a new car and then suddenly starts noticing the same kind of car everywhere on the road. It's not that there are suddenly more of those cars on the road; it's that their awareness is enhanced.

One watch-out in declaring intent is to always be sure that you're being honest and real about it. To do otherwise is to come across as duplicitous and deplete trust. You also want to ensure that your intent is not merely self-serving. The very process of considering how to declare your intent will help you improve it.

3. Choose Abundance

Abundance means that there is enough for everybody. The opposite—scarcity—says that there is only so much to go around, and if you get it, I won't. While scarcity may be a reality in some areas (such as competitive sports or forced grading curves), in most of the important things in life—such as love, success, energy, results, and trust—abundance is not only a reality, it is an attractor and generator of even more.

According to former New York University economist Paul Zane Pilzer, "economic alchemy" is derived from principles of abundance—not scarcity—and technology has liberated us from the zero-sum game of traditional economics into the new world of unlimited abundance.

The important thing to understand is this: *Abundance is a choice!*

I am personally convinced that, regardless of our economic status, abundance is a choice that each of us can make. It is not the exclusive domain of the well-to-do. I know wealthy individuals who are extremely scarcity-minded and much less fortunate people who are very abundance-minded.

> The measure of your life will not be in what you accumulate, but in what you give away.
>
> —DR. WAYNE DYER, AUTHOR, *THE POWER OF INTENTION*

In the previous chapter, I told you how Jon Huntsman (CEO of Huntsman Chemical) kept his word on a handshake deal, even though it cost him millions of dollars. Huntsman is one of the most abundant and philanthropic persons in the world. He is also one of the wealthiest persons in the world (#198 on the Forbes 400 in 2005). But interestingly, he decided to be abundant and to share significantly with others when he was poor. Perhaps one of the reasons for his success was his decision—and behavior—to be abundant, even when he didn't have any economic reason to be. His son Peter, who now runs Huntsman Chemical, says, "Our whole goal is to make money faster than Dad can give it away."

Abundance is a mind-set, a way of being and becoming. It is also a foundational element of improving intent, which will make us more credible—believable—with others.

So how do you create abundance?

First—as with the other accelerators in this chapter—I suggest that you examine your current thinking. Ask yourself:

- When I'm in the middle of a negotiation, do I really believe it's possible to come up with a solution that will provide benefit for us both—or deep down, do I believe that the other person can gain benefit only at my expense?
- When I'm in a meeting and ideas are being tossed around, do I really believe there's enough credit and recognition for everyone—or do I feel like someone is going to get it, and I want to make sure that someone is me?
- Do I believe that if I love other people, my own supply of love will be replenished—or diminished?
- Do I believe that there's room for other people to see things differently than I do . . . and still be right?
- Do I believe that, whatever my economic circumstances, I can share with and benefit others?

Questions such as these will help you explore whether you currently have an abundance or a scarcity mind-set. To whatever degree you do have scarcity thinking, recognizing it is the first step toward creating a mind-set of abundance.

Once again, great role models will help. Some excellent role models seem to come by abundance naturally. Mother Teresa devoted her entire life to lifting the less fortunate. At one point, entrepreneur Ted Turner pledged one billion dollars, one-third of his net worth, to United Nations charities and then challenged other well-off people to do the same. In our own neighborhoods, many schoolteachers elevate the lives of our children through their skill, dedication, and belief in their students. And community volunteers give their time and energy to create and sustain literacy centers, youth sports programs, senior citizens events, and other projects that benefit many.

Some role models show us clearly that whatever our past experience—even if it includes a painful and unfair childhood—we can rescript ourselves to create abundance in our lives and in the lives of others. Consider Oprah Winfrey, who was raised in rural Mississippi by her grandparents and abused by a relative as a youth. She chose to reframe her circumstances and rise above them. As she put it:

> *I don't think of myself as a poor deprived ghetto girl who made good. I think of myself as somebody who from an early age knew I was responsible for myself, and I had to make good.*

From her first media job where she earned $100 a week, Oprah created abundance for herself and for others, and she has become one of the wealthiest, most influential, and most generous people of our time. Her generosity is evidenced by her support of causes and charities too numerous to mention, including her own Angel Network and her personal service in South Africa. Years ago—despite a temporary drop in ratings—Oprah transformed the very nature of her show from a generic "talk show" into one that makes an enormous positive difference. A few years ago, after wrestling with whether to continue her show, she ended a particularly inspiring show with the comment, "Now that is worth staying on the air for."

As noted psychologist and author Dr. Laura Schlessinger observes in her book *Bad Childhood—Good Life: How to Blossom and Thrive in Spite of an Unhappy Childhood:*

> *You should not be satisfied with being a victim, nor with being a survivor. You should aim to be a conqueror. There is an extraordinary quality of spirit that leads one to aspire to conquering rather than surviving. I hope you discover that spirit in yourself.*

Role models, insightful thought leaders, and practitioners such as these serve as powerful reminders that we can do something about even the very deep, personal, character-based issues that impact our credibility. And remember, credibility is the prerequisite for trust.

We can increase our integrity. We can improve our intent. And we can likely do it faster than we imagine.

CORE 3—CAPABILITIES
ARE YOU RELEVANT?

[People] of capability inspire us.

—SAMAVEDA (SACRED HINDU TEXT)

In this chapter, we move from the cores of credibility that focus on character to those that focus on competence. The first dimension of competence is *capabilities*—the talents, skills, knowledge, capacities, and abilities we have that enable us to perform with excellence.

Going back to the metaphor of the tree, capabilities are the branches that produce the fruits or results. With regard to our example of the expert witness, capabilities are a glaring necessity. Who would even begin to pay attention to the testimony of an "expert" who had no capability in her supposed area of expertise?

My father tells of an experience he had some years ago making a presentation to generals in the air force of a small country. He asked one of the generals about the effectiveness of their 360-degree feedback process where the pilots rated one another's capabilities. He wanted to know how they kept it from becoming a "you scratch my back, I'll scratch yours" situation in which pilots would praise one another's capabilities so that both could get promoted. Evidently, the general was completely taken aback by the question. In essence, he said, "Don't you realize that we are surrounded by our enemies on every side, and our very survival as a nation depends upon our skill? No one would even think of misrepresenting the capabilities of anyone on this force."

As this experience clearly shows, capabilities are vital to creating credibility—both personally and organizationally. Our capabilities inspire the trust of others, particularly when they are specifically those needed for the task at hand. Our capabilities also give us the self-confidence that we can do what needs to be done.

Think about the difference between a child who has learned to play a musical instrument or excel in sports or drama or some area of academics, compared to one who has essentially wasted his time. Think about the difference in the confidence and discipline he has—not only that he can do what he has learned to do well, but also in his ability to learn and do other things in life. As he reaches his teenage years and applies for a job, think of the confidence potential employers will have in him. Even if the job doesn't require his currently developed talents or skills, employers will recognize his desire and ability to develop skills as demonstrated by his past. As he moves on into higher education, family, career, and contribution, his capabilities—and the desire and ability to develop his capabilities—will be a huge trust builder and will have a dramatic, positive impact throughout his life.

Capable people are credible. They inspire trust. It's that simple. You can have the other three cores—you can have integrity and good intent, and you can have even produced good results in the past. But at the end of the day—especially in this rapidly changing knowledge worker economy—if you don't have current capabilities, if you are not relevant, you will not have credibility. You'll be taxed. You won't get the dividends of trust.

An example of someone who has the other three cores—but not capabilities—would be someone who is honest and caring and produces the results necessary to be promoted to a new level of responsibility that he doesn't have the competence to handle. This is the Peter Principle in action—of promoting people to the level of their incompetence. If he simply relies on the skills that got him to where he is—if he isn't involved in constantly learning, growing, and developing new skills—he won't have what's necessary to succeed in his new situation. He's like a family doctor who is asked to perform brain surgery; he may be very competent in the practice of family medicine, but he doesn't have what it takes to perform with excellence in his new assignment.

On the flip side, you could have enormous capabilities, but be lacking in integrity, intent, or results. For instance, you might have tremendous potential but never become able to translate it into results, so it remains just that—potential. Or you might use your great intelligence and skill to accomplish unworthy goals or to accomplish goals through unworthy means. To sever capacities from their character roots is to engage in corruption and manipulation. It won't build credibility; it will destroy trust.

Again, all four cores are vital. And capabilities are particularly essential in today's changing economy, where technology and globalization are outdating skill-sets faster than ever before. The half-life of our current knowledge and skills is much shorter than it has ever been, and suddenly someone who was very competent and even had a great track record in yesterday's world may no longer be competent in today's world.*

> *Left untended, knowledge and skill, like all assets, depreciate in value—surprisingly quickly.*
>
> —DAVID MAISTER, BUSINESS AUTHOR AND CONSULTANT

The main message here for both individuals and organizations is that to remain credible in today's world, we need to constantly improve our capabilities. I have one colleague who maintains that it's vital to "reinvent yourself" every three years to significantly upgrade your skill-set and knowledge so that you can remain relevant and able to make new contributions in a world of constant change. This three-year reinvention may be important for organizations, as well. As the American Express *Next Chapter* book asserts, "Reinvention is the key to longevity." This is probably never more vital than in today's changing global economy, where new competitors often emerge from a standing start and technology can make a once-successful strategy obsolete overnight.

As you prepare to consider Core 3—Capabilities, you might want to ask yourself:

- What capabilities do I have that make me credible and that inspire the trust and confidence of others?
- What experience have I had (or not had) in developing capabilities that affects the confidence I have in myself?
- What impact are factors such as technology and globalization having on the relevance of my current capabilities?
- What is my attitude and approach toward improving my current capabilities and gaining new ones?

---

* To access my free audio discussion on why high trust is *the* critical career skill in the new global economy, go to www.speedoftrust.com.

In the first part of this chapter, we'll take a look at what we'll call our "technical abilities"—those skills that are specific to our job or situation or particular task at hand. In the last part, we'll focus on the one capability that is vital in every situation—the ability to establish, grow, extend, and restore trust, which I refer to as "trust abilities."

TASKS

One way to think about the various dimensions of capabilities is to use the acronym "TASKS."

T alents
A ttitudes
S kills
K nowledge
S tyle

Talents are our natural gifts and strengths. *Attitudes* represent our paradigms—our ways of seeing, as well as our ways of being. *Skills* are our proficiencies, the things we can do well. *Knowledge* represents our learning, insight, understanding, and awareness. *Style* represents our unique approach and personality.

These are all parts of what we call our capabilities. They are our means to produce results. By breaking them down into these components, we are able to more fully explore them, both independently and interdependently.

Here are some questions to consider:

> **TALENTS:** What are my unique strengths or talents? What is the highest and best use of my talents? How can I better maximize the talents I have? What talents might I have that I have not yet developed?

> *True happiness involves the full use of one's power and talents.*
>
> —JOHN GARDNER, AUTHOR OF *EXCELLENCE* AND *SELF-RENEWAL*

"Talents" are those things that come to us naturally. I have one colleague who has a talent for public speaking. Where most people find it stressful, Barry finds it energizing and renewing. He has a natural ability to engage with people, to make learning fun, and to connect people and ideas. Skills and knowledge are helpful to him, but what's at the heart of his ability and passion is talent.

Another acquaintance, Christi, had experience running home-based businesses, but was looking for something that more fully engaged her unique talents. Meeting with a coach who helps people discover their talents, she found that she loved organizing, so she ran with it. Today Christi is the president of her state chapter of the National Association of Professional Organizers and runs a home and office organizing business. Christi attributes her success not to hard work as much as to her talent and passion. She says, "I can't believe I'm getting paid to do this!"

As we think about our talents, we need to realize that we may have talents within us that we don't currently know we have. Maybe we haven't really thought deeply about our talents. Or maybe we've allowed the demands of employment or other circumstances or people to identify our talents for us. Going through a deep, introspective, personal process of talent identification may reveal surprising and exciting avenues to pursue.

We might do well to consider the well-known parable of the talents. In this story, a man who is leaving on a journey entrusts his servants with his goods. To one servant, he gives five talents (meaning a sum of money). To another, he gives two. To the last, he gives one. In the man's absence, the servants with the five and two talents trade with them and double them. The servant who is given only one talent, fearing that he might lose it, goes and buries it in the earth. When the man returns and calls for an accounting, he praises the two servants who increased their talents and tells them that because they were faithful over a few things, he would entrust them with many things. When the third servant tells the man he buried his talent out of fear, the man reprimands him and calls him an "unprofitable servant." He takes the talent away, gives it to the servant who increased his five talents to ten, and casts the unprofitable servant out.

Whatever other purposes this parable may serve, it is a good reminder to us all of the importance of developing the talents we've been given and of the credibility we create and the trust we inspire when we do. In the end, our greatest work and contributions flow from our talents.

ATTITUDES: What are my attitudes about work? About life? About learning? About myself, my capabilities, and my opportunities to contribute? Are there more productive attitudes and paradigms I could embrace that would help me create better results?

With regard to attitudes, consider the extraordinary way Eugene O'Kelly, former CEO of KPMG, chose to see the last 100 days of his life. Diagnosed at age 53 with incurable brain cancer, O'Kelly was told he had three months to live. How he approached his imminent death is a tale of courage and inspiration, described in his book, *Chasing Daylight: How My Forthcoming Death Transformed My Life.* He said:

> *I was blessed. I was told I had three months to live. . . . The verdict I received the last week of May 2005 . . . turned out to be a gift. Honestly. . . . In short, I asked myself to answer two questions:* Must the end of life be the worst part? *And,* Can it be made a constructive experience—even the best part of life? *No. Yes. That's how I would answer those questions, respectively. I was able to approach the end while still mentally lucid (usually) and physically fit (sort of), with my loved ones near. As I said: a blessing.*

O'Kelly died on September 10, 2005, but not before being able to "beautifully resolve" personal relationships and experience an abundance of what he called "Perfect Moments" and "Perfect Days."

Consider the difference the following attitudes might make in your personal enjoyment of life and your ability to perform:

I *have* to go to work.	or	I'm genuinely excited to go to work, where I can use my talents and skills to contribute and add value.
I work like crazy and live for the weekends. I can hardly wait until I can retire and do what I want to do.	or	I have a balanced life in which work, recreation, and rich relationships are all important parts. I expect to have this kind of balance throughout my life.

| My partner isn't meeting my needs in this relationship. | or | What can I do to help my partner be happy and fulfilled? |
| I can hardly wait until my kids are grown. | or | I enjoy each day with my kids because I know we're building meaningful relationships that will last throughout our lives. |

As well as the difference these attitudes might make in your own life, consider the difference it would make over time in the lives of your children. What would happen if they were to grow up constantly hearing comments like the ones on the left? How would their lives be different if they constantly heard comments like those on the right?

One attitude I believe we especially need to beware of is the "entitlement" mentality: "I'm the manager, I've got this position, so I can just coast while everyone else does the work." This depletes credibility fast and is a huge trust buster. When the manager coasts, the competence of the reports rapidly exceeds his/her own, and this creates dramatic tension that often leads the manager into a downward cycle of mediocrity. As Apple and Pixar CEO Steve Jobs has said, it's B grade managers hiring C grade reports and C grade managers hiring D grade reports.

Keep in mind that A grade managers (without such an "entitlement" mentality) hire A+ reports, which leads to greater capabilities, greater credibility, greater trust, and greater results all around. This practice demonstrates a leadership philosophy espoused by many excellent managers: Always surround yourself with people who are even more talented and competent than you. It takes tremendous self trust to do this—a confidence born of high integrity, positive intent, and an attitude of continuous improvement—but the results are incomparable.

SKILLS: What skills do I currently have? What skills will I need in the future that I do not currently have? To what degree am I involved in constantly upgrading my skills?

After winning the Masters tournament by a record 12 strokes in 1997 early in his career, Tiger Woods—widely recognized at the time as the best golfer in the world—decided that he wanted to improve his swing, and he was willing to pay the price of a year-and-a-half "slump" to make it happen. Why? Because he believed that in doing so, he would be able to play better longer. He said:

*You can have a wonderful week . . . even when your swing isn't sound.
But can you still contend in tournaments with that swing when your
timing isn't good? Will it hold up over a long period of time? The answer
to those questions, with the swing I had, was no. And I wanted to
change that.*

Tiger emerged from his slump to win what's been called the "Tiger
slam," holding all four major titles at once—a feat accomplished only
one other time in golf history by golf legend Bobby Jones.

Then, unbelievably to almost everyone, Tiger decided to reinvent
his swing yet again. He said:

*I'd like to play my best more frequently, and that's the whole idea. That's
why you make changes. I thought I could become more consistent and play
at a higher level more often. . . . I've always taken risks to try to become a
better golfer, and that's one of the things that has gotten me this far.*

Although the jury is still out on Tiger's second major overhaul, he is
clearly a great example of continuous improvement. *Golf Digest* referred
to Tiger's relentless desire to improve as "the Tiger creed: *I improve,
therefore I am.*" According to *Time* magazine:

*What is most remarkable about Woods is his restless drive for what the
Japanese call* kaizen, *or continuous improvement. Toyota engineers will
push a perfectly good assembly line until it breaks down. They'll find and
fix the flaw and push the system again. That's kaizen. That's Tiger.*

Tiger Woods demonstrates the kind of attitude and motivation that is
vital to success in today's flat, global economy. Unless you're continually improving your skills, you're quickly becoming irrelevant. And
when you're irrelevant, you're no longer credible. And without credibility, you won't sustain trust—which will dramatically impact both
speed and cost.

One thing to be careful of with regard to skills is what author Jim
Collins calls "the curse of competence." It's the idea that sometimes we
become good at doing something we're not really talented in or pas-
sionate about. As my father often says, "Your current skill-set may or
may not correspond with your natural talents." We need to make certain that the skills we develop don't limit or define us. At the end of the
day, talent provides a deeper well than skills.

KNOWLEDGE: What is my current level of knowledge in my specific field? What am I doing to stay current? What other areas of knowledge am I pursuing?

> *I am still learning. That is an important mark of a good leader . . . to know you don't know it all and never will.*
>
> —ANNE MULCAHY, CHAIRMAN AND CEO, XEROX

I'll never forget what one CEO said about the risk of investing in a focused training initiative for his company. Someone asked him, "What if you train everyone and they all leave?" He responded, "What if we don't train them and they all stay?"

Clearly, increasing knowledge is vital in today's global economy, where the world's fund of information now doubles every two to two and a half years. One way to accelerate the rate of learning, both individually and organizationally, is to learn with the intent to teach others what you learn. As Peter Drucker has observed, "Knowledge workers and services workers learn most when they teach." When leaders structure opportunities and processes so that people teach what they learn to others within the organization, it dramatically increases individual and organizational learning and knowledge transfer. Mentoring, coaching, and other training processes can facilitate such learning, and becoming a teacher of whatever you learn becomes a new life paradigm for many individuals who have experienced the power of such a process.

This point is well illustrated in the story told by Marion D. Hanks of an obscure woman in London. After attending a lecture by the distinguished naturalist Dr. Louis Agassiz, she complained that she never had a chance to learn. In response, he asked her what she did. She replied that she helped her sister run a boardinghouse by skinning potatoes and chopping onions.

He said, "Madam, where do you sit during these interesting but homely duties?"

"On the bottom step of the kitchen stairs."

"Where do your feet rest?"

"On the glazed brick."

"What is glazed brick?"

"I don't know, sir."

He said, "How long have you been sitting there?"

She said, "Fifteen years."

"Madam, here is my personal card," said Dr. Agassiz. "Would you kindly write me a letter concerning the nature of a glazed brick?"

She took him seriously. She looked it up in the dictionary. She read an article in the encyclopedia and discovered that a glazed brick is vitrified kaolin and hydous aluminum silicate. Not knowing what that meant, she looked it up. She went to museums. She studied geology. She went to a brickyard and learned about more than 120 kinds of bricks and tiles. Then she wrote a 36-page treatise on the topic of glazed brick and tile, which she sent to Dr. Agassiz.

He wrote back, offering to pay her $250 if she would allow him to publish the article. Then he asked: "What was under those bricks?"

She replied, "Ants."

He said, "Tell me about the ants."

She then researched ants in depth, after which she wrote 360 pages on the subject and sent it to Dr. Agassiz. He published it as a book, and with the proceeds she was able to travel to places she had always wanted to see.

In commenting on this experience, Hanks asks:

> *Now as you hear this story, do you feel acutely that all of us are sitting with our feet on pieces of vitrified kaolin and hydrous aluminum silicate—with ants under them? Lord Chesterton answers: "There are no uninteresting things; there are only uninterested people."*

STYLE: How effective is my current style in approaching problems and opportunities and interacting with others? Does my approach facilitate or get in the way of accomplishing what needs to be done? What can I do to improve the way in which I go about doing things?

> *Leaders come in many forms, with many styles and diverse qualities. There are quiet leaders and leaders one can hear in the next county. Some find strength in eloquence, some in judgment, some in courage.*
>
> —JOHN GARDNER, AUTHOR OF
> *EXCELLENCE* AND *SELF-RENEWAL*

In the midst of the dot-com boom in the late 1990s, Candice Carpenter, cofounder, chairman, and CEO of iVillage, implemented a style of what she called "radical mentoring"—a hard-line, no-nonsense approach to teaching and training young employees. According to an article in *Fast Company* during that time, Carpenter liked to compare herself and business partner, Nancy Evans, to "drill sergeants who are running a boot camp for young leaders."

> *Every few months, Carpenter and Evans choose a different rising star to coach. There are lunches, private meetings, occasional late-night phone calls. More important, they give the staffer feedback—direct, sustained, brutally honest: "People don't grow if you're soft with them."*

Operating in what some might consider the opposite end of the leadership universe is John Mackey, founder and CEO of Whole Foods (which, incidentally, topped Wal-Mart—the largest grocer in the U.S.—in both overall and comparable-store sales growth for four years in a row).

According to *Fast Company*, Mackey wears shorts and hiking boots to work. He closes every business meeting with a round of "appreciations" or nice expressions about those who attend. He publicly posts everyone's pay. He makes decisions by majority vote (including decisions concerning new hires), and he rarely overrules the majority decisions.

> *[John Mackey] doesn't just delegate; in fact, he can seem almost diffident about his company. Asked how 140 cashiers can function as a single team . . . he looks like an anthropologist who has just had a student ask a great question.*
>
> *"That does sound like a problem," he says. "A team that large could confound the basic operating principle. But I'll tell you, I don't have the faintest idea how they've solved that problem. That's not my job anymore. But call them up, ask. I guarantee they have found a solution. I'd be curious to know what it is."*

Obviously, Candice Carpenter and John Mackey have totally different "styles," but both have been enormously effective in creating credibility and trust.

Clearly there is a wide variety of effective styles. The challenge is to match the style to the highest effectiveness for the task. The problem comes when you have a "style" that gets in the way and creates distrust. For example, several years ago, Al Dunlap—called "Chainsaw Al" by some and "Rambo in Pinstripes" by himself—gained the attention of Wall Street with his "slash and burn," "flatten the structure, fire half the company" approach. While he was a hero for a while on Wall Street, he was never a hero with the people. His "style"—getting short-term results in a way that destroyed trust—also destroyed long term-sustainability and morale.

MATCHING T-A-S-K-S TO TASKS

The end in mind here is to develop our TASKS and to match them to the tasks at hand—to create the best possible alignment between our natural gifts, our passions, our skills, knowledge, and style and the opportunity to earn, to contribute, to make a difference.

According to the research from the Gallup organization, only 20 percent of employees working in large organizations surveyed feel their strengths are in play every day. Thus, eight out of ten employees surveyed feel somewhat miscast in their role.

In *Good to Great*, Jim Collins talks about the importance in success-ful companies of having "the right people on the bus" and also of hav-ing "the right people in the right seats" on the bus. As a leader, you want to have capable people in your organization, but you also want to create the right match between a person's specific capabilities and the job you're asking that person to do.

More and more, organizations have become aware of the impact of the Peter Principle. Smart companies engage in practices such as compe-tency modeling, training, mentoring, and coaching to help ensure that those who are promoted have the TASKS that will help them establish the credibility they need to succeed.

On the individual level, the problem is that many people aren't into the idea of continuous improvement. So they're working in a company—maybe they've been there for ten or fifteen years—but instead of having fifteen years of experience, they really have only one year of experience repeated fifteen times! They're not adapting to the changes required by the new global economy. As a result, they don't develop the credibility that would inspire greater trust and opportunity. Often they become obsolete. Their company and/or the external markets outgrow them.

The same is true of corporations that simply rely on what has been successful in the past and fail to respond to the needs and challenges of the new global economy. If corporations aren't engaged in contin-uous improvement, and in some cases radical improvement, they risk becoming irrelevant and obsolete. They demonstrate the truth of the words spoken by the great historian Arnold Toynbee: "Nothing fails like success." In other words, they keep doing the things that made them successful in yesterday's market, but those same things don't create success in today's global economy.

> If you don't like change, you're going to like irrelevance even less.
>
> —GENERAL ERIC SHINSEKI, U.S. ARMY CHIEF OF STAFF

Companies that do invest in continually learning, growing, and reinventing themselves have a different story to tell. Consider the success of Michael Dell and Kevin Rollins of Dell Inc. As leaders of one of the best-performing companies in the world, they have a massive 360-degree feedback process in place. And paying attention to this feedback to reinvent themselves—even when it has been hard—has been a big part of their success.

According to a 2003 article in *BusinessWeek*, Dell and Rollins had received disappointing personal feedback:

> [S]ubordinates thought Dell, 38, was impersonal and emotionally detached, while Rollins, 50, was seen as autocratic and antagonistic. Few felt strong loyalty to the company's leaders. Worse, the discontent was spreading: A survey taken over the summer, following the company's first-ever mass layoffs, found that half of Dell Inc.'s employees would leave if they got the chance.

Instead of ignoring the feedback (which would have been easy and typical behavior for highly successful leaders such as these), they took immediate corrective action. Dell met with his top managers, critiqued his own shortcomings as a leader, and committed himself to making closer connections with his team. Dell's self-critique was videotaped and shown to every manager in the company, and Dell and Rollins both made serious efforts to improve. Dell used a "desktop prop"—a plastic bulldozer—to remind him not to bulldoze his way through ideas without involving others, and Rollins got a Curious George doll to help him remember to listen to others before making decisions.

By 2005, Dell Inc. was ranked the Most Admired Company in America and the Third-Most Admired Company in the World by *Fortune* magazine. *BusinessWeek* continues:

What's Dell's secret? At its heart is his belief that the status quo is never good enough, even if it means painful changes for the man with his name on the door. When success is achieved, it's greeted with five seconds of praise followed by five hours of postmortem on what could have been done better. Says Michael Dell: "Celebrate for a nanosecond. Then move on."

The attitude and habit of continually improving is one of the prime differentiators between companies that remain relevant and succeed and those that fall by the wayside in today's global economy.

> The complacent company is a dead company. Success today requires the agility and drive to constantly rethink, reinvigorate, react, and reinvent.
>
> —BILL GATES, CHAIRMAN, MICROSOFT

HOW TO INCREASE YOUR CAPABILITIES

In working with clients, I've come across some excellent ideas to enhance credibility by increasing capabilities, but the three accelerators that make the greatest difference are the following:

1. Run with Your Strengths (and with Your Purpose)

The idea here is simply to identify your strengths (whether they be Talents, Attitudes, Skills, Knowledge, or Style), and then focus on engaging, developing, and leveraging what's distinctly yours.

Peter Drucker encourages leaders to "feed opportunities and starve problems." In the same vein, I contend that we need to "feed strengths and starve weaknesses." It's not that we ignore our weaknesses; rather, we make our weaknesses irrelevant by working effectively with others so that we compensate for our weaknesses through their strengths and they compensate for their weaknesses through our strengths. That's making sure that everyone is on the right seat on the bus.

One well-known example of running with one's strengths is the amazing athlete Michael Jordan. At one point, he decided to retire from his highly successful basketball career to play baseball, a sport he had always loved and wanted to prove he could play at a high level. However, in leaving basketball for baseball, he moved from "best in the world" to "mediocre." So Jordan decided to go back to basketball, where he won three additional championships on top of the three he had previously won. He ran with his strengths. As a result, not only was his own career more successful and enjoyable, he was able to make a unique and much appreciated contribution to basketball and to the world of sports at large.

For a business example, I once had a salesperson who was the "Michael Jordan" of salespeople. He was fantastic—extraordinary at sales and great with clients. He was truly world-class. But this man didn't want to be a salesperson; he wanted to be a general manager. Finally, he persuaded me to let him try—despite the fact that he had tried the same thing in two prior companies and had failed. He was mediocre at best—Michael Jordan playing baseball—and I offered to put him back into sales. But he didn't want to go there. This man became a powerful example to me of the personal and organizational loss created when people don't run with their strengths.

It's important to realize that there are times when the importance of running with whatever personal strengths we may have is outweighed by another kind of strength—strength of purpose. It may be something that's conscience-driven or some purpose we feel compelled to pursue. And we may not yet have developed the TASKS strengths we need to do it.

In my own life, I have found great satisfaction in pursuing education and opportunities to work and contribute in fields in which I feel I have natural strengths. But I have also felt a sense of excitement and pleasure in responding to an inner voice that has urged me at times into undeveloped territory, forcing me—sometimes even uncomfortably—to discover new strengths or to build new skills to face the task at hand.

2. Keep Yourself Relevant

For years, people have recognized the value of a four-year degree, but to succeed in today's economy, you really need a forty-year degree. In other words, you need to be engaged in lifelong learning. The four-year degree may teach you how to read, write, think, and reason, but its main purpose is to set you up for ongoing learning.

I know of one extraordinary man who for years would get up very early every morning and read for two hours. His goal was to learn everything possible about organizational behavior and development, human behavior, management, and leadership. And he did. I watched him become extremely competent. Each time he was given more responsibility, he raised his competence to the level of his promotion—what I call the Reverse Peter Principle in action.

Going back to the Dell/Rollins example, it would have been easy, even justifiable, for Michael Dell and Kevin Rollins to ignore the feedback they had been given. After all, they were already eminently successful as leaders. But instead they were driven to relentlessly improve. Not only did this result in their increasing their already high credibility, it enabled them to increase trust and improve results.

> *I am always learning and working at the margin of my ignorance.*
>
> —HARVEY GOLUB, CHAIRMAN OF CAMPBELL SOUP COMPANY AND FORMER CEO OF AMERICAN EXPRESS

3. Know Where You're Going

In a recent conversation with strategist and marketing expert Jack Trout, I asked him what, in his view, was the key to leadership. I'll never forget his simple and resounding response: "At the end of the day, people follow those who know where they're going."

> *It is a terrible thing to look over your shoulder when you are trying to lead and find nobody there.*
>
> —FRANKLIN DELANO ROOSEVELT

I remember years ago when my father decided to give up his teaching position at the university to form his own training and consulting company at the age of 50. Many of his friends thought he was crazy to do so and advised against it. He had a good life at the university. He was contributing, and he could always consult on the side. But my father had a clear, distinct vision of where he was going—a vision of a different-in-kind contribution that he believed he could make only by having an organization behind him. So he took the leap . . . and others followed. And together, they ultimately built the Covey Leadership Center—and later FranklinCovey—into one of the largest and most influential leadership development companies in the world.

To know where you're going and to have the capabilities to get there is another way of demonstrating competence. And that competence, coupled with character, creates a credible leader whom others will follow—not because they're forced, but because they're inspired to do so.

> *The people you lead want to know where they're going.*
>
> —CHRISTOPHER GALVIN, CHAIRMAN AND CEO, MOTOROLA

TRUST ABILITIES

As I mentioned earlier, while character is constant, competence—at least most competence—is situational. It depends on what the circumstance requires.

However, there are a few areas of competence that are vital in every situation, and what I call "trust abilities" are at the top of the list. This is basically what this book is all about—your ability to establish, grow, extend, and restore trust. I would go so far as to say that your technical capabilities are taxed dramatically—sometimes even becoming irrelevant—in direct relation to your trust abilities. And because of this, I once again affirm that it is not only vital to individual success, it is the key leadership competency of the new global economy.

Even considering how important technical abilities are with regard to trust, I am convinced that the most important thing you can get out of this chapter is the awareness of the supreme importance of trust abilities. To get a better grip on these abilities, you could once again overlay the template of TASKS—talent, attitude, skills, knowledge, and style—and assess where you can work to create the most effective improvement in your trust abilities. You might ask yourself:

- To what degree do I have some degree of natural *talent* in the area of trust abilities? Do things such as integrity and good intent come naturally to me? Do I naturally seek for mutual benefit? Do I inherently know and do things that inspire trust?
- What are my *attitudes* in this area? Do I recognize and respect the need for trust? Do I approach issues and try to get things done in ways that build trust?
- Do I have trust-building *skills*? Do I interact with others in ways that build trust?
- What *knowledge* and understanding do I have about establishing, growing, extending, and restoring trust?

- Is my *style* of action and interaction one that inspires trust? Is my style one that extends trust to others?

The best "accelerator" I can think of to improve your trust abilities is to immerse yourself in the content of this book. As you learn to establish, grow, extend, and restore trust from the inside out, you will be amazed at the credibility this will give you, the confidence you will feel, and the results you will get in every dimension of life.

CORE 4—RESULTS
WHAT'S YOUR TRACK RECORD?

You can't create a high-trust culture unless people perform.
—CRAIG WEATHERUP, FORMER CEO, PepsiCo

In December of 1994, I was asked to step in as president and CEO of the Covey Leadership Center. Within the first week, I had a difficult meeting with the bank. The good news was that the company had been creating value for clients quite well, as was evidenced by our growth. The bad news was that we hadn't yet figured out our own business model, as was evidenced by our lack of profit and cash.

Despite the great intellectual capital, some terrific people, and amazing growth, the company was in dire straits. We'd had 11 straight years of negative cash flow. We had no outside capital, no margins, and nothing in the bank. We were totally extended on our accounts payable and our credit lines were maxed out. Our "debt to tangible net worth" ratio was 223 to 1. Basically, we were growing ourselves out of business, and the bank's confidence and trust was practically nil. They demanded that we go back on personal guarantees, and they were in the process of deciding whether or not to pull the plug.

Fortunately for us, and for our clients, they didn't.

Within two and a half years of that meeting, we established a sustainable business model that made it possible for us to increase the value of the company from $2.4 million to $160 million. We increased profit by 1,200 percent. We decreased day's receivables from 87 to 48. We decreased the "debt to tangible net worth" ratio from 223 to 1 to less than 2 to 1. Not only were we high growth; we were also high profit.

One of the most interesting things about this whole experience was seeing the effect those results had on our relationship with our bankers. As they saw us reaching milestone after milestone during those two and a half years—producing, hitting the numbers, increasing the margins, and increasing the cash as we had committed to do—we could see their confidence in us grow. They began to see us as a good risk. They significantly increased our credit line—again and again and again. They wanted to give us more business.

What made them want to extend more trust? Results!

RESULTS MATTER!

Results matter! They matter to your credibility. They matter to your ability to establish and maintain trust with others. In the words of Jack Welch, having results is like having "performance chits" on the table. They give you clout. They classify you as a producer, as a performer. Without the results, you simply don't have that same kind of clout.

Returning once again to the metaphor of the tree, results are the fruits—the tangible, measurable end purpose and product of the roots, trunk, and branches. To have the other three cores without results is like having a barren tree. It won't create credibility, no matter how strong the other three cores may be. And it won't inspire confidence because the tree doesn't produce what it was intended to produce.

Let's come back to the idea of establishing the credibility of an expert witness in a court of law. A witness may be seen as an honest person with no hidden agenda and plenty of credentials. But if she doesn't have a good track record—a solid history of results—her credibility will be called into question and her testimony significantly discounted.

Bottom line, without results, you don't have credibility. It's like the old Texas saying "All hat, no cattle" or the California racing phrase "All show and no go." People don't trust you because you don't get things done. And there's no place to hide here—either you produce or you don't. You may have excuses. You may even have good reasons. But at the end of the day, if the results aren't there, neither is the credibility and neither is the trust. It's just that simple; it's just that harsh.

On the other hand, if you are getting results but you're violating one of the other three cores—say you get the numbers in a way that violates integrity, or creates a "lose" for others—your production will not be sustainable, nor will the fruit be good. It will taste bad. It will smell bad. Even if it looks good on the outside, it will be rotten inside, and it won't create long-term credibility and trust. You simply can't get a sustainable yield of good fruit if the results are severed from the character roots.

This creates a huge issue for organizations today. What do you do with someone who gets the results, but in ways that violate company values? The GE approach, which illustrates the dynamic between "getting results" and "living the values," recognizes four possibilities. They say it's fairly easy to know what to do with the first category of people, who both deliver results and live the values. They should be retained and promoted. It's also fairly easy to know what to do with the second category, who neither deliver results nor live the values. They should be let go.

The other two categories, however, are tougher to deal with. Those who live the values but achieve low results can often be trained, coached, or moved to another role. If they don't improve, they may need to be let go. The hardest of all to deal with are those who have high results but are poor in living the values. They achieve the end that everybody wants, but they do it a way that blatantly defies organizational values. According to GE, people in this category need to learn to operate within the company's values—or be let go, despite their results. To keep them on as they are is not only unsustainable, it is damaging to the organization and destroys credibility and trust.

According to Jack Welch:

Clarity around values and behaviors is not much good unless it is backed up. To make values really mean something, companies have to reward the people who exhibit them and "punish" those who don't. Believe me, it will make winning easier. I say that because every time we asked one of our high-performing managers to leave because he didn't demonstrate the values—and we said as much publicly—the organization responded incredibly well. In annual surveys over a decade, employees would tell us that we were a company that increasingly lived its values. That made people even more committed to living them too. And as our employee satisfaction results improved, so did our financial results.

There's no doubt that results will cover a multitude of shortcomings. If you're a top producer, for example, management will likely be more lenient in dealing with expense reports that don't make it in on time. We've all seen the equivalent of this in our companies—where it sometimes creates a double standard that produces its own cynicism. But in the long run, even top results will not offset a lack of integrity.

On the other hand, strength in integrity will also not offset an absence of results. Again, *all* four cores are vital to personal and organizational credibility, which is the basis for establishing trust.

As we prepare to explore this fourth core, you may want to ask yourself:

- What kind of results am I currently producing? Do those results increase or diminish my personal credibility?
- If I were considering hiring someone, to what extent would that person's track record and current performance influence my decision?
- How good is my own track record? How likely would someone be to hire me based on it?
- How good am I at identifying desired results and executing effectively to accomplish those results? Does my performance inspire confidence and trust?

RESULTS—PAST, PRESENT, AND FUTURE

I have worked briefly on Wall Street and been an executive in a public company, and it's clear to me that there are three key indicators by which people evaluate results. One is past performance—your track record, your reputation, the things you've done, and the results you've already achieved. Another is current performance—how you are performing today. And the third is anticipated performance—how people think you will perform in the future.

You see these three dimensions come into play clearly when outside entities place a value on a company. They look at historical earnings (past performance). They may put a multiple on that and come up with a value. Or they look at current, real-time data and results (present performance), and they may put a multiple on that and come up with a value. Or (as is effectively the case with Wall Street) they take the anticipated, expected results (future performance) and then discount them back to arrive at a present value. All three dimensions of results—past, present, and future—are important in considering a company's worth.

These three dimensions also come into play with each of us as individuals. Our credibility comes not only from our past results and our present results, but also from the degree of confidence others have in our ability to produce results in the future.

At one time I worked with a person who was honest, had great intent, and was extremely talented, but for the life of him, he couldn't seem to make anything happen. We were part of a team that was working on a rotation system to follow through on leads. When a big opportunity came along and it was time for this person to get it, I was hesitant—in fact, everyone on the team was hesitant—to give it to this person because he hadn't produced results. As we projected his past track record on his future anticipated performance, we didn't feel we could trust him to come through for the team. Over time, in spite of his talents, he became increasingly irrelevant and left the company.

On the other hand, when you have a person or a company that builds a reputation of always delivering results, it's a whole different story. Just think about the overnight delivery industry many years ago when reliability was good, but not 100 percent. FedEx came along with the tagline, "When it absolutely, positively has to get there overnight!" Not only did they have the tagline, they had the service to back it up. They performed. They consistently produced the results. As their founder, Frederick Smith, said, "We thought that we were selling the transportation of goods; in fact, we were selling peace of mind." In consequence of their performance, they earned credibility . . . and trust . . . and business. Today, people anticipate that FedEx will deliver on time because they *have* delivered on time—time and time again.

Many companies, such as The Hartford, use their track record to build trust and court new business. Even advertising references such as "serving you for over 50 years" or "in business since 1925" are designed to communicate a track record that inspires trust. One of the more exciting developments of this new global economy, however, is the fact that a relatively new business such as JetBlue can establish a successful track record quickly. Started in 2000, JetBlue was one of the few U.S. airlines to make a profit during the sharp downturn following 9/11, and is recognized for its customer service. Similarly, Google, established in 1999, has been recognized as the third-strongest brand in the U.S. according to the *Wall Street Journal*'s 2006 Reputation Quotient survey. Examples such as these confirm the fact that, through results, you can establish trust faster than you think.

The experience of one of JetBlue's competitors, Continental Airlines, confirms another point—that through results, you can also *restore* trust faster than you think. Following their declaration of bankruptcy in 1991, Continental significantly improved performance and went on to earn recognition for highest on-time performance and lowest rate for mishandled baggage. They have also won more J.D. Power awards for customer service than any other airline. In 2005, Continental was recognized as the Most Admired Global Airline by *Fortune* magazine.

Bottom line, whether you're dealing with restoring trust or establishing it in the first place, it is results that will convert the cynics.

The impact of results on trust plays out in every dimension of life. I have a friend who was going on a trip for a few days and planned to leave his home in the care of his teenage daughter and her friend. He said he felt perfectly comfortable doing this, but confided that he never would have even thought about doing such a thing with his son when he was a teenager. Why? Both his daughter and his son were "good" kids. However, the daughter had a track record of maturity and responsibility; the son did not. The degree of confidence this man had in each child—and thus the degree of trust that he was willing to extend—was a projection of past performance on future results.

"WHAT" AND "HOW"

In considering results, you always need to ask two critical questions: *What* results am I getting? and *How* am I getting those results? Most people only ask the *what*. They have no idea that the answer to the *how* may be doing them in.

For example, suppose you get your team to hit the numbers, but in the process you create an adversarial win-lose competition between team members, push them until they reach burnout, and take all the credit for your team's performance. What's going to be the attitude of those team members the next time you challenge them to hit the numbers? Will it be easier—or harder—for you to get results?

On the other hand, suppose you hit the numbers, but you do it by creating a team spirit of abundance and collaboration. You help team members work together so that everyone succeeds, no one reaches burnout, and the credit is freely shared. What's going to be their attitude the next time the challenge comes up? What if you can get the same great results—only this time, it's going to be 30 percent faster and easier?

That's why you have to ask the question: *How* am I getting the results? The *how* can generate huge roadblocks to future results—or it can grease the skids. It's so much easier to get results the next time around if people trust you . . . if they know you're going to give credit, to seek mutual benefit, to not place blame. They will want to engage with you, to give you information, to help you because you've become credible with them. They trust that you will go for results in a way that will benefit them and everyone involved.

This is why the trust abilities I mentioned in the last chapter are so important. And this is why I define leadership as *getting results in a way that inspires trust.* I am convinced that with regard to results, the *how* matters every bit as much as the *what.* And you see it manifest on every level—individual, relationship, team, organizational, and societal.

In this rapidly changing economy, I've seen a lot of companies that have had to change their business model, pare back their cost structure, and lay off employees in order to get sustainable results. Some have created a huge tax in the process—not only with those they let go, but also with those who remained and saw what happened to those who were let go.

I've also seen some outstanding companies that have actually built trust in the process. In one instance, I advised a company that was in the process of having to radically undergo a painful transformation to remain relevant and viable. After making many cost-cutting changes, they had reached a point where, in order to regain profitability, they needed to significantly downsize. At that point, they were open, transparent, and honest with their people. Through creating generous severance packages and help with placement, they demonstrated such concern for the people who were leaving that it actually increased confidence and trust with them and also with those who were staying. Everyone realized that they were confronting reality, but they were doing it in a principled way that demonstrated care and concern for all.

Keep in mind that "results" can't always be measured in dollars and cents. In fact, to ignore the trust tax or dividend in any analysis is to skew the results. The greatest profit may not be in the current transaction, but in the credibility and trust that comes from that transaction that paves the way for even greater results in the future.

DEFINING "RESULTS"

On Wall Street, I learned that "results" are bottom line and the connection between results and credibility is often brutal. A company can get consistently good results, but if they miss one quarter—even by a small amount—it can be as if the prior results weren't even there. In some ways it's worse because the organization is now seen as unpredictable.

Off Wall Street, however, I've learned that wisdom suggests that we sometimes look at "results" in other ways. As Robert S. Kaplan and David P. Norton point out in *The Balanced Scorecard,* there are multiple stakeholders and measures that serve as indicators of the sustainability of financial results. One vital thing to consider is the trust tax or dividend we just discussed. There's no way to get an accurate picture of the result of anything you do without taking that multiplier or divisor into consideration.

Another thing to consider is your definition of results. It's possible that you could do everything right—you could have integrity, good intent, and capabilities and you could do everything in a principled way to achieve a good result—but still your business might fail, your spouse might walk out on you, your children might make bad choices, or you might have a tsunami or a Hurricane Katrina that wipes out your home and everything you've worked for. There are some things that are simply not in your control, and there are times when you have to define "results" in a different way than you might have thought:

> *Yes, my business is going through a rough time. But what am I discovering? What strengths am I gaining? What increased capacity will I have to apply to future efforts?*

> *Yes, my marriage failed. But what is the result? What have I learned? Did I do my best? Have I come through it with my integrity intact? Am I a better, stronger person because of it? Am I modeling the kind of behavior I want my children to see?*

> *Yes, this disaster has wiped out my home and my business. But what new opportunities do I have as a result? Is there some better way I can now use my talents and abilities to make a difference? What strengths do I have that will enable me to work with others to rebuild?*

Even when the observable results appear to be negative, you can still make huge progress in increasing your self-trust and self-confidence by recognizing, defining, and evaluating yourself on results that are not only positive, but are, perhaps, even more important in the long run.

I had the opportunity to coach Little League flag football for nine years, and I saw the impact on young kids whose parents and coaches thought that winning was the only legitimate desired result. In my mind, there were other results that—particularly at that age—were even more important. So I worked with the teams I coached to come up with a list of six objectives:

1. To play hard
2. To have fun

3. To be a good sport
4. To be a good team player
5. To learn something
6. To win

You'll notice that "to win" was the last objective on the list. There were plenty of good results, plenty of things to celebrate, even if the other team won the game. And those results needed to be celebrated. They were things that would benefit those kids throughout their lives.

On the flip side, you see marriages or families who appear to have it all together—but really don't. You have businesses or enterprises that seem to be profitable and thriving—but they're not. You have students who get all As but have no real education. We need to be careful that we don't become superficial in defining or evaluating results, both in our own lives and in the lives of others. And when we're in the evaluating role, we also need to exercise wisdom in projecting past performance on future results. Like the standard investment prospectus says, "Past performance is no guarantee of future results."

As reported in the *Wall Street Journal*, at one time, David Sokol, CEO of MidAmerican Energy (a wholly owned subsidiary of Berkshire Hathaway) had to face Berkshire Hathaway's CEO—Warren Buffett—with some highly disturbing news. It appeared that the Iowa utility needed to write off some $360 million for a zinc project that had gone south. Sokol braced himself to be fired, but he was totally unprepared for Warren Buffett's response. "David," he said, "we all make mistakes. If you can't make mistakes, you can't make decisions. I've made a lot bigger mistakes myself." The entire meeting was over in 10 minutes.

In our businesses, relationships, families, and personal lives, there is wisdom in recognizing the capacity of people to learn from their mistakes and to change. There is also wisdom in creating a culture that makes it safe for that to happen. A transparent culture of learning and growing will generally create credibility and trust, even when the immediate results are not the best. The more important desired result is growth, and growth cannot happen without risk. To always make decisions and give opportunity based on past observable performance is to severely limit our ability to achieve great results in the future.

Finally, we need to be aware and appreciate the value of playing a supporting role in achieving results that may be primarily attributed to others. The reality is that no results ever come exclusively from the work of one individual or organization; they represent the efforts of many. You can see it in the world of science, where most new "discoveries" clearly come out of the work, and even sometimes the mistakes, of those of the past. You see it recognized in sports such as basketball, where statisticians measure not only points but also assists, and baseball, where they measure sacrifices as well as runs. Understanding and appreciating the importance of a supportive role in getting results helps us all to more appropriately value our own contributions, as well as the contributions of others.

COMMUNICATING RESULTS

As a teenager, I worked in an organization that had a set of requirements I needed to pass off before I could be considered for promotion. Excited about the work and wanting to do well, I worked hard to prepare ahead of time and passed them off my first day there. As it turned out, my first day there was also the first day for the new boss, and in the midst of all that was going on (and unknown to me), it never reached his attention that I had passed the requirements off.

During the next eight months, no matter how hard I worked, others were advanced, but not me. I wondered about it, but I didn't say anything. I just tried to work even harder. Finally, this leader said to me, "Stephen, I just can't understand it. You're an excellent worker. You're doing everything else right. I don't understand why you won't pass off these requirements so we can put you in a position to manage others."

Shocked, I exclaimed, "But I did pass them off—the first day I was here!" We were both dismayed to realize all that could have happened if he had known. I had delivered results, but the fact that they were not appropriately recognized affected his perception of me and my credibility, and therefore the level of trust he was willing to extend. However, once those results were recognized—and particularly when they were combined with the results I'd had even in the limited opportunities of the past few months—the whole perception changed. Trust was extended in abundance, and I was able to contribute in far more meaningful ways.

In creating credibility with others, it's not just the results that count; it's people's awareness of the results. Thus, it's important to be able to appropriately communicate results to others.

HOW TO IMPROVE YOUR RESULTS

Given the importance of results in establishing credibility and trust both with ourselves and with others, the question is: How can we improve our results? I believe the three accelerators below are most effective.

1. Take Responsibility for Results

As my father taught me when I was seven years old, a real key to success is in taking responsibility for results—not activities. He told me I was responsible to keep the yard "green" and "clean"; he didn't tell me I was to water the lawn twice a week, mow it on Saturdays, or pick up the garbage and put it in the can. In fact, he told me I could get the yard "green" and "clean" any way I liked. The point was that when I accounted to him, I had to account for results.

That lesson turned out to be the beginning of a major learning in my life: It's vital to take responsibility for results—not just activities. This approach unleashes creativity. It helps you understand that if you can't get results one way, you try another way—you don't just sit there and whine, "Well, I did what you told me to do!" It's helped me to release ingenuity in working with coworkers and children alike.

Just consider the contrast:

ACTIVITIES	RESULTS
I called the customer.	I made the sale.
I did the research, I wrote the report.	I got the grant.
I took the class.	I learned how to give an effective presentation.
I stayed on my diet.	I lost 13 pounds.
I tried.	*"Do or do not; there is no try."* —Master Yoda

A results focus is a way of thinking. It's a different mentality than an activities focus. Kozo Ohsone of Sony once brought a small piece of wood to his engineering team and told them he wanted a personal stereo built to that size. As a result, the Walkman was born. In his book, *Thriving on Chaos*, Tom Peters tells the story of how Lee Iacocca, former chairman and CEO of Chrysler, wanted to add a convertible to Chrysler's line. He writes:

> *Following standard operating procedures, he* [Iacocca] *asked his chief engineer to craft a model. The engineer, consistent with industry standards, replied, "Certainly. We can put together a prototype in nine months." Several bystanders report Iacocca's furious response: "You just don't understand. Go find a car and saw the top off the damn thing!"*

Iacocca got his prototype in short order, and it resulted in a huge success. Regarding the development of both the Discman and the Chrysler convertible, the focus was clearly *not* on activities, but on results.

In addition to the benefit of differentiating between results and activities, there's another positive dimension to taking responsibility for results. As I've emphasized over and over in this chapter, *accomplishing* results will build credibility and trust. But simply *taking responsibility for results* will also build credibility and trust—sometimes even when the results are not good . . . and sometimes when they were not even your fault.

You may remember the situation in 1982 when seven people in the U.S. died from ingesting Tylenol that had been laced with cyanide. The nation panicked. Some predicted that Johnson & Johnson would never be able to sell another product under that name. But Johnson & Johnson took responsibility for the situation. They immediately alerted consumers to stop using Tylenol until they could determine the extent of the tampering. They recalled approximately 31 million bottles of Tylenol, retailing at more than $100 million. They offered to exchange all Tylenol capsules that had already been purchased for Tylenol tablets, which cost them millions more. They established relations with law enforcement officers on every level to help search for the person who laced the medication and to help prevent further tampering. They put up a reward of $100,000 for the person who committed the crime. When they reintroduced the product back in the market, it had new triple-seal, tamper-resistant packaging. As a result of their actions, they turned what could have been a disaster into a victory in credibility and public trust.

Interestingly, the basis for their decision making was a "credo" written in the mid-1940s by Robert Wood Johnson, the company's leader for 50 years. Their values were clear, and they were clearly "mutual benefit." As one observer reported:

Johnson outlined his company's responsibilities to "consumers and medical professionals using its products, employees, the communities where its people work and live, and its stockholders." Johnson believed that if his company stayed true to these responsibilities, his business would flourish in the long run. He felt that his credo was not only moral, but profitable, as well.

And so it turned out to be. By focusing on mutual benefit and accepting responsibility for results and even bad results and even when they were not Johnson & Johnson's fault—the company was able to restore credibility and trust.

It's amazing how the impact of taking responsibility for results plays out in personal and family life—where instead of blaming and accusing, a spouse will say, "I'm sorry for my part in this. What can I do to make it better?" Or a parent will say, "Maybe I didn't communicate clearly on this issue. Let me try to explain a little better." Or an estranged brother or sister will accept responsibility for the breach and take the initiative to mend it. When you say, "I accept responsibility for my part in this, whatever it may be . . ." and also "I accept responsibility to help find a solution," you build credibility and trust . . . and get better results all around.

> It's no use saying, "We are doing our best." You have got to succeed in doing what is necessary.
>
> —WINSTON CHURCHILL

2. Expect to Win

According to Greek mythology, Pygmalion, the king of Cyprus, carved an ivory statue of the ideal woman. He named her Galatea. She was so beautiful that Pygmalion fell in love with her, and because of his deep desire and will for her to be real, with the help of the goddess Venus, he was actually able to bring her to life, and they lived happily ever after.

This ancient myth has come to serve as a metaphor that illustrates the power of expectation. While this phenomenon is commonly referred to as "the Pygmalion effect," it's also been called the Galatea effect, the Rosenthal effect, self-fulfilling prophecy, positive self-expectancy, confidence, optimism, or just plain faith. In modern times, it's been made popular through the musical *My Fair Lady*, a modern Pygmalion story in which a speech professor's expectations become the catalyst that inspires the transformation of a Cockney flower girl into a lady.

The principle is simply this: We tend to get what we expect—both from ourselves and from others. When we expect more, we tend to get more; when we expect less, we tend to get less.

This phenomenon was clearly manifest in a 1968 study by Dr. Robert Rosenthal in which teachers were told that, based on IQ testing, students in a control group were high achievers—though in fact they had been randomly assigned. When the students were tested several months later, the control group students performed measurably better than their peers. Higher teacher expectations of students had been translated into increased student learning.

In our own lives, having a mind-set of expecting to win increases our odds of winning. It helps us get better results. And better results help us increase our credibility and self-confidence, which leads to more positive self-expectancy, and then more winning—and the upward cycle continues. It becomes a self-fulfilling prophecy.

As Harvard Business School professor and writer Rosabeth Moss Kanter has observed, "Confidence consists of positive expectations for favorable outcomes . . . winning begets winning, because it produces confidence at four levels." The first of those levels, she says, is "self-confidence: an emotional climate of high expectations." The second level is "confidence in one another."

So if you want to increase your results, expect to win—not only for yourself, but also for your team. Not at all costs, but honorably. Not at the expense of others, but in conjunction with others. Expecting to win—and expecting others to win—is a fundamental approach of helping to bring it about.

3. Finish Strong

One year my son Stephen, who was an outstanding football player and captain of his high school team, decided that he wanted to go out for basketball. He made the team, but to his disappointment, he was only average and spent most of the year on the bench. A month before the season ended, he hurt his shoulder, and the doctor said he would not be able to play anymore that year. His initial response was to quit the team. He was injured and he wasn't going to play, so in his mind, there was no reason to stay.

But Jeri and I had another view. To us, there was a principle involved. Stephen was on a team, and the team was still playing. Whether he played or not was irrelevant; the team needed his support.

At first, Stephen grumbled. He said it would be a waste of time. He even went for the ultimate parental "button": "But, Dad, I could be *studying!*" But in the end, he hung in there and stayed on the team until the season was over. He helped out at practices. He supported the team. And both his coaches and his teammates commended him for it.

After he graduated from high school, he gave a speech in which he thanked his coaches and said that as a result of sports, he had learned two great lessons in life: The first was to work hard; the second was to finish strong. And we've seen the positive results of those lessons play out in everything he's taken on since.

Results are all about finishing. You're probably aware of the old adage, Beginners are many; finishers are few. Increasingly, it seems, we live in a society of victims and quitters. The sheer number of people quitting their jobs, fathers abandoning children (both physically and financially), couples divorcing, and teenagers who don't even graduate from high school indicates, that at least in some situations, when the going gets tough people simply quit. Of course, there are circumstances in which making some of these decisions may be the best thing to do. But in many situations and for no good reason, people just don't have the motivation and stamina to finish strong.

Clearly, finishing strong is a powerful antidote to a culture of quitting. But have you ever thought of it in terms of its even greater impact on credibility and trust?

My motto is: Whenever possible, finish, and finish strong. A colleague of mine who was training for a marathon shared some excellent advice he received from a world-class runner. "When you 'hit the wall,'" the runner said, "and you feel like you can't go on, instead of focusing on your exhaustion and going into the 'survival shuffle,' lift up your head and *pick up your pace.*" At first glance, that advice may sound counterintuitive. But on reflection, it makes great sense. By picking up the pace, you're really saying to yourself that you're not just going to finish; you're going to finish strong.

A SUMMARY OF THE FOUR CORES

In this section, we've explored the First Wave of Self Trust. We've looked at the Four Cores that create credibility—the character and competence necessary for us to trust ourselves and to be deserving of the trust of others. We've talked about ways to build character by increasing integrity and improving intent. We've talking about ways to build competence by increasing capabilities and improving results. In doing these things, we build credibility and inspire trust.

As I mentioned earlier, in our Speed of Trust workshops, one of the exercises we do with the participants is send out a 360-degree trust feedback tool to get input from their boss, peers, reports, and others whose names they provide. The feedback is then compiled and run through an analysis by an independent firm—we don't even see it. The following day, we allow time for those who would like to discuss the feedback with their coaches and to share with the group.

For many, it is very surprising to see how others rate them on these 4 Cores.

At one recent workshop, one CEO said:

> *I graded myself very hard, but my perception was that I was terrific at getting results. But they said, "You don't deliver," and that was eye-opening. My company's doing great, but I started to think, If I listen to them more and I step aside and stop micromanaging—if I just move over and get out of the way—think of how big the company could be!*

A leader in a nonprofit entity said:

> *One of the things that really shocked me was one of the comments that I was selfish. I thought, Selfish? How can someone say that I'm selfish? But as I met with my coach and started talking through some of the issues, I had to stop and say, "Well, maybe I am selfish because my whole thing is 'cover your tail at all costs.' Maybe I need to change that so they realize, 'Hey, this is a win for all of us.'"*

Whether you're aware of it or not, people notice the 4 Cores. They affect your credibility. Understanding them will give you conscious competence. It's like putting on your trust glasses. It will enable you to see beneath the surface, to see specifically why you—or others—are trusted or not. It will also enable you to pinpoint what you can do in your own life to increase trust, and also how you can work with others to help them increase trust in your organization or at home.

THE SECOND WAVE— RELATIONSHIP TRUST

The Principle of Behavior

The Second Wave—Relationship Trust—is all about behavior . . . *consistent* behavior.

It's about learning how to interact with others in ways that increase trust and avoid interacting in ways that destroy it.

More specifically, it's about the 13 Behaviors that are common to high-trust leaders and people throughout the world. These behaviors are powerful because:

They are based on principles that govern trusting relationships. (They are not based on fads or techniques or even practices, but rather on enduring principles that have proven successful in all thriving civilizations throughout time.)

They grow out of the 4 Cores. (They are based on personal credibility—on both character and competence. They flow out of what you are, not what you might pretend to be.)

They are actionable. (They can be implemented immediately.)

They are universal. (They can be applied in any relationship—with your boss, peers, associates, customers, spouse, children, extended family, or friends. They can also be applied in any organization—business, government, education, medicine, or nonprofit—and in any culture, although specific cultural applications may vary.)

I can promise you that these 13 Behaviors will significantly enhance your ability to establish trust in all relationships—both personal and professional.

THE 13 BEHAVIORS

You can't talk yourself out of a problem you've behaved yourself into.

—STEPHEN R. COVEY

No, but you can <u>behave</u> yourself out of a problem you've behaved yourself into . . . and often faster than you think!

—STEPHEN M. R. COVEY

A few years after we married, Jeri and I moved to Boston, where I attended business school. Our son Stephen was one year old at the time. One weekend, my parents flew out to visit us. They took us out for a buffet dinner, and I was so excited to be with them that I'm afraid I reverted back to my childhood. I quickly loaded my plate with food, sat down, and began laughing and reminiscing with my parents, who had gone ahead to get a table. In doing so, I virtually ignored Jeri, who was still in line struggling with our one-year-old and his diaper bag and trying to serve his plate and hers. Finally she joined us, but throughout the evening, she remained focused on the baby and didn't say much.

When we got home, I sighed with satisfaction and said, "It's so great to have my parents here, isn't it?" Then I turned to her and said, "I sure do love you!"

She said, "No, you don't."

Surprised, I replied, "Of course I do!"

She said, "No you don't—Freddy!"

"Freddy!" I exclaimed. "Who's Freddy?"

"He's the guy in *My Fair Lady*," she replied with some disdain, "You know . . . the one who talks about love but doesn't do anything about it?"

"What?" I said incredulously. "What are you talking about?"

She looked me straight in the eye. "When we were in that restaurant tonight, you were completely clueless! Here I was trying to take care of little Stephen, to get his plate and feed him and keep him happy and quiet, and all you could think of was having fun with your parents. You were no help at all—Freddy!"

With that, she reminded me of the words that Eliza—the main character in *My Fair Lady*—sang (somewhat disparagingly) to Freddy: "Don't talk of stars burning above; If you're in love, *show me!*" Eliza didn't want words; she wanted demonstrative behavior. And so did Jeri.

As I thought about the evening's events from her perspective, I felt terrible. She was right—I had been clueless. I should have been sensitive and aware. My actions—even more than my words—should have clearly demonstrated my love for her.

> *People don't listen to you speak; they watch your feet.*
>
> —ANONYMOUS

BEHAVIOR MATTERS

The truth is that in every relationship—personal and professional—what you *do* has far greater impact than anything you say. You can say you love someone—but unless you demonstrate that love through your actions, your words become meaningless. You can say you want to engage in win-win negotiation—but unless your behavior shows that you really mean it, you will come across as insincere. You can say your company puts the customer first. You can say that you recognize people as your most important asset. You can say that you will comply with the rules, that you won't engage in unethical practices, that you will respect a confidence, keep a commitment, or deliver results. You can say all of these things, but unless you actually *do* them, your words will not build trust; in fact, they will destroy it.

Good words have their place. They signal behavior. They declare intent. They can create enormous hope. And when those words are followed by validating behavior, they increase trust, sometimes dramatically. But when the behavior doesn't follow or doesn't match the verbal message, words turn into withdrawals.

> *Trust is established through action. . . .*
>
> —HANK PAULSON, CHAIRMAN AND CEO, GOLDMAN SACHS

This section is about the 13 Behaviors of high-trust people and leaders worldwide. These behaviors are powerful because they are based on the principles that govern trusting relationships. They grow out of the 4 Cores. They are actionable and universal. And as you will see, they are validated by research and experience.

Undoubtedly you're already living some of these behaviors and getting the high-trust dividends that grow out of them. There are others you're probably not living as well, and as a result, you're paying a tax. As you go through the following short chapters that describe these behaviors, you can choose the ones you feel will make the greatest difference to you.

However, before we get into these chapters, I want to briefly share a few important ideas that will help you understand and apply these behaviors in your unique situation.

YOU CAN CHANGE BEHAVIOR

Some people say you can't change behavior. But there is clear evidence to indicate that people can and do change behavior—sometimes dramatically—and that doing so often produces extraordinary results.

Look at Anwar Sadat, who changed his anti-Israel behavior so dramatically that he brought Egypt and Israel, two long-standing enemies, together to the negotiation table to work for peace. Look at Nelson Mandela, once the head of the ANC's armed wing, who ended up leading his nation through a dramatic transition with an almost unparalleled spirit of nonviolence, forgiveness, and reconciliation. Look at the many parents who become "transition" people, refusing to pass their own parents' poor behavior on to their children, transforming a heritage of abuse into a legacy of love. Look at those who successfully go through alcohol and drug rehabilitation programs. Think about your own life. Haven't there been times when you have consciously chosen to change your own behavior—and have been successful?

For the most part, the difference between those who change behavior and those who don't is a compelling sense of purpose. When your purpose is to accomplish results in a way that builds trust, suddenly the behaviors that build trust are no longer just nice "to do's"; they become powerful tools that enable you to enjoy rich, satisfying relationships, greater collaboration and shared accomplishment, and more just plain fun.

In recent years, much emphasis has been placed on the importance of "paradigm shifts"—changes in the way you see or think about things that create significant changes in behavior. I hope this book will help you create valuable paradigm shifts in your life regarding trust.

But I also hope it will help you create significant "*behavior* shifts"—shifts in *doing* that actually change the way you see and think. I love the story credited to minister George Crane about a woman who came into his office one day so angry at her husband that she wanted not only to divorce him, but to cause him pain. Dr. Crane said to her, "Go home and act as if you really loved your husband. Tell him how much he means to you. Praise him for every decent trait. Go out of your way to be as kind, considerate, and generous as possible. Spare no efforts to please him, to enjoy him. Make him believe you love him. After you've convinced him of your undying love and that you cannot live without him, then drop the bomb. Tell him that you're getting a divorce. That will really hurt him." The woman thought that was a brilliant idea, so she set out to totally convince her husband that she deeply, sincerely, completely loved him. Every day, she did everything she could think of to make him believe it. But by the time several months had passed, she was astonished to suddenly realize that she really *did* love him. She had actually behaved her way back into love.

The lesson from the story is this: If you're not a caring person now—but you *desire* to be a caring person—then go out and behave in caring ways. If you're not an honest person now—but you *desire* to be honest—then go out and behave in honest ways. Just do what caring and honest people do. It may take time, but as you do these things, you can behave yourself into the kind of person you want to be.

BUILDING TRUST ACCOUNTS

As you work on behaving in ways that build trust, one helpful way to visualize and quantify your efforts is by thinking in terms of "Trust Accounts." These are similar to the "Emotional Bank Accounts" my father introduced in *The 7 Habits of Highly Effective People*. By behaving in ways that build trust, you make deposits. By behaving in ways that destroy trust, you make withdrawals. The "balance" in the account reflects the amount of trust in the relationship at any given time.

One of the greatest benefits of the Trust Account metaphor is that it gives you a language to talk about trust. It's also valuable because it helps you become aware of several important realities:

Each Trust Account is unique. There is a great deal of difference in the account I have with my three-year-old daughter and the one that I have with my nineteen-year-old son. While my three-year-old trusts me implicitly, my nineteen-year-old constantly reminds me of the words of Mark Twain: "When I was a boy of 14, my father was so ignorant I could hardly stand to have the old man around. But when I got to be 21, I was astonished at how much the old man had learned in seven years!" Recognizing uniqueness can help you build each account more effectively.

All deposits and withdrawals are not created equal. Often the little things can be disproportionately large. When Hurricane Katrina hit the southeastern coast of the U.S., one of my associates sent a brief e-mail of concern to a client who had to evacuate her island home. He said that he hoped she was doing well, that she was in his prayers, and that he would talk to her when she was able to return. She later said, "That was the only e-mail I got that expressed concern from anyone outside of my family, and it meant a lot to me. Thank you." On the other hand, little things such as forgetting a family member's birthday (or worse, your own wedding anniversary!), not saying "thank you," or failing to attend to other small courtesies or customs can create huge withdrawals, particularly with some people, or with most people in some cultures around the world.

What constitutes a "deposit" to one person may not to another. I may think it's a deposit to take you and your partner out to dinner. But to you, it may be a withdrawal. Maybe you don't like to eat out with business associates, or you're on a diet, or you really want to spend the evening at home, but you feel obligated because you don't want to offend me. Or I may think it's a deposit to publicly acknowledge you for some positive thing you did. But to you, it may be a withdrawal— even a huge withdrawal—because you wanted your deed to remain anonymous. Always remember: It's important to know what constitutes a deposit to a person when you're trying to build trust.

Withdrawals are typically larger than deposits. As Warren Buffett has said, "It takes twenty years to build a reputation and five minutes to ruin it." In general, withdrawals can have 10, 20, or even 100 times more impact than deposits, but there are some withdrawals that are so significant that they completely wipe out the account in one stroke. I once heard the analogy that trust is like a big bucket that gets filled with water (making deposits) one drop at a time, and some withdrawals (the massive ones) are like "kicking the bucket"—in other words, because of a single action, you simply don't have anything left. The important thing to remember here is that it's not smart to kick the bucket! You're going to make mistakes—everybody does—but try not to make the ones that completely destroy trust, and work hard to build trust and to restore whatever trust has been lost.

Sometimes the fastest way to build trust is to stop making withdrawals. When I assumed the challenge of turning the Covey Leadership Center around, we had five different businesses, four of which were profitable. The fifth was losing money, taking 20 percent of my time and providing only 2 percent of our revenue. Although this business had been popular with some of the company's leaders, I recognized that the quickest way to improve the overall profit was not to focus on improving the other four, but to eliminate the fifth. So we sold it, and that made a huge difference in turning the center around and restoring the trust of bankers and others who were involved. As this experience affirms, to raise the level of performance (or, in this case, trust) you not only need to strengthen the driving forces, you also need to remove the restraining forces. If you don't, it's like trying to drive a car with one foot on the gas pedal and the other foot on the brake. Sometimes the fastest way to achieve results is to simply take your foot off the brake.

Recognize that each relationship has two trust accounts. The way you perceive the amount of trust in a relationship and the way the other person perceives it may be different. So it's generally wise to think of any relationship in terms of two accounts—not one—and to try to be aware of the balance in each account. I've often thought it would be helpful if we could see "signal bars" over people's heads (like those in the Cingular cell phone commercials showing the bars going up and down to reflect varying cell phone reception). Instead of cell phone reception, these bars would show the effect of every interaction—whether it made a deposit or a withdrawal, and the resulting balance. But without such graphic help, it's best to make a sincere effort to understand what makes a deposit or withdrawal to another person and always try to act in ways that build trust.

> *There are no facts, only interpretations.*
>
> —FRIEDRICH NIETZSCHE

THINGS TO KEEP IN MIND

As we move now into the 13 Behaviors, I'd like to call your attention to a few ideas that will help you with understanding and implementation.

First, all the 13 Behaviors require a combination of both character and competence. The first five flow initially from character, the second five from competence, and the last three from an almost equal mix of character and competence. This is important to recognize because generally, the quickest way to decrease trust is to violate a behavior of character, while the quickest way to increase trust is to demonstrate a behavior of competence.

Second, like any good thing, it's possible to take any one of these behaviors to the extreme. And any strength pushed to the extreme becomes a weakness. As we discuss each of the behaviors, it will be helpful to keep the following visual in mind. I will point out specific ways you can use the 4 Cores and strengthen your judgment to hit the "sweet spot" on the curve for each behavior.

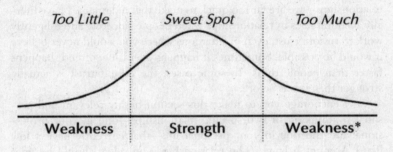

*Any strength used to an extreme can become a weakness.

Third, these 13 Behaviors work together to create balance. For example, "Talk Straight" must be balanced by "Demonstrate Respect." In other words, you don't want to talk so straight that you're like a bull in a china shop, showing blatant disregard for the worth or ideas or feelings of others.

Fourth, along with each behavior, I will note the *principles* upon which it is based. I will also give the *opposite* and the *counterfeit* for each behavior. It's these opposites and counterfeits (often unrecognized) that create the biggest withdrawals.

Fifth, at the end of each chapter, I'll suggest a few "Trust Tips." This will include ideas for strengthening your 4 Cores to hit the "sweet spot" on the curve, and also a few specific suggestions for ways to apply the behavior. Keep in mind that the behavior itself is the real "to do" in each chapter; the application suggestions are designed to stimulate "next step" thinking.

MAKING IT PERSONAL

At the end of one of my presentations, a man came to me with tears in his eyes. He said, "I wish I had heard all of this ten years ago. That Warren Buffett quote, 'It takes twenty years to build your reputation and five minutes to ruin it,' is so true. In five minutes, I ruined my reputation with my wife, and it's been a battle ever since."

As I acknowledged to him, there are situations where the withdrawals have been so huge and the pain is so great that trust cannot be restored. In effect, the account is closed. But I firmly believe that in the vast majority of cases—particularly in personal friendships and family relationships—we are far too quick to make that judgment. I have literally seen miracles in relationships when people sincerely and diligently work to restore trust, even in situations where you would never believe it would be possible. Sometimes it happens over time; often it happens faster than people think. In some cases, the rebuilt trust is actually stronger than it was before.

So I encourage you to make this section highly relevant and personal by thinking of two specific relationships—one in your professional life and one in your personal life—that currently have a low Trust Account balance. The relationships you select should be ones where you would like to increase trust, and where, by improving trust, you would get far better results professionally and find far greater happiness personally.

At the end of this section, I'll give you the opportunity to look back, identify the two or three behaviors that would make the greatest difference for you, and create an actionable plan for change.

> *The only relationships in this world that have ever been worthwhile and enduring have been those in which one person could trust another.*
>
> —SAMUEL SMILES, BRITISH AUTHOR AND BIOGRAPHER

As you think about behaving in ways that build trust, keep in mind that every interaction with every person is a "moment of trust." The way you behave in that moment will either build or diminish trust. And this opportunity is geometric. How you behave with one family member is noticed by other family members. How you behave with one report gets discussed with other reports. How you interact with one client is observed by other clients. This is the stuff by which corporate legends are created. It's the ripple effect—once again, the opposite of the mafia creed: By behaving in ways that build trust with one, you build trust with many.

BEHAVIOR #1:
TALK STRAIGHT

The people who I have trouble dealing with . . . are people who tend to not give full information. They purposefully leave out certain parts of the story—they distort facts.

—SHELLEY LAZARUS, CHAIRMAN AND CEO,
OGILVY & MATHER

At one time I worked with a person who would never let you know where he stood on an issue until the decision was made and the wisdom of the decision was either validated or shown to be in error. You could never pin him down. However, once the decision was finally made and the results were in, he rode the winning horse and energetically asserted that that had been his opinion all along.

At one point a very important proposal came up in our executive meeting. I knew that if we acted on this proposal, it would either be fantastic or it would bomb. As usual, this person said a lot in the meeting, but he really didn't commit one way or the other.

Tired of his sidestepping, I wanted to have him on record as committing one way or the other. So that night I went to his home to talk with him. He knew that I was against the proposal. So when I asked him where he stood, he said, "Oh, I am totally against it."

The next day, in front of the entire group, I said to him, "Yesterday in our meeting it wasn't clear to me where you stood on this issue. Would you please share your views?" The chairman of the company was at this meeting, and because this man knew that the chairman wanted to accept this proposal, he postured entirely differently than he had with me the night before.

Somewhat exasperated, I said to him, "That's not at all what you said last night to me. You told me straight up that you are against this proposal." He hemmed and hawed and said, "Yes, well, that's what I was thinking at that point, but . . ." He was masterful at skirting commitment and playing to the preferences of the key players involved.

TELL THE TRUTH *AND* LEAVE THE RIGHT IMPRESSION

In your personal life or your professional life, have you been in situations where you wish people would just be honest and up-front, tell it like it is, say what they think, give you the facts, make their agenda clear?

What happens to trust when they don't?

What happens to trust when they do?

"Talk Straight" is honesty in action. It's based on the *principles* of integrity, honesty, and straightforwardness. As I said earlier, it means two things: to tell the truth and to leave the right impression. And both are vital to building trust. It's possible to tell the truth and to leave the wrong impression. Leaving the right impression means communicating so clearly that you cannot be misunderstood.

> *What we say is true and forthcoming—not just technically correct.*
>
> —DELL INC.'S CODE OF CONDUCT

A good example of Talk Straight is a man I know who is president of a large division of a public company. Whenever he has to give formal feedback to someone who is not performing and whose job is on the line, this man will always say very clearly, "Here are the specific things you need to do, and if you do not do these things, *you will be fired.*" He doesn't allow people to think they are just going to get some slap on the wrist or be transferred to another division. They clearly know: if they don't perform, they will be f-i-r-e-d. This is hard for people to hear. Undoubtedly it's hard for him to say. But saying it is a lot kinder than leaving the impression that there is any other option in mind.

Another excellent example of Talk Straight is Warren Buffett. Every year he writes a management letter for his company's annual report. His letters are descriptions of things as they really are, without spin. For example, he writes:

- *I've made this kind of deal a few times myself—and, on balance, my actions have cost you money.*
- *I didn't do that job very well last year. My hope was to make several multibillion acquisitions that would add new and significant streams of earnings to the many we already have. But I struck out.*
- *Rather than address the situation head-on, however, I wasted several years while we attempted to sell the operation. . . . Fault me for dithering.*

In contrast, many management letters in annual reports read like public relations blather, positioning their companies to look as good as legally possible. When a letter begins with a statement such as, "2005 was a challenging year for XYZ Corp. . . ." you know that the company probably had a lousy year, but will try to "put makeup on the pig." Buffett would just straight out call a pig a pig.

Another example is Abraham Lincoln, whose ability to inspire trust in others—even in his former rivals—is legendary. Undoubtedly, there are many reasons for this, but clearly one of his most defining characteristics was his method of communication. He was often described as being "plainspoken," which is another way of saying he talked straight. And while some people disagreed with him, no one saw him as being duplicitous. Said Lincoln with his characteristic wit: "If I were two-faced, would I be wearing this one?"

The *opposite* of Talk Straight is to lie or to deceive. Such behavior creates a huge tax on interactions—either immediately or at some later time when the deception is discovered. The U.S. presidential Watergate scandal of the early 1970s is a powerful example of the impact of lying and deceiving and attempting to cover up. When people lie, they destroy trust. Period. They make it so that no one going forward can take them for their word.

> What upsets me is not that you lied to me, but that I can no longer believe you.
>
> —FRIEDRICH NIETZSCHE

Most people don't flat-out lie—at least not blatantly. Instead, they engage in the *counterfeit* behaviors of Talk Straight. These counterfeits include behaviors such as beating around the bush, withholding information, double-talk (speaking with a "forked tongue"), flattery, positioning, posturing, and the granddaddy of them all: "spinning" communication in order to manipulate the thoughts, feelings, or actions of others. Another dangerous counterfeit is "technically" telling the truth but leaving a false impression. This is mincing words and legally splitting hairs. All these behaviors invariably diminish trust.

THE IMPACT ON SPEED AND COST

According to a 2005 Mercer Management Consulting study, only 40 percent of employees trust that their bosses communicate honestly—which means that six in ten believe their bosses are not honest about what they're saying.

What kind of impact do you think that has on speed and cost?

Instead of straight talk, much of organizational life is filled with spin. This creates what I call a "spin tax," and is one of the main reasons why trust is low in so many organizations. When people keep hearing spin from their leaders, they tend to become skeptical and cynical—much in the same way that many people respond to politicians and their perpetual spin. Then when the tough changes take place—the layoffs, restructurings, or mergers—people don't give the benefit of the doubt to what top management says or does. Instead, they tax it all right off the top.

Sometimes entire cultures are held hostage by a downward cycle of spin and posturing. This diminishes trust and creates an additional "withholding tax" where people withhold information and keep things "close to the vest." As a result, companies often have three meetings instead of one: the premeetings (to prepare and position), the meetings themselves (where, because of all the spin and withholding, very little discussion of the real issues take place), and then the "meetings after the meetings" (the smaller meetings where the real discussion happens and the real issues are aired).

When a culture is caught up in a downward cycle of spin and withholding, it requires great courage to Talk Straight. Perhaps you remember the Hans Christian Andersen story "The Emperor's New Clothes." An emperor is sucked into a scheme by two charlatans who claim they can weave a magical cloth that is invisible to all who are either stupid or unfit for their positions. Not wanting to appear stupid or unfit, everyone who comes to see the cloth (including the emperor) praises its excellence. Soon—despite the obvious—everyone gets caught up in spinning and flattering and following the "company line."

When the emperor finally wears the "clothes" made out of this cloth in a public processional, all the people lining the streets begin to "oooh" and "ahhh." But finally, one little child says, "But he doesn't have anything on!" As the people realize the truth, they all begin to shout, "But he doesn't have anything on!"

When people do have the courage to stop the cycle of spin and Talk Straight instead, amazing things happen. Communication is clear. Meetings are few, brief, and to the point. Trust increases. Speed goes up. Cost goes down.

WHEN TALK STRAIGHT IS TAKEN TOO FAR

Like all of the other behaviors, Talk Straight can be taken too far. I knew one leader who, in the name of talking straight, justified cruel, brutal communication. Either he didn't recognize the harmful impact his approach was having on others and on trust, or else he recognized it and did it anyway—and in this case, his "straight talk" became an extreme weakness.

While straight talk is vital to establishing trust, in most situations, it needs to be tempered by skill, tact, and good judgment. I had this point burned indelibly into my own mind one time when our family was on a vacation at the beach and I decided to go for a swim. When I took off my shirt, my three-year-old daughter looked at me and exclaimed, "Whoa, Daddy! You have a big tummy!" Unfortunately, that was straight talk—but it was not tempered by any tact or consideration whatsoever!

These simple examples affirm how the behaviors need to balance each other out, and how the 4 Cores provide the judgment that will keep you on the "sweet spot" of the bell curve. When you blend courage (Integrity) with an agenda that is truly mutual benefit (Intent), with the ability to address situations directly (Capabilities), and a focus on building trust (Results), you have the discernment that enables you to Talk Straight in a way that significantly increases trust.

TALKING STRAIGHT AT HOME

Talk Straight is important not only in organizational life, but in personal and family relationships, as well. Particularly in such close relationships, it is often helpful to preface your discussions by declaring your intent—especially if you have difficult things to say or to hear.

Good examples of talking straight in homes include:

- A parent who is appropriately straightforward and clear in teaching or helping a child, even in dealing with difficult topics, such as drug abuse, choosing friends, or sex.
- Couples who kindly but clearly express their thoughts and feelings to each other and work toward win-win solutions, even in dealing with difficult topics such as child discipline, in-laws, or money.
- Family members who take the responsibility to say, "Hey, I've done something here I'd like you to notice" instead of feeling belittled and victimized or accusing others of being insensitive or uncaring.

As you think about Talk Straight, think about the powerful difference it could make in your relationships with the most important people in your life.*

TRUST TIPS

When you put Talk Straight on the bell curve, you will notice that behaviors on the left—which represent not talking straight enough—might typically be caused by Integrity issues (a lack of courage), Intent issues (a self-focused agenda—you care more about avoiding discomfort than acting in someone's best interest), Capability issues (a lack of verbal or interpersonal skills), or Results issues (a failure to focus on outcomes that build trust). Obviously, behaviors on the left side of the curve will not maximize moments of trust.

But neither will excessive behaviors on the right. This is where you find examples like the ones I mentioned under "When Talk Straight Is Taken Too Far." It would also include the married couple who go to counseling to learn how to be more skilled communicators, only to come out better fighters. Or the person who, in the name of "straight talk," constantly bad-mouths and puts down others behind their backs. Excessive behaviors such as these also reflect the 4 Cores issues—perhaps a lack of humility (Integrity) or caring (Intent), or an overbearing style (Capabilities), or insensitivity to the consequences (Results).

---

* Does this work with teenagers? Find out about this and other challenging personal relationships at www.speedoftrust.com.

Again, the key to optimization is to make sure that each behavior is at its highest point of connection with the 4 Cores. This will maximize judgment in applying the behavior and ensure alignment with the principles that govern trusting relationships. As a result, it will enable you to create the biggest trust dividends and avoid trust tax.

Following are a few suggestions for improving in your ability to Talk Straight:

- Ask yourself: What keeps me from talking straight? Is it fear of the consequences? Fear of pain? Fear of being wrong? Fear of hurting others' feelings? Is it a desire for popularity? A lack of courage? The challenge of living or working in an environment where people don't Talk Straight? Identify the dividends of being honest and straightforward and the cost when you're not. Then work to strengthen your 4 Cores and your ability to Talk Straight.

- Become aware of your conversation. In the middle of an interaction, stop and ask yourself, Am I talking straight—or am I spinning? If you're spinning, figure out why, recognize you're paying a tax for it, and work on Integrity and Intent.

- Learn to get to your point quickly. Avoid long prologues and giving excessive context. Recognize that in most cases, "less" is "more." In the legal world vernacular, "If you're explaining, you're losing." The personal discipline of talking straight helps create a precision of language, an economy of words, and a lack of spin.

Though I won't list it in every behavior, I have one more suggestion I believe is good to keep in mind with them all:

- Involve other people. Tell them, "I'm really trying to improve my ability to Talk Straight in my communications with others. Would you be willing to help me by giving me feedback to let me know how I'm doing in my relationship with you?"

Involving others will do two important things:

First, it will make it easier for you to change. By enlisting others in your growth and development, you transform a culture that typically resists change to one that encourages it.

Second, it will enable you to better see your current situation and your progress. When it comes to our own behavior, we often have "blind spots"—things that we can't see but others can. Getting feedback helps us see those blind spots.

If you do decide to involve others, however, you need to be aware that you will be held to a higher standard. By engaging others in your efforts to improve, you raise their expectations. If you don't follow through, you'll definitely be making withdrawals. But if you do follow through, this is another great way to build trust.

SUMMARY: BEHAVIOR #1—TALK STRAIGHT

Be honest. Tell the truth. Let people know where you stand. Use simple language. Call things what they are. Demonstrate integrity. Don't manipulate people or distort facts. Don't spin the truth. Don't leave false impressions.

BEHAVIOR #2:
DEMONSTRATE RESPECT

You can judge a person's character by the way he treats people who can't help him or hurt him.

—Anonymous

Synovus Financial Corporation is one of *Fortune* magazine's 100 Best Companies to Work for in America, and has been every year since these rankings began, achieving the number one position in 1999. Their chairman, James Blanchard, shared what he believed was the main reason why his company—and others like it—are able to succeed in the marketplace and to be such great places to work:

> There's a common thread that runs through those very few organizations who are just busting out on top all the time. They're meeting and exceeding their goals. They're realizing their visions and aspirations. They're always over and above their expectations. . . . And yet this group of robust, energized, enthusiastic, continually successful organizations, they seem to have a secret. And frankly, we have studied it, we have gone to school, we have consulted, we've done everything we can to try and find that formula that says, "We'll be one of these in this very small, select group that seems to achieve perpetual success."
>
> The secret, the clue, the common thread is simply how you treat folks. It's how you treat your fellow man, and how you treat your team members and how you treat your customers, your regulators, your general public, your audiences, your communities. How you value the worth of an individual, how you bring the human factor into real importance and not just a statement you make in your annual report.

Behavior #2 is Demonstrate Respect. There are two critical dimensions to this behavior—first, to behave in ways that show fundamental respect for people, and second, to behave in ways that demonstrate caring and concern. In many cultures—particularly Eastern cultures—this behavior is highly valued as evidence of a person's good upbringing. As a result, the casualness of much of the West is considered by some to be abrasive or rude. Understanding a cultural difference such as this becomes critically important in seeking to build Trust Accounts in today's global economy.

Demonstrate Respect is based on the principles of respect, fairness, kindness, love, and civility. The overarching principle, however, is the intrinsic worth of individuals—the importance of each human being as a part of the human family. This behavior is the Golden Rule in action—a rule that is actually recognized by almost every culture and religion worldwide. Consider the following examples:

Christianity: *"Do unto others as you would have them do unto you."*

Judaism: *"What you hate, do not do to anyone."*

Islam: *"No one of you is a believer until he loves for his brother what he loves for himself."*

Hinduism: *"Do nothing to thy neighbor which thou wouldst not have him do to thee."*

Buddhism: *"Hurt not others with that which pains thyself."*

Sikhism: *"Treat others as you would be treated yourself."*

Confucianism: *"What you do not want done to yourself, do not do to others."*

Aristotle: *"We should behave to our friends as we wish our friends to behave to us."*

Plato: *"May I do to others as I would that they should do unto me."*

The *opposite* of Demonstrate Respect is to not respect other people. This is commonly experienced as showing disrespect, which is a huge issue, both at work and at home. The opposite also includes *not* showing people you care—either because you really don't care, or because you don't know how or don't take the time to do it.

The *counterfeit* of Demonstrate Respect is to fake respect or concern, or, most insidious of all, to show respect and concern for some (those who can do something for you), but not for all (those who can't). This incongruence is becoming known as the "Waiter Rule." It's based on the idea that you can learn a lot about a person by the way he or she treats the waiter in a restaurant. Sara Lee CEO Brenda Barnes, herself a onetime waitress, says, "Sitting in the chair of CEO makes me no better of a person than the fork-lift operator in our plant. If you treat the waiter, or a subordinate, like garbage, guess what? Are they going to give it their all? I don't think so."

> I try to treat people as human beings. . . . If they know you care, it brings out the best in them.
>
> —SIR RICHARD BRANSON, FOUNDER AND CHAIRMAN,
> THE VIRGIN GROUP

I particularly like the story of the business student who did well on her final exam until she came to the last question: "What is the name of the person who cleans your dorm?" She was incredulous. How could she be expected to know the answer to that? And what in the world did it have to do with her business degree? Finally, she asked the professor if the question really counted on their final grade. "Indeed it does!" he replied. "Most of you dream about being the president and CEO of a successful company. But success is a team effort. A good leader takes nothing for granted and recognizes the contributions made by everyone on the team—even those people who appear to do the most insignificant jobs."

On the job, problems such as discrimination and sexual harassment have elevated respect to a major focus of organizational excellence, both as the right thing to do and as a better way of doing business. The Great Place to Work Institute, which partners with *Fortune* magazine to produce the 100 Best Companies list, names respect as one of the three pillars of trust in organizations. Sirota Survey Intelligence recognizes respect as one of the key defining characteristics of superhigh morale organizations and observes that in these top 10 percent of organizations, lower-level employees are treated the same as senior managers. Many employers are taking action to at least ensure compliance with respectful behavior. The real opportunity, of course, is to move beyond compliance and into people's minds and hearts.

THE LITTLE THINGS

Demonstrate Respect is a clear example of the disproportionate impact of the "little things" in building Trust Accounts. I remember what it meant to my executive assistant one time when I visited her mother in the hospital. This was just a little thing, but to my assistant it was a demonstration that I cared, and it really meant a lot to her that I would do that. Her response was similar to that of our client in Texas to whom my colleague sent an e-mail during the Hurricane Katrina evacuation. As the expression goes, "There are no little things."

One of our workshop participants who served as executive assistant to the president of a university for about ten years shared the following experience:

> *One afternoon, we were preparing for a special dinner in the president's home. The following day was commencement, and that night we were hosting a dinner for major donors to the university and the honorary doctorate recipient, a prominent government official from Latin America.*
>
> *As we were setting up the tables, a delivery of beautiful floral centerpieces arrived, obviously ordered by the university development office. The wife of our university president came over to him in a dither and said, "We have a problem." She held up a plain-looking margarine tub containing violets from the garden. As it turned out, Lola—an older woman from Europe who had been their housekeeper for many years— had already prepared the "centerpieces" for the event.*
>
> *The president looked at his wife and said, "No, we don't have a problem. Just send back the flowers to the florist. We'll use the centerpieces Lola made."*
>
> *That was a hugely defining moment for me. It taught me that no matter how small a contribution is to an activity or to an effort, that contribution needs to be honored and respected.*

Just think about the deposit this "little" demonstration of concern and respect made in the housekeeper's account. And think about the geometric impact it had on the Trust Accounts this university president had with everyone involved, including the staff, the guests, the people who worked in the university development office, and our workshop participant. In fact, I'm sure that everyone with whom she has shared this story (including me) has been influenced by this moment of trust. And it hasn't stopped there. After sharing this experience at the workshop, this woman went on to tell us of ways in which she has integrated the learning of this moment in her current job (which is totally unrelated to the university), and the effect it's had on the Trust Accounts she has with the people with whom she currently works.

Just think of the trust that was created as a result of that one defining moment!

DEMONSTRATING RESPECT AT HOME

At home, the "little things" are even more important. Simply saying "please" or "thank you," sincerely listening to someone, cleaning up after yourself, sharing the remote, or surprising someone with flowers or some other token of love make huge deposits in family Trust Accounts.

Growing up, I remember my mom and dad taking their daily half-hour ride around the neighborhood on a Honda trail bike so they could have special private time together to talk. I remember how family members would often stop and greet me with warmth and love when I walked through the front door. I remember times when my mom or dad would tell all of us to work really hard to surprise the other parent by cleaning up the kitchen, the garage, or the yard before the other one got home, and what fun it was to see the surprise and appreciation on that parent's face. In our own home now, I see how our three-year-old daughter's eyes light up when her thirteen-year-old brother takes her for a ride on the four-wheeler in our backyard, or how they used to light up when her nineteen-year-old brother was at home and would dress up like a prince to join the "princess" for a tea party on the floor.

I know firsthand what a difference those "little things" can make!

> *The end result of kindness is that it draws people to you.*
>
> —ANITA RODDICK, FOUNDER AND CEO, THE BODY SHOP

However, I also know that seemingly little demonstrations of disrespect can lead to the bigger withdrawals that ultimately wipe those Trust Accounts right out. As one publication on abuse points out:

> *The beginnings of both spouse and child abuse can be found in seemingly insignificant things, such as belittling the abilities and competency of another, constantly criticizing, being insulting or calling names, refusing to communicate, manipulating, causing guilt feelings, repeatedly making and breaking promises, intimidating, threatening physical harm, making unfounded accusations, or destroying property.*

In a popular culture of television, music, books, and movies that often reflect, laugh at, and even elevate disrespectful attitudes and little abusive behaviors, it's easy to become numb to the effects they have on the relationships that mean the most. We must never forget that—for good or ill—the "little" things *are* the big things at home.

THE BOTTOM LINE

While Demonstrate Respect may come across as a "soft" behavior to some, I contend that it absolutely has a direct relationship to trust and therefore to the bottom line.

Think back to some of the research I've shared in this book. *Why is it* that only 29 percent of employees believe that management cares about them developing their skills? *Why is it* that only 42 percent believe that management cares about them at all? In too many cases, though management might *talk* about it, fundamentally, management does not *behave* in ways that demonstrate respect, and as a result, employees don't trust management.

> *What creates trust, in the end, is the leader's manifest respect for the followers.*
>
> —JAMES O'TOOLE, AUTHOR OF *LEADING CHANGE*

And what is the impact on speed and cost? When employees believe their managers really don't care, how willing are they to give their best? To be innovative? To collaborate? On the other hand, how quick are employees to complain, criticize, unionize, and strike?

From the perspective of the customer, Demonstrate Respect has a huge impact. Several years ago, there was a fierce competition among real-estate agents to represent the developer in the sale of some exclusive home sites near Park City, Utah. The 4,000-acre parcel involved had been owned by a sheep-ranching family since pioneer days.

The developer invited several of the top real-estate agents in Park City to make presentations. Among them was Tom Peek, who made his presentation pretty much the same as everyone else. However, Tom did one thing that was distinctly different. He sent a handwritten thank-you note to the developer for the opportunity to be considered. The developer said that that one act clinched the choice for him. For Tom, sending the thank-you note was a natural thing to do. He said, "It is important to show respect to others and think of them when you are not there."

This development, named The Colony, became the largest ski-in and ski-out development in North America, with minimum four-acre lots and homes of up to 30,000 square feet. And Park City became one of the sites of the 2002 Winter Olympics.

There are countless examples of economic choices that are made based on a (sometimes small) demonstration of concern. People in advertising know this, and they often seek to convince consumers that the production of a particular product is a demonstration of concern for them.

TRUST TIPS

With Demonstrate Respect on the bell curve, it becomes obvious that the behaviors on the left—which demonstrate too little concern—often derive from issues of Integrity (insufficient humility), Intent (too much ego; not caring enough), or Capabilities (not knowing how to demonstrate caring or respect). Excessive behaviors on the right—including overprotectiveness, jealousy, pandering, and unproductive worry—may come from issues of Intent (more focus on self than on acting in what is really someone's best interest), Capabilities (attitudes and style), and Results (taking too much responsibility; not being sensitive to the effects of the behavior).

Again, it's interesting to note that in this, as well as all the behaviors, the judgment that comes from strengthening and blending the 4 Cores is vital to hitting the "sweet spot" on the curve.

Below are a few ideas that might help as you seek to Demonstrate Respect:

- Apply the "Waiter Rule" to yourself in terms of how you treat people at work and at home. Do you like what you see? If not, focus on improving your Intent.

- Think about specific things you can do to show others you care about them. Call people. Write thank-you notes. Give acknowledgment. Send e-mails of concern. Try to do something each day to put a smile on someone's face—even if that someone is the janitor in the building where you work. Don't let there be a gap between how you feel and what you do.

• Never take existing relationships for granted—particularly relationships with loved ones, family, and friends. Avoid the common tendency to put more energy into new relationships and assume that people in existing relationships know you care. There is probably a greater need for demonstrations of concern in existing relationships than in new relationships.

SUMMARY: BEHAVIOR #2— DEMONSTRATE RESPECT

Genuinely care for others. Show you care. Respect the dignity of every person and every role. Treat everyone with respect, especially those who can't do anything for you. Show kindness in the little things. Don't fake caring. Don't attempt to be "efficient" with people.

BEHAVIOR #3: CREATE TRANSPARENCY

For some people, becoming a leader can be a real power trip. They relish the feeling of control over both people and information. And so they keep secrets, reveal little of their thinking about people and their performance, and hoard what they know about the business and its future. This kind of behavior certainly establishes the leader as boss, but it drains trust right out of a team.

—JACK WELCH

A few years ago, when Donald Carty was CEO of American Airlines, the company worked to get significant wage concessions from its unions in order to keep the airline afloat and out of bankruptcy. It ended up negotiating $1.8 billion in annual wage and benefit cuts from the unions.

During this process of negotiation, however, the company made arrangements to provide substantial "stay" bonuses for the top six American Airlines executives, and a special trust was established so that executive pensions would be paid for the top 45 executives even if the company went into bankruptcy. Nothing done was illegal, but it was not disclosed to the unions during negotiations.

However, these executive perks had to be revealed in an annual SEC filing, which came out on the day the union approved the pay cuts. The disclosure caught the unions completely by surprise. It immediately destroyed whatever trust Carty had—not only with the unions, but also with at least some members of the board. According to *BusinessWeek*,

"Suddenly, Carty's calls for 'shared sacrifice' rang hollow," and "[t]he price of Carty's bungling turned out to be his job." Within days, Carty resigned.

When Gerard Arpey came in as the new CEO, he immediately faced a huge "inheritance tax" created by this prior behavior. Arpey said that he would work to "restore the confidence of all employees." His approach was open rather than secretive, transparent rather than hidden. He created an open-door environment, began disclosing all financial matters to his unions, turned down a raise the board offered him, and sold the company's expensive art, which had become an inappropriate symbol in a difficult time. Most significantly, he involved the unions directly in the company's problems by putting union representatives on senior management committees so that they could see the challenges from the same vantage point as management. He said, "Some people think that the unions are the problem, but we think they are part of the solution."

> Try to be transparent, clear and truthful. Even when it is difficult, and above all when it is difficult.
>
> —JEAN-CYRIL SPINETTA, CHAIRMAN AND CEO, AIR FRANCE

Arpey's behavior was not a "show"; it was the extension of his real character and competence (his 4 Cores). He said, "The only way to build trust professionally and personally is by being trustworthy. I hope I'm living up to that standard." As a result, Arpey has been able to rebuild trust, and American Airlines has been able to avert bankruptcy, while the other four-largest U.S. traditional carriers have not. Union leader Campbell Little said, "I believe Gerard to be a sincere person, compassionate, and someone who wants to turn American around."

Several months ago, I ran into a pilot from American Airlines on an elevator and I asked him, "What do you think of Gerard Arpey?"

Without hesitating, he replied, "He's outstanding! I can trust him."

> Strong reputations result when companies are transparent in the way they conduct their affairs.
>
> —CHARLES FOMBRUN, AUTHOR OF *REPUTATION*

Behavior #3—Create Transparency—is about being open. It's about being real and genuine and telling the truth in a way people can verify.

It's based on the *principles* of honesty, openness, integrity, and authenticity. I also like to include the principle of light, because when something is transparent, light will flow through it. In the words of former U.S. Supreme Court Justice Louis Brandeis, "Sunshine is the best disinfectant." It cleanses. It dissipates the shadows. It casts out the darkness. It enables people to see. It gives them a sense of comfort and confidence because they know there's nothing being hidden.

The *opposite* of Create Transparency is to hide, cover, obscure, or make dark. It includes hoarding, withholding, having secrets, and failing to disclose. It includes hidden agendas, hidden meanings, hidden objectives. The antonym for transparent is opaque—meaning something that is impervious to light and through which images cannot be seen.

The *counterfeit* of transparency is illusion. It's pretending, "seeming" rather than "being," making things appear different than they really are. The Internet is a good example of both transparency and illusion. At the same time as it engenders extraordinary transparency, allowing people to get information and access truth wherever they live, it also creates a place where people can make up pseudonyms and interact with others inside an illusion—where nobody knows their true identity or intent.

BUILDING TRUST FAST

More and more in our global economy, transparency is gaining recognition as a critical value in high-trust organizations. According to PriceWaterhouseCoopers, the "spirit of transparency" is the first key to restoring public trust.

And transparency will usually establish trust fast. For example, when a certain charity recently fell into trouble, it took the quickest path to restore trust, which was simply to show people where their money was going. In situations where there is a conflict of interest, the best way to prevent it from turning into a concern is to simply be up-front about it and to address it in the spirit of complete disclosure. Transparent companies are constantly disclosing relationships, interests, and conflicts ahead of time so that everything is always out in the open and no one can question their agenda.

Particularly when trust is low, people don't trust what they can't see. By opening things up, you assure people that there's nothing to hide.

A good example of transparency is the way in which Toyota operates with their suppliers. In an industry where most automakers focus on getting the lowest price and telling suppliers what to do, Toyota models a different-in-kind approach. They focus on building long-term relationships with and among their suppliers, who, in turn, collaborate with Toyota and with one another. Although product knowledge is treated as proprietary, process knowledge is expected to be shared within the value chain. Toyota's approach could not work without abundant transparency from all participants, and it is this transparency that is at the core of all Toyota's supplier relationships.

Another great example—and one that made a huge deposit to me personally—was the way a CEO of a $500 million company negotiated with me on a particular deal. He and I met and laid out the potential framework for the deal, but didn't finalize it because the input and buy-in of this CEO's sales, product development, and legal teams was critical to its success. I wrote up the potential deal points and sent them by e-mail to the CEO as a deal term sheet. After meeting with his people, he received redlined markups of the term sheet from the heads of his team, describing their issues and concerns. Rather than summarizing their concerns, he simply forwarded those communications directly to me, *with no edits*. This stunned me. It allowed me to understand and address the real issues without guessing. I decided to reciprocate the transparency and sent a similar document to his people with my markup of their concerns. As a result, we were able to negotiate a better deal for both parties, and we did so in probably a third of the time it would have taken without such transparency.

From the standpoint of speed and cost, transparency makes enormous sense. You don't have to worry about hidden agendas. You don't have to second-guess. You don't have to waste time and energy trying to maintain an appearance or keep up with which approach you took with which person.

Many companies create transparency with their own employees by going to what is known as Open Book Management—opening up their financial statements for the entire company to see. I worked with one CFO who said that this built trust faster than anything the company had ever done. He said, "Initially, there was some skepticism about whether what we had shared were the real numbers. But we sustained the approach, and it soon resulted in a palpable excitement and an enormous increase in trust. That's when the company started becoming highly profitable."

> We adopted a philosophy that we wouldn't hide anything, not any of our problems, from the employees.
>
> —Rollin King, founder, Southwest Airlines

Creating transparency also creates buy-in. In a family, for example, being transparent with children about finances and inviting their participation in spending decisions not only helps them understand why you sometimes have to say "no," it also helps them become more sensitive to the appropriateness of asking for certain things in the first place, so you don't have to waste time and emotional energy dealing with inappropriate requests. As an added bonus, transparency gives children an understanding of family economy and helps them become more responsible in their own spending decisions as they mature.

To negotiate with transparency does not mean you always have to lay all your cards on the table. But it does mean that you are transparent with appropriate information and with what you're trying to accomplish.

TRUST TIPS

In Create Transparency, as in all of the behaviors, there must be responsible balance. Particularly in public companies, there are certain things the law does not allow you to disclose to anyone unless it can be disclosed to everyone. There are other things that are confidential and inappropriate to disclose. Good, common sense would tell you that you don't talk about confidential matters, private conversations, or other things you don't have a right to talk about.

I was in one situation where a CEO attempted to create transparency in a management meeting by disclosing the salaries of everyone, including the management team in the room. This quickly changed the tenor of the meeting, and people suddenly began to look around wondering why some of their peers were making two times more than they were. Unbalanced by other behaviors such as Demonstrate Respect, this action was a shock to the system. It was on the far right of the bell curve. It was irresponsible transparency—too much, too fast. Most often, this kind of behavior comes from a lack of one or more of the following: humility (Integrity), mutual benefit agenda (Intent), trust abilities and leadership skill (Capabilities), or appropriate definition of and sensitivity to outcomes (Results).

On the left side of the curve, though, why would you limit appropriate transparency? Why would you withhold information? Why would you not put at least all your objectives, if not all your cards, on the table? Failure to create transparency usually indicates a lack of honesty or courage (Integrity), a hidden rather than open agenda (Intent), or a lack of Trust Ability to discern the importance of transparency and create it (Capabilities).

Again, keep in mind that strengthening the 4 Cores will keep you in the "sweet spot" on the bell curve, and that all of these behaviors work together to balance one another out.

As you work to Create Transparency, here are some tips to consider:

- At work and at home, periodically ask yourself, Am I withholding information that should be shared? If so, ask yourself why. Consider the tax you may be paying as a result. Think about the dividends you could be getting by being more transparent.

- If you're in a position of leadership at work, rate the transparency of your organization with regard to your various stakeholders. Then consider each situation and ask yourself: If we were more transparent, what difference would it make? Look for ways to appropriately increase transparency—and trust dividends!

- If you share a financial stewardship with someone—for example, a spouse—consider how transparent you are in dealing with financial issues. Keep in mind that money matters are still listed by many as a primary cause of divorce. If you're not transparent concerning your financial priorities, decisions, and spending, ask yourself why. Strengthening your 4 Cores will not only help you act and interact with your partner in more transparent ways, it will also increase your ability to work toward a unified approach.

SUMMARY: BEHAVIOR #3—
CREATE TRANSPARENCY

Tell the truth in a way people can verify. Get real and genuine. Be open and authentic. Err on the side of disclosure. Operate on the premise of "What you see is what you get." Don't have hidden agendas. Don't hide information.

BEHAVIOR #4:
RIGHT WRONGS

To know what is right and not to do it is the worst cowardice.

—CONFUCIUS

As we were growing up, my brothers and I loved sports and were extremely competitive. This enthusiasm has remained strong, and I'm sorry to say that at one game a few years ago, I got carried away and totally lost it with my teenage nephew, Kam.

It was the day of the big BYU–Utah basketball game—the biggest game in the state of Utah. This rivalry is legendary, and regardless of past wins and losses, the competition is always intense. Because my sister's husband had gone to the University of Utah, he and Kam were big Utah fans. Kam had been told to cheer conservatively so as not to embarrass the extended family there, especially since all but Kam and his dad were cheering for BYU.

Kam contained his enthusiasm until, at a crucial point in the game, the referee made an extremely questionable call in Utah's favor. Kam spontaneously jumped to his feet in celebration, waving his arms in the air. As he sat back down, I simply couldn't contain myself. I grabbed my water bottle and dumped the water on his head! Kam's grin turned to shock, then disappointment, then hurt. It was obvious that he couldn't believe I would do that to him.

Instantly, I was ashamed and felt deep regret for my immature actions. I knew I had taken a big withdrawal from our relationship. I wanted to make up for it, so I did the only thing I could think of at the time. After apologizing profusely, I bought a soft drink and demanded that Kam throw it in *my* face! Kam was embarrassed and refused. He said he knew I just got carried away, and he forgave me. But I didn't forgive myself.

Over the next two months, I called Kam almost every week. Every time I talked with him I'd say, "Hey, I just wanted you to know I'm really sorry about dumping that water on your head. Please forgive me!" When the next BYU–Utah game came around, I bought tickets for Kam and my sister. The game was at the "U" this time, and I forced myself to sit in the arena there without yelling at all. I bought Kam some Utah logo wear and all the junk food he could eat, and I repeated again, "Just wanted to mention once more, Kam, I'm so sorry for what I did." The poor kid finally responded, "All right, already! I really forgive you! Let's forget it!"

Interestingly, through all of this, my relationship with Kam actually became stronger. My repeated efforts to apologize and make restitution convinced him that I really did care deeply about him and about our relationship. As an added bonus, the experience helped me subdue my temper. Though I still get into the games and I care a lot that my team wins, I have never lost it again.

GOING THE EXTRA MILE

Behavior #4—Right Wrongs—is more than simply apologizing; it's also making restitution. It's making up and making whole. It's taking action. It's doing what you can to correct the mistake . . . and then a little more.

In business, Right Wrongs includes "service recoveries" or rectifying mistakes made with customers—hopefully so well that customers are not only satisfied, they are also given incentive to develop even greater loyalty to the company. The "little more" a company might add to encourage such loyalty could be a small thing, such as including a free product or gift certificate with a corrected order to apologize for the inconvenience. Or it could be a big thing, like JetBlue not charging customers any fees for missing their flight.

In a personal or family relationship recovery, that "little more" could be an extra-mile effort to express love, such as accompanying a sincere apology and restitution with a thoughtful gesture, such as flowers or breakfast in bed.

HUMILITY AND COURAGE—OR EGO AND PRIDE?

Right Wrongs is based on the *principles* of humility, integrity, and restitution. Its *opposite* is to deny or justify wrongs, to rationalize wrongful
behavior, or to fail to admit mistakes until you're forced to do so. It
involves ego and pride. It's being humbled by circumstance instead of
by conscience.

The *counterfeit* of Right Wrongs is to cover up. It's trying to hide a
mistake, as opposed to repairing it. In the case of Right Wrongs, the
counterfeit actually creates a double trust tax, one tax when you make
the mistake, and another—usually a far greater tax—when you try to
cover it up and get caught. The reality is that everybody makes mistakes. The issue isn't whether you will make them, it's what you will do
about them. It's whether you will choose the path of humility and
courage or the path of ego and pride.

Consider some examples of those who have chosen the path of
humility and courage. Recently Oprah Winfrey helped put James
Frey's book, *A Million Little Pieces*, on the *New York Times* bestseller list
by naming it as her book club selection. When accusations were raised
that Frey had embellished incidents in the supposedly "nonfiction"
book, Oprah initially defended the author. However, when she discovered the truth, she brought him back on her show. She sincerely apologized to her viewers, and she publicly chastised Frey for betraying both
his readers and her television audience. She said, "I feel duped. But
more importantly, I feel that you betrayed millions of readers." She
also acknowledged that she made a mistake when she had called in to
Larry King's talk show and defended the author. "I regret that phone
call," she said. "I made a mistake and I left the impression that the truth
does not matter, and I am deeply sorry about that. That is not what I
believe. To everyone who has challenged me on this issue of truth, you
are absolutely right." Oprah's behavior affirmed people's confidence in
her integrity and her genuine concern for others, which has been the
hallmark of her brand and reputation.

In Adrian Gostick and Dana Telford's excellent book, *The Integrity
Advantage*, the authors relate the experience of Wayne Sales, president
and CEO of Canadian Tire, who shared the following:

> *Chrysler let executives drive their new vehicles. They would turn them
> in with a few thousand miles on them, but someone was turning back
> the odometer and selling them as new. When this was discovered, I can*

only imagine what was happening within the organization. . . . In doing the right thing, Lee Iacocca took out a full-page ad in the Detroit Free Press *and said, "Look, we made a mistake. We breached the trust and integrity of our customers. We acknowledge we did this and we promise it will never happen again." And you know what? Life went on.*

In March of 2005, Doug Wead, a former special assistant to President George W. Bush, issued a letter of apology for writing a book containing material from discussions that had been tape-recorded without the president's knowledge. Wead shared the contents of this letter in a television interview with Chris Matthews and also a letter to the editor in *USA Today*.

In this letter, Wead said that he had first begun taping Bush back in 1987 with Bush's permission. Wead continued:

When our conversations began again in 1997, I first started taking notes. Many options were discussed and discarded in those conversations. Eventually, I was asked to carry a sensitive message to a reporter or even to a political opponent's camp. The exact wording was critical and I felt inadequate to the task. And so, the following year, my secret tape-recording of George W. Bush began. At first, it was only to make sure I was doing the right thing, what he wanted. But it was prideful and arrogant of me to think my good intentions justified my actions. I taped a man without his permission and he happened to win the presidency. My decision to release a portion of the tapes has come at a terrible price for my family and has deeply hurt many others.

I was foolish and wrong to tape-record Mr. Bush without his permission. I was wrong to play any part of the tapes for my publisher, regardless of the circumstances. I was wrong to play any part of them for a journalist. I apologized to the president before the story appeared and again afterward. He has been typically patient, in spite of the personal hurt.

Today, the work of reparation has begun.
* *My book promotion has been cancelled.*
* *Future royalties from the book have been assigned to charity.*
* *The hours of tapes, which prompted offers of millions of dollars, have been turned over to the president.*
* *The work of rebuilding relationships, with God, the president and friends, has begun.*

*If I could live my life over again, there are many things I would do
differently. I cannot undo the hurt I have caused but I can, with God's
help, take the heat I deserve and move on.*

The interesting thing about this situation is that it never really became
a huge political issue—due, in good part, I believe, to the fact that the
apology was made quickly, humbly, and sincerely, and was followed by
behavior (including giving up royalties and possible gain from the
tapes) that clearly confirmed his words.

Often the stories I hear about the power of righting wrongs in
building trust do not come from the key players; they come from
employees who have been asked about the trust in their organizations.
In other words, the trust-inspiring behavior of the leaders in these organizations has become an organizational symbol. This is yet another
example of the geometric growth that impacts the speed of trust:
When you build trust with one, you build trust with many.

Now contrast the results of these positive experiences with those
where people have chosen the other path of ego and pride. One striking example is the Watergate scandal of the early 1970s. When it was
discovered that U.S. President Richard Nixon's administration had
been involved in illegal efforts to access confidential information, those
involved—including the president—failed to take responsibility and
apologize for their misdeeds; in fact, they tried to cover them up. As a
result, trust was entirely destroyed, and, on threat of impeachment,
Nixon was forced to resign.

> Watergate wasn't so much a burglary as it was the failure
> to recognize mistakes, to take responsibility for them,
> and to apologize accordingly.
>
> —JON HUNTSMAN, CHAIRMAN, HUNTSMAN CHEMICAL

In a more recent example, former Philadelphia Eagles wide receiver
Terrell Owens made comments to the media that came across as critical
of his quarterback and management. Through the first half of the season, according to the media, he persisted in boorish, noncollaborative
behavior and continued to take subtle swipes at management and others on his team. Finally, despite his immense talent, the team decided
that the harm had been too great. They suspended him for the rest of
the season for "conduct detrimental to the team." Immediately after

the suspension, Owens came out and apologized, saying, "I know in my heart that I can . . . be a team player." But it was too little, too late, too halfhearted. Trust had already been lost. He couldn't talk his way out of the problem he'd behaved himself into.

Notice how in each of the positive examples in this chapter, people have been *quick* to admit a mistake and make an effort to repair it. When wrongs happen, and you quickly acknowledge them and apologize, in most cases you're able to move on. What damages credibility and trust the most is when, once something has gone wrong, people don't acknowledge it or apologize. This causes small incidents to blow up into far bigger issues, and when people try to cover it up, it gets even worse. While apologizing later is clearly better than not apologizing at all, apologizing and rectifying mistakes *immediately* will do far more to build and restore trust.

THE BOTTOM LINE

Right Wrongs powerfully affects the bottom line. Despite the fact that most insurance companies will tell doctors to not apologize to patients when they make mistakes, there's increasing evidence that shows that those who do apologize and are respectful and empathetic get sued less. People are more likely to sue when they're mad. People stay mad when they're owed an apology and don't get one. Giving a heartfelt apology in many cases takes the sword out of people's hands. As evidenced by the trust dividends Johnson & Johnson continues to receive 25 years after righting wrongs in the Tylenol scandal of 1982, "wrongs" can create geometrically significant moments of trust.

Even when you're on the other end—when someone else has wronged you—there are important things you can do to help Right Wrongs and build trust. By being forgiving, for example, you enable others to more easily apologize and make restitution to you. And acknowledging your own mistakes gives freedom to others to do the same, which is extremely ennobling and enabling for a culture, both at work and at home.

TRUST TIPS

If your behavior is too far left on the bell curve—if you're not going far enough in righting wrongs—you may want to work on honesty, humility, or courage (Integrity), or caring (Intent), or alignment between behavior and desired outcomes (Results). If you're too far on the right—apologizing too profusely or apologizing repeatedly for the same mistakes—you may want to work more on congruence (Integrity), or motivation (Intent), or on the judgment that comes from strengthening and blending all 4 Cores.

As you work to increase your ability to Right Wrongs, here are a few ideas:

- The next time you make a mistake, pay attention to your response. Are you trying to ignore it, justify it, cover it up? Or are you quick to admit it and do what you can to make restitution? If you don't now have the humility and courage it takes to quickly Right Wrongs, work on behaving yourself into the person you want to become.

- Give some thought to your past. Are there wrongs that haven't been righted? Are there estranged relationships that are waiting to be made whole or become "beautifully resolved"? Even though making the attempt may seem insurmountably difficult, I can assure you that whatever acute pain you may feel as you attempt to right a past wrong is not nearly as hard to live with as the chronic pain of distrust. And the relief that comes when you truly make an effort to right past wrongs is immense.

- The next time someone has wronged you, be quick to forgive. Try to make it easier for others to Right Wrongs. Not only will this help them, it will also help you.

SUMMARY: BEHAVIOR #4—RIGHT WRONGS

Make things right when you're wrong. Apologize quickly. Make restitution where possible. Practice "service recoveries." Demonstrate personal humility. Don't cover things up. Don't let pride get in the way of doing the right thing.

BEHAVIOR #5:
SHOW LOYALTY

*It's been my experience that the people who gain trust,
loyalty, excitement, and energy fast are the ones who
pass on the credit to the people who have really done the
work. A leader doesn't need any credit. . . . He's getting more credit than he deserves anyway.*

—ROBERT TOWNSEND, FORMER CEO, AVIS

Many years ago, I worked in a company where I would go to
lunch almost daily with a group of about 12 coworkers.
When they finished eating, a couple of people in the group
would get up and leave, and the others would immediately start talking
about them. When two or three more would leave, the group would
talk about them. It got to where I didn't dare leave the table because I
knew the minute I left, they'd start talking about me!

My experience with this lunch group was an example of the *opposite*
of Behavior #5. It showed disloyalty, and it made huge withdrawals—
not only with the people who were being discussed at the time, but also
with everyone else who was there. We all knew that the treatment of
those not present was an indication of the way we would be treated
when *we* were not present. And that certainly didn't build trust!

To Show Loyalty, on the other hand, is a way to make huge deposits
in the Trust Account—not only with the person you show loyalty to,
but also with everyone who becomes aware that you do it.

In John Marchica's book, *The Accountable Organization*, Colleen Barrett, president and COO of Southwest Airlines, demonstrates a way to

show loyalty to employees that clearly builds trust in the organization. She says:

> *It's all very logical to me, but I think it's sometimes a surprise with some other customer service–driven companies that will say the customer is always right. We don't subscribe to that. And we have said that publicly, too, which has caused me a letter or two! But that is one of the ways that we earn the trust of our employees. I'm not saying that if the employee makes a mistake, and it's a serious enough mistake, that they won't be disciplined or talked to. But I am saying that if the customer was wrong, and if the customer behavior was bad, then I am going to defend and support the employee. We haven't done this often, but we have, on occasion, told a customer that we don't want him or her back on our airline.*

Show Loyalty is based on the *principles* of integrity, loyalty, gratitude, and recognition. There are many ways to show loyalty—big and small—but in this chapter we will focus on two dimensions: giving credit to others, and speaking about people as though they were present.

GIVE CREDIT TO OTHERS

One important way to Show Loyalty is to give credit to others, to acknowledge them for their part in bringing about results. By giving credit, you not only affirm the value of an individual's contribution, you also create an environment in which people feel encouraged to be innovative and collaborative and to freely share ideas, kicking in the geometric trust multiplier.

With regard to giving credit, I like to think of "the window and the mirror" metaphor articulated by Jim Collins. He basically says that when things go well, you look through the window; in other words, you look at everyone out there and all they did to contribute, and you give them the credit, attribution, recognition, acknowledgment, and appreciation. When things don't go well, you look in the mirror. You don't look out there and blame and accuse others; you look at yourself.

The *opposite* of giving credit is to take the credit yourself. In one of our programs, a salesman told about how he found a choice client, ran with the opportunity, did all the work, and in the final stages of the deal, went to his boss for help. When his boss saw how big the account was, he took it over. He kept all the revenues and all the recognition. This created enormous distrust—not only with the person from whom he took the account, but also to everyone else on the team. No one wanted to ask the boss for help anymore because they knew he could do the same thing to them. This is yet another example of how when you build (or destroy) trust with the one, you build (or destroy) trust with the many.

> Leaders also establish trust by giving credit where credit is due. They never score off their own people by stealing an idea and claiming it as their own.
>
> —JACK WELCH

The *counterfeit* of giving credit is to be two-faced: to appear to give credit to someone when they're with you, but then downplay their contribution and take all the credit yourself when they're not there. This kind of duplicity is seldom hidden, and it damages trust with all.

Business author Dottie Gandy makes the point that it is not only important to give credit to people for *what they do*, but also to acknowledge people for *who they are*. There are many ways to acknowledge people and give credit for contributions, both at work and at home. You can celebrate. You can create legends and lores by the stories you tell. You can send thank-you's (letters, cards, or flowers). You can publicize success stories in company or family newsletters. You can go out of your way to catch people doing things right.

A senior executive at one of our workshops shared this idea:

> *Whenever our department is asked to provide input to those higher up, I share the request with the appropriate staff. When the good suggestions come back, instead of synthesizing them or sending them forward under my signature, I attach their e-mail and just say, "Our comments follow." This gives people recognition for their work. It also creates a huge credibility and loyalty factor between me and my staff because they know that wherever possible I will give them recognition and credit where it's due.*

However you do choose to do it, I guarantee that giving credit to others will significantly increase trust and economic results—as well as other positive results—on all levels. And I encourage you to give credit abundantly. To "give credit where credit is due" is a judgment, but to give credit abundantly flows out of an abundant heart.

> *You can accomplish anything in life provided you don't mind who gets the credit.*
>
> —HARRY S. TRUMAN, FORMER U.S. PRESIDENT

SPEAK ABOUT OTHERS AS IF THEY WERE PRESENT

The second dimension of Show Loyalty is to speak about others as if they were present. I learned the importance of this behavior firsthand in my experience with the lunch group I mentioned earlier. I saw how the lunchroom discussions that focused on those who had left ended up damaging trust with everyone involved.

Obviously this was an example of the *opposite* of speaking about others as if they were present—of selling people out or not representing them fairly when they're not in a position to do so themselves. The *counterfeit* of this behavior, which is equally destructive, is sweet-talking people to their faces and bad-mouthing them behind their backs. Often we're not even aware that we're involved in these opposite or counterfeit behaviors—or of the impact it has on trust. One CEO of a software company shared her feelings about some insightful feedback she received from her 360-degree Trust Audit. She said:

> *Under the "comments" section, one person wrote: "When someone leaves the company, do not bad-mouth them in front of your current employees. It makes me feel like no matter what I contribute to this company, it will be forgotten the moment I leave, no matter the circumstances." Ouch! I had no idea I was doing that and no idea of the impact it was having. It was very humbling for me to hear it.*

Interestingly, people who talk about others behind their backs often seem to think that it will build some kind of camaraderie and trust with those who are there. But the exact opposite is true. When you talk about others behind their backs, it causes those who are present to think you'll do the same to them when they're not there. So it clearly has a negative geometric impact on trust.

In contrast, my wife, Jeri, has a friend about whom she has said, "I trust Karen implicitly with anything. I've never heard her bad-mouth or criticize another soul. She just won't do it." What I also hear Jeri saying is, "And I know she won't criticize me."

An excellent example of this behavior occurred when Sam Alito was appointed U.S. attorney for New Jersey. He inherited a case from his predecessor that ended up going south, causing him to experience a defeat. Under the circumstances, it would have been easy for him to point fingers, but, according to an article in *USA Today*, "Alito refused to blame his predecessor, who had brought the case, or his assistants." As a result, "The new U.S. attorney scored 'huge points' with his staff."

> To retain those who are present, be loyal to those who are absent.
>
> —STEPHEN R. COVEY

I'm aware of a man who had a similar experience some years ago when he replaced the former president of a midsize company. Although this new president inherited significant problems from the former president's administration, he made the decision that he would not bad-mouth this man—publicly or privately—under any circumstance. This was an immense challenge for him. There were many times when he wanted to do it, but he didn't, and his approach helped him establish trust much faster in the organization. It also allowed him to create an excellent relationship with the former president's talented son, whom he wanted to stay in the company, and who did stay because of the new president's respectful treatment of the prior administration.

On the home front, one young acquaintance of mine said that as she was growing up, she always knew that what she said to her parents in private would never be discussed with anyone else in the family. They would never say to her brother, "Oh, you should have heard what your sister said the other day!" And neither would they talk about their private conversations with other family members with her. That demonstration of loyalty created high-trust relationships between parents and children in the home.

Obviously, for good or ill, the way we talk—or don't talk—about others when they're not there has geometric effect. It can build or destroy trust . . . fast.

WHEN YOU HAVE TO TALK ABOUT PEOPLE

So what happens when you're in a situation where your job involves talking about people? You can't just bury your head in the sand and say, "I just won't talk about anyone." So what do you do?

One former HR executive shared the following experience:

At one point, I was in a job where I had to talk about people all day. Managers would come to me and say, "I'm having a problem with Jim or Lori. What do I do?" Obviously we needed to discuss the individual, and sometimes what we had to talk about was not very complimentary. So I had to ask myself, How can I show loyalty to this person who is not present, and still do my job well?

I finally realized that the difference in showing loyalty and not showing loyalty is in intent. If the purpose was to improve the performance or the relationship and if the conversation was fair and respectful toward the person, then I could feel that I was showing loyalty. Most of those conversations ended up focusing on the manager and what he or she could do instead of on the faults (real or imagined) of the person we were talking about.

The key is to talk in a way that shows respect. Again, you're building trust with those who are present by communicating that you would speak with respect about them, too, if they were not there.

Another key is to have the courage to go directly to the person with whom you have a concern. Sometimes the person who needs to change is the last to know. To exercise courage—to go to the person and talk to him/her about the concern—is also a demonstration of loyalty.

TRUST TIPS

Let's take a look at the bell curve for this behavior. On the left side, you behave in ways that show loyalty only in minimal ways. Perhaps you're loyal as long as it's convenient. Or maybe you show some degree of loyalty, but not to the extent that you're willing to take a firm stand when others disagree.

On the right side of the curve, you might behave in ways that appear to be extremely loyal to someone at the moment, but which are not loyal to their future well-being or to principles. For example, you might agree to keep quiet about a person's committing a criminal act, or you might remain fiercely "loyal" to an idea or belief system, even when additional information clearly shows it to be outdated or incomplete.

Integrity (particularly courage and congruence), Intent (motive and behavior), and Capabilities (trust abilities) play a big role in helping you stay in the area of maximization. Keep in mind that often loyalty to principle is the best way to demonstrate loyalty to people.

In working to improve in this behavior, you might want to consider the following ideas:

- The next time you're in a conversation where people start bad-mouthing someone who's not there, consider your options. You can participate in the discussion. You can leave. You can stay, but remain silent. You can say something positive about the person to try to balance out the conversation. Or you can say, "I really don't feel comfortable talking about this person like this when he/she is not here. If we have a concern, let's go talk with this person directly." Consider what would be the most principled behavior in the situation and do it.

- The next time you work with others on a project at work or at home, go out of your way to give credit freely. Help create an environment in which everyone's contributions are recognized and every person is acknowledged. Give credit generously.

- Make it a rule to never talk about family members in negative ways. Be thoughtful about how you talk with your partner about family members, including children. Catch your children doing things right—and share your excitement about their good deeds with others.

SUMMARY: BEHAVIOR #5—SHOW LOYALTY

Give credit freely. Acknowledge the contributions of others. Speak about people as if they were present. Represent others who aren't there to speak for themselves. Don't bad-mouth others behind their backs. Don't disclose others' private information.

BEHAVIOR #6:
DELIVER RESULTS

Future leaders will be less concerned with saying what they will deliver and more concerned with delivering what they have said they would.

—DAVE ULRICH, BUSINESS AUTHOR
AND PROFESSOR

People frequently ask me, "If you want to establish a relationship with a new client, what is the one thing you can do to build trust the fastest?" Without hesitation, I reply, "Deliver results!" Results give you instant credibility and instant trust. They give you clout. They clearly demonstrate that you add value, that you can contribute, that you can perform. As well as being an integral part of your personal credibility (one of the 4 Cores), results provide a powerful tool for building trust in your relationships with others.

With Deliver Results, we move from those behaviors that are based primarily on character to those based primarily on competence. This behavior grows out of the *principles* of responsibility, accountability, and performance. The *opposite* of Deliver Results is performing poorly or failing to deliver. The *counterfeit* is delivering activities instead of results.

I've worked with a lot of people over the years—particularly salespeople—who are long on talk, but short on delivery. They make all kinds of fantastic presentations and exciting promises of all the wonderful results they are going to achieve. But when it comes down to it, they either never deliver or deliver far short of what they promise. I finally learned to look for people who are short on talk and long on delivery. It's not that they don't make excellent presentations or anticipate high-level success. They do. But they don't overhype. They just consistently deliver results. I learned it's most effective to give the best opportunities to the big producer who doesn't talk instead of the big talker who doesn't produce.

> *We judge ourselves by what we feel capable of doing, while others judge us by what we have already done.*
>
> —HENRY WADSWORTH LONGFELLOW

When I think of delivering results, I think of the movie trilogy *Lord of the Rings*. You watch nine hours of film, but in the end, it's all about Frodo getting that ring in the volcano. Without that, not much else really matters.

THE IMPACT ON TRUST ACCOUNTS

When I came in as CEO of Covey Leadership Center, there was one division that was perceived by the culture as a "hobby," or a business that people like being in, but that doesn't now (and likely never will) make money. Although there had been a lot of talk for three years, this division had not yet delivered any products or results, and the feeling was that the division was being carried. I met with the leader of this unit, and together we mutually agreed that there *would* be a product, that they *would* deliver results within six months—no exceptions. We set up a clear goal and accountability to that goal.

Along the way, I began getting feedback from the people in the division that the deadline was too aggressive and they just couldn't do it. I said, "Look, our credibility is on the line here. Until there is a product, this division is just a hobby. We've been talking about a product for years; we are going to hit this deadline."

They all hated me. They wanted me to give them more time. But I felt strongly that we needed to hold them accountable to the agreement. And in the end, they came through. The product was released on the agreed-upon date, and within the first several months it brought in millions of dollars.

This totally changed the perception that this division was just a hobby. They had delivered results! And that delivery built trust—trust in the people in that division, trust in the culture, and self trust and team trust in the lives of those who got that product out and made it happen.

On the home front, Jeri and I recently gave our twelve-year-old son, Christian, the job of taking out the garbage cans and bringing them back in. That's a big job at our house because the heavy cans have to be taken down a long, steep driveway to the street, which can be difficult when it's snowing. As parents, we have been thrilled with the way Christian has carried out this responsibility. We only told him once. He never talks about it. But every Wednesday night when I come home, the cans are out. When I come home on Thursday, they're in. He just delivers.

Part of the reason why we're so thrilled with Christian's behavior is that we've known the opposite. When his brother had the same job, we had to remind and remind and remind—and it still didn't get done half the time.

Both when this job has been handled responsibly—and when it hasn't—the impact on the Trust Account (and on speed and cost) has been huge. We've found that we are much quicker to listen to requests and to extend privileges when a child delivers results and the account is high.

And the same dynamic plays out at work, where producing results almost always gives a person more choices, more options, more flexibility. Jack Welch speaks of this flexibility as it relates it to a boss's willingness to support work-life balance:

> *Yes, bosses are agreeable to giving people the flexibility to come and go as they please—but only after they have earned it with their performance and results. In fact, I would describe the way work-life balance really works as an old-fashioned chit system. People with great performance accumulate chits, which can be traded in for flexibility. The more chits you have, the greater your opportunity to work when and where and how you want.*

Deliver Results is how you convert the cynics. It's how you establish trust fast in a new relationship. It's how you gain flexibility and choices. It's how you can restore trust quickly when it has been lost on the competence side. It's also the first half of the way I define leadership: *getting results* in a way that inspires trust.

> I don't think you have a full trusting relationship until you are actually at the point that you deliver success repeatedly. When one of my major suppliers says we want to have a trusting relationship, I think, "What a lot of rubbish that is!" I turn around and say, "I don't trust you. I am not going to trust you until you repeatedly deliver success to me."
>
> —PETER LOWE, IT DIRECTOR, HOME OFFICE, UK

CLARIFY "RESULTS" UP FRONT

At times, I talk with people who deliver results, but fail to get the response they expect. They anticipate a $1,000 deposit in the Trust Account, but end up with a $10 deposit, or worse—a withdrawal. And they wonder why.

In almost every case, it's because they didn't take the time up front to establish clarity around what was expected. What they considered "good" or even "great" results were only "mediocre" to the people to whom they delivered. Either that, or their "results" were in a completely different ballpark than the one in which they should have been playing—like the parent who works 80 hours a week to provide a lot of extras for a child, thinking it should make a huge deposit, when what the child really wants most is the parent's time. Or like the product development team that works feverishly to create product features the customer doesn't even care about.

At a recent conference in the United Kingdom, chief information officers and other IT professionals discussed technology and trust in organizations. One of the key takeaways was that while technology creates many exciting promises, unless basic results are delivered day in and day out, these promises don't mean a thing. At the conference, Paul Coby, CIO for British Airways, said:

> *My perspective on trying to build trust is that I don't get in the door to talk about the next great thing we're going to do in BritishAirways.com, or some other great new development, unless I'm delivering 24/7 IT operations. . . . [W]hen you've done that, you can then talk to them about more creative ideas.*

In today's economy, taking time to define results up front is particularly vital because a large percentage of the workforce is employed in jobs where it's often difficult to demonstrate measurable results. Thus, it's important in each situation to define the results that will build trust, and then deliver those results—consistently, on time, and within budget.

> [T]he first thing you do is deliver statistics—results. If you don't have mission-critical systems up and nothing else happens, you don't get to vote.
>
> —JP RANGASWAMI, GLOBAL CIO,
> DRESDNER KLEINWORT WASSERSTEIN

TRUST TIPS

Now on the bell curve, we see the competence cores coming more fully into play. On the left side of the curve, you see below-expectation delivery, revealing the need to strengthen Integrity, Capabilities, and, of course, Results—most often by defining them up front. On the right side, you see the delivery of plenty of Results, but with no consideration as to whether those results are even the ones you should be focused on (e.g., an employee working like crazy, but not on the boss's priorities . . . or that parent working extra hours instead of spending time with a child). Again, a focus on Integrity (particularly congruence), and on aligning Capabilities and defining Results, will help you move toward the "sweet spot" on the curve.

As you work to Deliver Results, you might try one of the following:

- The next time you plan to Deliver Results, make sure you thoroughly understand the expectation. Don't assume that just because you deliver what you may think are good results, you're going to hit the mark. If you really want to build trust, you have to know what "results" mean to the person to whom you're delivering.

- The next time you plan to make a commitment to Deliver Results, stop and ask yourself if the commitment is realistic. To overpromise and underdeliver will make a withdrawal every time.

- With customers or with coworkers, try to anticipate needs in advance and deliver before the requests even come. The great Canadian hockey player Wayne Gretzky said, "I skate to where the puck is going to be, not to where it has been." Anticipating needs will give an added dividend to the deposit in the Trust Account.

SUMMARY: BEHAVIOR #6— DELIVER RESULTS

Establish a track record of results. Get the right things done. Make things happen. Accomplish what you're hired to do. Be on time and within budget. Don't overpromise and underdeliver. Don't make excuses for not delivering.

BEHAVIOR #7:
GET BETTER

The illiterate of the 21st century will not be those who cannot read and write but those who cannot learn, unlearn, and relearn.

—ALVIN TOFFLER

As a young boy growing up, I used to snow ski every winter. I worked really hard at it and I got better and better every year. I knew I was getting better, not only because I could perform better, but also because I was regularly falling down. That might sound counterintuitive, but I came to realize that if I wasn't falling, I wasn't pushing myself hard enough to improve.

At age eighteen, I hit my peak as a skier. That's when I started to become more conservative. I had different motivations. I didn't want to fall anymore. I didn't want to break a leg. So I quit taking risks.

I'm still a good skier, but I haven't improved in over 25 years. I'm completely living in the past, relying on the skills I learned years ago. Skiing is one of those sports where there is a "degree of difficulty" variable, represented by green circles (easy runs), blue squares (difficult runs), and black diamonds (most difficult runs). Today if you put me on a simple green run, or a moderate blue run, I'd still look pretty good. But if you put me on a double-black-diamond run with the steep hills and moguls, I'd look ridiculous. I tried it just last winter, and quickly realized that I could no longer keep my balance or stay in control.

> *One of the reasons people stop learning is that they become less and less willing to risk failure.*
>
> —JOHN GARDNER, AUTHOR OF *EXCELLENCE*
> AND *SELF-RENEWAL*

Today we live in a double-black-diamond world. Technology, globalization, and the knowledge worker economy have increased the degree of difficulty and put us in a more challenging context. To try to apply the same skills we've always had in this demanding new context is like trying to apply green-run capabilities on a black-diamond run.

Unless we improve our capabilities dramatically, we're going to be inadequate to the challenge. And in today's increasingly competitive environment, it will be very obvious. It's like my skiing: On the green runs, I may look the same as another more competent skier. But if you put us both on the double black diamonds, we're obviously worlds apart.

Clearly it's the double-black-diamond skiers (and leaders) who really inspire trust.

GET BETTER BUILDS TRUST

Get Better is based on the *principles* of continuous improvement, learning, and change. It is what the Japanese call *kaizen*, and it builds enormous trust. Like Deliver Results, this behavior is an example of how one of the 4 Cores (Capabilities) can be turned directly into a powerful relationship-building tool. When people see you as a learning, growing, renewing person—or your organization as a learning, growing, renewing organization—they develop confidence in your ability to succeed in a rapidly changing environment, enabling you to build high-trust relationships and move with incredible speed.

The *opposite* of Get Better is entropy, deterioration, resting on your laurels, or becoming irrelevant. With the pace of change in today's world, if you aren't making a conscious effort to Get Better, you're not just standing still; you're getting farther and farther behind. You're becoming less and less relevant because those around you are moving rapidly ahead. Thus, simply staying where you are will not inspire trust; it will diminish it.

Get Better has two common *counterfeits*. The first is represented by the "eternal student," the person who is always learning but never producing. The second is represented by author Frank Herbert's observation: "The people I distrust most are those who want to improve our lives but have only one course of action." It's trying to force-fit everything into whatever you're good at doing. It's the manifestation of psychologist Abraham Maslow's thought: "He that is good with a hammer tends to think everything is a nail."

EXAMPLES OF GET BETTER

A good example of Get Better is the manager I mentioned in the chapter on Capabilities who studied for two hours early every morning until he became highly competent and an expert in his field. Other examples include Jack Canfield, coauthor of the *Chicken Soup* book series, who reads at least one book a day, and founders Bill Gates of Microsoft, Fred Smith of FedEx, and Mary Kay Ash of Mary Kay Cosmetics, who, as fast, constant learners, were relevant not only when they founded their companies but also through changing times.

> *Anyone who stops learning is old, whether this happens at twenty or eighty. Anyone who keeps on learning not only remains young, but becomes constantly more valuable regardless of physical capacity.*
>
> —HARVEY ULLMAN

A good athletic example of Get Better is Karl Malone, the power forward who played for 20 years in the NBA. In Malone's rookie season, he shot a poor 48 percent from the free throw line. Recognizing that he would be shooting many free throws throughout his career, he decided to turn this weakness into a strength. He worked hard at it, and became a 75 percent foul shooter for the rest of his career, which is outstanding for such a big man.

In addition, after his rookie season, Malone decided to train with weights with a different-in-kind level of intensity that had never been seen before. When he showed up for the following year's camp, it quickly became obvious that he had been working out to the extreme and was in far better shape than when the prior season had ended. It also became obvious that his teammates were still playing at the same level. As a result of his efforts to Get Better, Malone not only vastly improved his own game and became a certain Hall of Famer, he was likely the catalyst for elevating the level of strength and conditioning for the entire league. Jerry Rice, the great NFL football player, had a similar impact on football, and Tiger Woods has had the same on golf.

An excellent business example of Get Better is the Finnish company Nokia, considered the most trusted brand in Europe and now the largest mobile phone company in the world, with sales of $40.5 billion in over 130 countries. But Nokia didn't start out in mobile phones. Almost a century and a half ago, Nokia was a paper manufacturing company. At that time, its leaders built innovation into the company's culture as their key capability. They called it "renewal," and have been practicing it for the past 140 years. As *Fast Company* has said:

> *[Nokia] has gone from manufacturing paper to making rubber boots, then raincoats, then hunting rifles, and then consumer electronics, until finally betting the farm on mobile phones. It's all part of an ongoing emphasis on renewal. . . . Nokia is a company that refuses to grow big, grow old, or grow slow.*

Today Nokia is in a challenging industry, and its leadership recognizes that if the company doesn't constantly innovate and improve according to market demands, it will be surpassed. Thus, Nokia remains relentlessly innovative.

Whether it's called renewal, reinvention, re-creation, innovation, continuous improvement, or getting better, the need for this behavior has become a requirement for succeeding in a double-black-diamond world. As Jeffrey Imelt, GE's CEO, said, "Constant reinvention is the central necessity at GE. . . . We're all just a moment away from commodity hell."

HOW TO GET BETTER

In seeking to Get Better, there are two strategies that are particularly helpful in maximizing your effort: seek feedback, and learn from mistakes.

Seek Feedback

Seeking and effectively utilizing feedback are vital to quality improvement. In my own life, feedback has been a part of every successful endeavor I've been involved in, from internal surveys and external customer visits at work to regularly asking Jeri, "What can I do to make life better for you?" at home.

When I think of how Michael Dell and Kevin Rollins of Dell Inc. sought and responded to feedback, when they could have justifiably ignored it based on their track records, it inspires me to do the same. I remember one time I did not want feedback on a particular product development project, and when I got it anyway, I ignored it. Imagine my chagrin later when the tepid market response validated what the feedback had been saying!

Appropriately seeking feedback and acting on it is the hallmark of a learning, growing, innovating company. Marriott International sends me an e-mail feedback request nearly every time I stay at one of their hotels. Amazon.com asks me to rate every order I place through a third-party seller, and my feedback becomes part of that affiliate's performance rating. Almost all large organizations do some type of employee feedback survey, asking questions about employee satisfaction, engagement, etc. What differentiates the best from the good companies is not whether they ask the questions, it's how they respond to the answers.

Feedback is so vital to improvement that, as I've said, we've included an in-depth 360-degree trust feedback instrument as part of our Speed of Trust programs. It's always fascinating to watch people learn how to work through the process—comparing their own perceptions of their strengths and weaknesses to the perceptions of others, and sometimes hearing things that startle them, cause them to reframe their paradigms, help them open their minds and hearts, and create a path to positive change.

As we tell our participants, it's possible to put too much emphasis on feedback or overreact to it, and in the process, discount your own instinct and vision. In addition, feedback often tells you more about the person who is giving it than about you. However, even this information can be enormously helpful in building trust because it gives you insight into the meaning others are bringing to the relationship and what behaviors make deposits in the Trust Account you share with them.

You also need to be sure and thank those giving the feedback and let them know how you plan to implement it. When people see you taking their input seriously, it not only inspires trust in you, it also creates an environment of growth and change. As we discussed in Deliver Results, however, you need to always be responsible in following through. Otherwise your expression of intent will create a withdrawal, and you'll be worse off than had you not solicited feedback in the first place.

Learn from Mistakes

As I discovered on the ski slopes, if you're not willing to make mistakes, you're not going to improve. Often people aren't willing to make mistakes because they're either afraid to fail or they're focused on looking good. But smart people and smart companies realize that making mistakes is part of life. They see mistakes as feedback that will help them improve, and they become expert in learning how to learn from mistakes.

Most often, in fact, it is the failures that bring about the break-throughs and insights. Albert Einstein said, "I think and think for months and years. Ninety-nine times the conclusion is false. The hundredth time I am right." In commenting on the process of perfecting the lightbulb, Thomas Edison said, "I didn't fail ten thousand times. I successfully eliminated ten thousand materials and combinations that didn't work."

World-class companies have adopted similar ways of thinking regarding innovation. Soichiro Honda, the founder of Honda Motor Co., said: "To me success can only be achieved through repeated failure and introspection. In fact, success represents the one percent of your work that results from the ninety-nine percent that is called failure."

> *You learn nothing from your successes except to think too much of yourself. It is from failure that all growth comes, provided you can recognize it, admit it, learn from it, rise about it, and then try again.*
>
> —DEE HOCK, FOUNDER AND FORMER CEO,
> VISA INTERNATIONAL

Smart leaders create an environment that encourages appropriate risk-taking, an environment that makes it safe to make mistakes. A good example is IBM founder Tom Watson Sr. In *Leaders: Strategies for Taking Charge*, Warren Bennis and Burt Nanus recount the following story about Watson:

> *A promising junior executive of IBM was involved in a risky venture for the company and managed to lose over $10 million in the gamble. It was a disaster. When Watson called the nervous executive into his office, the young man blurted out, "I guess you want my resignation?" Watson said, "You can't be serious. We've just spent $10 million educating you!"*

It's this type of learning that caused Watson to say, "If you want to increase your success rate, double your failure rate."

TRUST TIPS

On the bell curve, to Get Better most effectively clearly involves all 4 Cores. You need Integrity to make and keep improvement commitments. You're at the peak when your Intent is to improve your ability to make a contribution to the lives of others—whether those others are the beneficiaries of your sharpened talents and skills or (as in the case of your family) those who benefit from your ability to earn. Get Better involves Capabilities. Aside from the obvious, this includes the capability to set and achieve meaningful goals and also the ability to establish, grow, extend, and restore trust. It also involves Results, both in terms of maximizing the input/output ratio of the effort you invest in getting better, and also seeing the relationship between the focus of improvement and the results you're trying to achieve.

In order to Get Better, you might consider doing one of the following:

- Send out a "Continue/Stop/Start" inquiry to your direct reports, to your customers, to members of your team, or members of your family. Ask three simple questions:

  1. What is one thing we are now doing that you think we should *continue* doing?
  2. What is one thing we are now doing that you think we should *stop* doing?
  3. What is one thing we are *not* now doing that you think we should *start* doing?

  Thank people for their input, tell them what you're planning to do, and report on your progress.

- The next time you make a mistake, rather than agonizing over it, reframe it as feedback. Identify the learnings from it and ways you can improve your approach to get different results next time.

- If you have a leadership role in an organization, on a team, or in a family, take steps to create an environment that makes it safe to make mistakes. Encourage others to take appropriate risks and to learn from failure so that you create high trust, high synergy, and high-level productivity.

SUMMARY: BEHAVIOR #7—GET BETTER

Continuously improve. Increase your Capabilities. Be a constant learner. Develop feedback systems—both formal and informal. Act on the feedback you receive. Thank people for feedback. Don't consider yourself above feedback. Don't assume today's knowledge and skills will be sufficient for tomorrow's challenges.

BEHAVIOR #8: CONFRONT REALITY

The first responsibility of a leader is to define reality.
—Max DePree, Chairman and CEO,
Herman Miller

Have you ever been a participant in those "meetings after the meetings"—those informal discussions where smaller groups of people talk about all the things that should have been addressed in the formal meeting, but were not? How much time and money do you think was wasted because the real issues weren't directly addressed and resolved?

Have you ever been in a family situation where it was obvious that everyone was avoiding what business author Kathleen Ryan has called the "undiscussables"—those things that get in the way of open, trusting relationships, but that no one ever seems to have the courage to bring up? How much difference do you think it would make if there were no "undiscussables"—if people felt free to interact about any subject with openness and respect?

Behavior #8—Confront Reality—is about taking the tough issues head-on. It's about sharing the bad news as well as the good, naming the "elephant in the room," addressing the "sacred cows," and discussing the "undiscussables." As you do these things appropriately, you build trust—fast. People know you're being genuine and authentic. You're not shying away from the tough stuff. You're directly addressing the difficult issues that are in people's minds and hearts and affect their lives.

Confront Reality is based on the *principles* of courage, responsibility, awareness, and respect. An outstanding example of Confront Reality is U.S. Admiral James Stockdale. In dealing with the harsh realities of surviving eight years as a prisoner of war in Vietnam—and earning enormous trust and respect from all who were incarcerated with him— he demonstrated what Jim Collins has called the "Stockdale Paradox." In his book *Good to Great*, Collins quotes Stockdale as saying:

> *You must never confuse faith that you will prevail in the end—which you can never afford to lose—with the discipline to confront the most brutal facts of your current reality, whatever they might be.*

Collins goes on to say that "the Stockdale Paradox is a signature of all those who create greatness, be it in leading their own lives or in leading others."

Another good example of Confront Reality is Anne Mulcahy. As reported in *Fortune* magazine, when she became CEO of Xerox in August 2001, the brutal facts were just that: brutal. Not only was Xerox losing money, they had enormous debt, high costs, and declining sales. They were in the midst of a liquidity crisis, and there had been a significant exodus of talent. On top of all that, they were facing an SEC accounting scandal, an outdated business model, and a staid product and service line. Prior leadership had put off the tough decisions the company needed to make in technology, product development, and services. In addition, the overall economy was lousy. Xerox operated in a highly competitive industry, and in the prior year, the stock had fallen from $63.69 to $4.43 per share.

These were brutal facts, indeed. But rather than skirt them, Mulcahy confronted them head-on. She went to work first on surviving and avoiding bankruptcy—despite input from workout experts who advised against it. She said, "Whatever you think the advantages [of bankruptcy] are from a financial standpoint, I think they are dismal and demoralizing for a company that desperately wants to turn around and regain its reputation."

Then Mulcahy made the tough calls. She shut down the desktop division. She pared down the cost structure. She resolved the accounting scandal. She transitioned the product and service line. Above all, she told the truth, even when it was unpopular and others didn't want to hear it. On one occasion, she said honestly that the Xerox business model was unsustainable and needed to be re-created. Wall Street didn't want to hear that, and the stock dropped 26 percent in one day. But while the stock dropped, her own credibility with her people soared. Here was a leader willing to take on issues that had been neglected for years. Her trust increased—first with Xerox coworkers, then with customers and investors, including bankers. People saw in Mulcahy a leader who took on the issues prior Xerox leaders might have seen but were not able—or willing—to address.

Since that time, Xerox has improved significantly. The company is profitable. The debt has been significantly reduced. The stock is rebounding. Although the jury's always out on any current company, Anne Mulcahy is a real-time example of a leader who establishes trust by taking tough issues head-on.

The *opposite* of Confront Reality is to ignore it, to act as though it doesn't exist. It's burying your head in the sand, thinking that maybe it will go away or that it's not really there after all. The *counterfeit* is to act as though you're confronting reality when you're actually evading it. It's focusing on busywork while skirting the real issues.

One of the problems with both the opposite and the counterfeit is that whenever you fail to deal with the real issues for any reason, people tend to see you in one of two ways: They see you as lacking in character (you're not being open or honest, not being transparent, not talking straight) or lacking in competence (you're clueless, naïve, incompetent; you don't even know what the real issues are). Either way, it doesn't inspire trust.

SPEED AND COST

When you openly Confront Reality, it affects speed and cost in at least two important ways. First, it builds the kind of relationships that facilitate open interaction and fast achievement. Second, instead of having to wrestle with all the hard issues on your own while trying to paint a rosy picture for everyone else, you actually engage the creativity, capability, and synergy of others in solving those issues. Ideas flow freely. Innovation and collaboration take place. Solutions come much faster and better, and are implemented with the understanding, buy-in, and often the excitement of others involved in the problem-solving process.

My own experience in the wake of the FranklinCovey merger was a powerful affirmation to me of the trust dividends that come from confronting reality. That day in Washington, D.C., when I offered to set aside the meeting's agenda and talk about the issues people really wanted to talk about, I could feel the initial shock. I could feel the disbelief. But within an hour, it was like a huge dam had burst. I could feel openness and trust flooding the room and the enormous relief and appreciation of everyone there. It was truly a watershed experience, and it made a quantum difference in our ability to work together—and eventually in our ability to create more value for our customers—from that point on.

SO WHY DON'T WE CONFRONT REALITY?

In his book, *Open Book Management*, veteran business writer John Case suggests that the key to successful management is in treating people like adults. "When treated like adults," he says, "people act like adults." That's the paradigm behind "opening the books," confronting the realities, and sharing the bad news as well as the good. According to Case, this kind of approach shows respect. It says to others, "You are an adult. You can handle this." To me it also says, "I value your input concerning how we can make this situation better."

You rarely gain anything by shutting out the very people who are in the best position to help you solve the challenges and problems you face. As American Airlines CEO Gerard Arpey said regarding his decision to openly involve his unions in confronting AA's reality, "If folks are not truly your business partners, they will undermine your strategy."

So why don't people confront reality?

In some cases, they want to be popular. They don't want to be the bearers of bad news. Sometimes leaders leave the bad news for their lieutenants to deliver, thinking they need to create some distance from what's going wrong in order to maintain credibility and trust. But in reality, such action has the opposite effect. It creates a huge tax because people feel their leader is not being honest and straightforward, that he's ducking from interacting with them on these tough issues and leaving the "dirty work" for others to do.

> Leaders need to be more candid with those they purport to lead. Sharing good news is easy. When it comes to the more troublesome negative news, be candid and take responsibility. Don't withhold unpleasant possibilities and don't pass off bad news to subordinates to deliver. Level with employees about problems in a timely fashion.
>
> —JON HUNTSMAN, CHAIRMAN, HUNTSMAN CHEMICAL

In some cases, people want to avoid discomfort. Sometimes, for example, parents don't want to hear that they have a child involved in drugs, or some other addictive behavior. It causes too much pain, so they overlook the clues, they look the other way, they don't confront the child—instead of acknowledging the problem and taking the quick action that might save the child from serious addiction.

In some cases, people don't want to lose face. I saw this clearly one time when I counseled with a family that had serious financial problems. Their income had suddenly taken a huge dip, but they persisted in living the kind of lifestyle their prior income would support. Bottom line, they were embarrassed. They were concerned about not appearing as successful as they had been and were worried about losing face with their friends, so they kept trying to cover up the situation by draining their savings and going into debt. But the reality was that if they continued on that path, they were going to bankrupt themselves and get into really dire straits. They didn't want to face that reality, so they had buried their heads in the sand. It took a lot of counseling, months of straight talk, but ultimately they acknowledged the reality of their situation and took the necessary steps to deal with it.

In my own experience, both personally and professionally, I've learned that you don't wait to confront reality. It doesn't get easier. It doesn't get better. And, in some cases, if you don't get the relevant information from people and act quickly, you start losing options. You're into damage control.

According to a study for Mercer Human Resource Consulting, only 39 percent of employees believe that senior management does a good job of confronting issues *before they turn into major problems*. Just think of the cost! How much more effective it would be to confront the issues early, when the cost of dealing with them is relatively low.

The bottom line is this: Don't be afraid to deliver bad news. Don't feel like you have to try to spin everything in a positive light. Of course, you don't want to be on the far right end of the bell curve saying, "Everything's terrible and we're all going to die!" But, as Jim Collins points out, you can "confront the brutal facts yet never lose faith." In fact, the companies (and leaders) he studied that went from good to great did precisely that, and their approach actually became a source of their strength. Collins said:

> *In confronting the brutal facts, the good-to-great companies left themselves stronger and more resilient, not weaker and more dispirited.*

There is a sense of exhilaration that comes in facing head-on the hard truths and saying, "We will never give up. We will never capitulate. It might take a long time, but we will find a way to prevail." Likewise, you can say, "Here are the facts. Let's deal with them. Let me also tell you why we'll prevail," or "Here's how I believe we can move this team forward."

TRUST TIPS

The "sweet spot" for Confront Reality clearly reflects the judgment that comes from the interaction of all 4 Cores. On the left side of the curve, confrontation is ignored or, at best, diluted. It's too mild to be effective. Or perhaps there's confrontation, but no follow-through. Movement toward the "sweet spot" comes by increasing courage (Integrity), improving Intent, working on trust abilities (Capabilities), and gaining confidence from experience with the Results of confronting reality.

On the right side of the curve, people are into confronting other people instead of issues—and sometimes brutally. Or they're into extremism ("This is terrible and we're all going to die!") or victimization ("This situation is awful, and there's absolutely nothing I can do"). Again, strengthening the 4 Cores is the key.

In your effort to improve in confronting reality, you may want to consider the following ideas:

- The next time you feel reluctant to confront reality at work or at home, explore your feelings. Are you hesitant because of fear of the outcome or fear of the pain? Consider the consequences of not confronting reality. If necessary, try to reframe your attitude toward others involved. See them as adults (or as strong, resilient children, if that's the case) who are capable of handling things as they are. Move ahead. Confront reality, and treat them with respect.

- Think about your financial life, your professional qualifications, or your health. Are you confronting reality or are you living in "la-la land"? Work on being completely honest with yourself. Take on the challenge of aligning your life with the principles that will create the results you want to have.

• If you feel uncomfortable in a personal or professional relationship, ask yourself why. Is there some issue that's getting in the way of creating an open, high-trust relationship? Consider confronting the issue head-on, with respect.

**SUMMARY: BEHAVIOR #8—
CONFRONT REALITY**

Address the tough stuff directly. Acknowledge the unsaid. Lead out courageously in conversation. Remove the "sword from their hands." Don't skirt the real issues. Don't bury your head in the sand.

BEHAVIOR #9: CLARIFY EXPECTATIONS

Almost all conflict is a result of violated expectations.
—BLAINE LEE, AUTHOR OF *THE POWER PRINCIPLE*

One night a few months ago, my wife, Jeri, told our 16-year-old daughter, "You can't go out with your friends tonight until you clean your room and the bathroom." Later, Jeri came to me and exclaimed, "McKinlee is grounded! She broke a commitment! I told her she could not go out until she cleaned her room and the bathroom, and she didn't do it but she left anyway."

"I'll call her," I said. She was at a dance, and when I got her on her cell phone, I said, "McKinlee, you have to come home right now. You promised Mom you would clean your room and the bathroom before you left, and you didn't do it."

"But I did do it, Dad!" she exclaimed.

"Evidently, you didn't."

"Yes, I did!"

"Then you didn't do a very good job of it."

"But, Dad, I did it like I always do."

My daughter thought she had been honorable. She thought she had done what her mother had asked her to do. For my wife, however, this was an issue of trust. In her view, McKinlee had made a commitment, and she had left to have fun with her friends without following through.

As Jeri and I processed the situation, we realized that the problem was that McKinlee's standard of "clean" and Jeri's standard of "clean" were not the same. And there had been no clearly defining discussion around what "clean your room and bathroom" meant. In the end, we allowed McKinlee to stay at the dance with the promise of a discussion when she got home.

EXPECTATIONS AND TRUST

Behavior #9—Clarify Expectations—is to create shared vision and agreement about what is to be done *up front*. This is one of those behaviors that people rarely pay enough attention to. I call it the behavior of prevention because if you focus on this one up front, you will avoid heartaches and headaches later on. In contrast, if you don't pay the price with this behavior up front, you *will* have trust issues later, and they will affect speed and cost.

Just think about your own experience, both at work and at home. How much time and effort are wasted because people are not clear on expectations? "You were supposed to do this . . ." "I thought you said to do that . . ." "You wanted it *when*?" "What do you mean this is over budget? You never told me . . ." "Well, you never said I couldn't . . ." How often do people get off track on a project because leaders have not been sufficiently clear in describing the right path? How much "poor performance" is really due to a lack of clarity around what is expected? And what is the effect of all of this on trust?

Clarify Expectations is based on the *principles* of clarity, responsibility, and accountability. The *opposite* of Clarify Expectations is to leave expectations undefined—to assume they're already known, or to fail to disclose them so there is no shared vision of the desired outcomes. This causes people to guess, wonder, or assume what expectations might be. Then, when results are delivered but not valued, everyone is disappointed and trust, speed, and cost all take a hit.

The *counterfeit* of Clarify Expectations is to create "smoke and mirrors"—to give lip service to clarifying expectations, but fail to pin down the specifics (results, deadlines, or dollars and cents) that facilitate meaningful accountability. Or it's going with the ebb and flow of situational expectations that shift based on people's memories or interpretations, or what is expedient or convenient at the time.

Clarifying expectations can be challenging. In our Speed of Trust programs, we sometimes do a small group exercise where we have the people at each table list the top ten words that come to mind as they answer the question, What is trust? Surprisingly, even though "trust" is a word we use all the time, typically the six or seven people at each table will not come up with more than one or two words in common. I believe this speaks to the difficulty of clarifying expectations. We each bring our own meaning to language and experience. Meaning is not in things; it's not even necessarily in words. Meaning is in people. So even if you and I agree on something, we need to make sure we understand the words we're using in the same way.

One of the reasons why the impact of Clarify Expectations is so pervasive is that in *every* interaction—explicitly or implicitly, understood or not understood—there are expectations. And the degree to which these expectations are met or violated affects trust. In fact, unclarified expectations are one of the primary reasons for broken trust because—as happened in the situation with Jeri and McKinlee—violated expectations almost always get translated into trust issues: "You didn't come through." "You didn't do what you said you'd do."

CLARIFYING EXPECTATIONS IN BUSINESS

Someone once asked me why we put business agreements in writing if we trust the other party. My response is that agreements identify and clarify expectations, which actually help preserve and even enhance trust over time. I've known of several "handshake" deals that went south because there never was clarification of expectations beyond the initial deal, or because when the players changed, so did the understanding of the deal. I'm not against handshake agreements, but I prefer that they also become written agreements so that expectations regarding both parties are clear.

However, even written agreements have their limitations and are not able to replicate trust. In fact, where I have problems with legal agreements is when they are written in one-sided, adversarial, nontrusting language, or where they are intended, de facto, to serve as a replacement for a relationship of trust.

In contrast, trust can bring life, meaning, and understanding into written agreements, and can improve performance overall. For example, in the first chapter of this book, I referred to a study sponsored by the Warwick Business School where the researchers analyzed 1,200 outsourcing contracts over a 10-year period of time. Those relationships which relied on trust as the primary driver (versus relying on the stringent service-level agreements written into the contract) outperformed the value of their contracts by 20 to 40 percent.

Talk about a trust dividend!

Marshall Thurber, a protégé of both W. Edwards Deming and Buckminster Fuller, made the very astute observation that "clarity is power." An example of this kind of power is seen in the illustration Jim Collins gives of "Cork" Walgreen III, CEO of Walgreens during the time of its transformation from good to great. The company had earlier decided that what they could be best in the world at was running drugstores, not restaurants, even though they had been in the food service business for generations. In Collins's book *Good to Great*, Dan Jorndt, the CEO who succeeded Cork, explained:

> *Cork said at one of our planning committee meetings, "Okay, now I am going to draw the line in the sand. We are going to be out of the restaurant business completely in five years." At the time, we had over five hundred restaurants. You could have heard a pin drop. He said, "I want to let everybody know the clock is ticking. . . ." Six months later, we were at our next planning committee meeting and someone mentioned just in passing that we only had five years to be out of the restaurant business. Cork was not a real vociferous fellow. He sort of tapped on the table and said, "Listen, you have four and a half years. I said you had five years six months ago. Now you've got four and a half years." Well, that next day, things really clicked into gear to winding down our restaurant business.*

In my own experience, I remember being in one meeting where an executive wanted to make sure that everyone recognized the sensitive nature of what we would be talking about. There had been some violations of confidentiality in this very group because people had been too casual, and it had created a low-trust environment. In an effort to make the expectation crystal clear, this executive went around the table and spoke directly to each person in the room individually—eye to eye—and he asked, "Do you understand that this is confidential, and will you agree to keep the confidence?" It was a dramatic—and effective—way of clarifying the expectation.

CLARIFYING EXPECTATIONS AT HOME

As I've said, Clarify Expectations makes a huge difference at home, as well as at work. If you're married, for example, consider how much disappointment and contention come as a result of unclear or differing expectations regarding roles and responsibilities. Maybe your spouse expects you to handle the finances, discipline the children, or take out the garbage because that's the way it was done in the home where he/she grew up—but you expect your spouse to do those things because that's the way it was in your home. You've never really gotten the issue out on the table and come to a resolution, so it's always a sore spot in the relationship.

If you're a parent, consider how much time and energy are wasted when you don't take time to clarify expectations concerning responsibilities or other issues at home. Following our experience with McKinlee, I talked with a friend of mine who said that when her children were young, she clarified expectations in her home by posting a list on the back of each closet door or bathroom cabinet door that defined specifically what she meant when she told a child to "clean" the room. Then she trained her children and held them accountable to the criteria on the list, so there was no question about what was expected. She said it didn't eliminate all the problems, but it went a long way toward decreasing wasted time and energy, increasing the quality of the work, and building an environment of confidence and trust.

IT'S A TWO-WAY STREET

According to a recent study by the AMA/HRI, the number one reason for unethical corporate behavior is unrealistic expectations. People are handed expectations, given deadlines, and told things have to be done by a certain time and for a certain cost. The pressure of delivering the result by the deadline becomes intense, so they start cutting corners. They start doing unethical things in order to meet the expectation.

Keep in mind that clarifying expectations effectively is always a two-way street. People have to have the opportunity to push back, to help come to an expectation that is realistic and will work from both points of view.

One time at the Covey Leadership Center, representatives from a company approached me with a proposal to form a strategic alliance around a particular idea. We seriously explored the possibilities, but ended up concluding that it didn't make sense for either party.

One of the people from this organization came back to me and said, with some energy, "I'm really disappointed in you. You don't even practice what your father teaches."

That took me aback. In an effort to not be reactive, I replied, "I'm sorry. Tell me more."

He said, "Your father teaches win-win. We came here to do a win-win deal with you, but you won't even do it!"

Somewhat relieved, I said, "Look, I completely agree with win-win. The problem is that what you're proposing is not a win-win; it's a win-lose. It would not be a win for us to do this deal, and to make it a win for us would make it a lose for you. That's not what my father teaches. He teaches 'win-win or no deal'—if it can't be a win for both of us, we don't do the deal. And that's where we are on this."

This person had conveniently left out the "no deal" part. But you can't leave out "no deal"; otherwise you're held hostage by negotiations that can only end up in lose-lose. Once this person understood what I was saying—once expectations were clarified (win-win or no deal)—he changed his view.

MAKING IT HAPPEN

Over the years I have learned several important things about clarifying expectations.

First, I have learned to quantify everything: What result? By whom? By when? At what cost? How will we measure it? How will we know when we have accomplished it? And when and to whom is the accountability—both in terms of benchmarks and end results? As I said in the 4 Cores chapter on Results, it's generally more effective to focus on results rather than activities, although with children you sometimes have to be a little more activity specific. However, even when I was seven, my dad told me I could get the yard "green and clean" any way I liked. He said I could use hoses or buckets or that I could even spit on it if I wanted. So he encouraged my creativity and gave me the freedom to achieve the results any way I liked. But he also told me about the sprinklers and showed me how to use them.

Second, I have learned that in most circumstances, it's wise to look at three variables—quality, speed, and cost—and realize that you can usually pick any two, but not all three. For example, if you want high quality and you want it fast, it's usually going to cost you more. If you want it fast at low cost, you're probably going to give up quality. If you want a quality product and a low cost, it's likely to take longer. It's almost always a choice: to get two, you have to give up one. This understanding has been helpful to me in clarifying expectations and understanding the trade-offs involved. However, there is one transforming variable that can alter this trade-off equation, and that is high trust. When the environment of trust is strong enough, the achievement of high quality (value), high speed, and low cost becomes a realistic possibility.

Finally, I've learned that even though it's hard sometimes to clarify expectations—for example, to give someone a realistic delivery date instead of giving them the false promise of what they want to hear—it's much better to do it up front than to disappoint them later.

TRUST TIPS

Reaching the "sweet spot" in Clarify Expectations takes Integrity (being honest and courageous about setting expectations and communicating with others). It takes Intent to create expectations that represent a "win" for all involved. It takes Capabilities, including the ability to organize the elements of the agreement, to set up accountability, and to execute with excellence. And it takes the ability to identify the desired Results in a way that everyone involved understands.

If you're on the left side of the curve, to some degree, you're not being sufficiently clear. On the right, you may be too detailed, too activity oriented, too closed to interim adjustment if needed, or too distrusting. For many people, for example, a prenuptial agreement would be on the far right. While it does clarify expectations, it's likely to undermine trust in the process.

Look at the 4 Cores and consider where you might need to improve. In addition, you might want to try one of the following:

• When you communicate with others, recognize that clarity is power. One way of checking to see if your communication has been clear is to "check for clarity" by asking a few simple questions:

  ○ What have you understood from this conversation?
  ○ As a result of our interaction, what do you see as your next steps? What do you see as mine?
  ○ Do you feel that others are clear regarding expectations?
  ○ What can we do to make things more clear?

• The next time you have a project at work, create a clear project agreement in advance. If you're in charge, call everyone together and encourage them to express any ideas and concerns. Work to come up with a clear agreement that is realistic and represents a win for all stakeholders. If you're not in charge, either suggest the idea to your team leader or write up an agreement on your own. Tell your team leader, "This is my understanding of what you expect and what I can do. Do you see it differently?" That will give you a chance to clarify expectations and to pin them down so that you don't run into problems later on.

• Clarify expectations at home. Plan some "marriage investment" time with your spouse. Without collaborating, both of you independently write down the three biggest frustrations in your marriage. Then look at each frustration and ask this question: What expectation do I have here that's not being met? Share any insights concerning your frustrations and expectations with each other, and work together to achieve clarity.

SUMMARY: BEHAVIOR #9— CLARIFY EXPECTATIONS

Disclose and reveal expectations. Discuss them. Validate them. Renegotiate them if needed and possible. Don't violate expectations. Don't assume that expectations are clear or shared.

BEHAVIOR #10: PRACTICE ACCOUNTABILITY

All power is a trust; and we are accountable for its exercise.

—BENJAMIN DISRAELI

Behavior #10 is Practice Accountability. The reason why Clarify Expectations precedes this behavior is that you can practice accountability far better when you've clarified expectations first. It's hard to hold someone accountable if they're not clear on what the expectations are.

Clearly this behavior has a significant impact on trust. In a 2002 Golin/Harris poll, "assuming personal responsibility and accountability" was ranked as the second-highest factor in building trust. Price-WaterhouseCoopers lists "a culture of accountability" as one of three keys in building public trust.

There are two key dimensions to this Practice Accountability. The first is to hold *yourself* accountable; the second is to hold *others* accountable. Leaders who generate trust do both.

HOLD YOURSELF ACCOUNTABLE

At a recent Speed of Trust program, one of the participants shared a story about another participant, "Matt," who was a buyer from a large beef supplier in the United States. One of Matt's people had been in an accident while driving a company vehicle. The accident wasn't serious, but the company policy is that anytime there is an accident involving a company vehicle—even if it's in a parking lot or hitting a tree—the person has to file a police report at the time. Matt wasn't aware of the policy. So when his boss came to him and said, "Your guy didn't fill out a police report, so you need to write him up," Matt said, "Well, he didn't know about the policy because I didn't know about the policy." Matt wrote up a report on his employee—and then he wrote up a report on himself. He turned both reports in. When his boss said, "I'm not going to accept this," Matt said, "It's my responsibility to make sure my employee knows the policy."

Matt's behavior is an excellent example of what it means to hold yourself accountable. It demonstrates one of the points Jim Collins makes in his metaphor of the window and the mirror. This was a time to stop looking out the window—to not look out at others and to blame and accuse—but to look in the mirror, to focus on your own responsibility in the situation.

This behavior is built on the *principles* of accountability, responsibility, stewardship, and ownership. The *opposite* of this behavior is to not take responsibility, to not own up, but rather to say, "It's not my fault." Its *counterfeit* is to point fingers and blame others, to say, "It's their fault."

To grasp the impact of this behavior on trust, consider the following examples.

On the final drive of an important game, Hall of Fame quarterback Steve Young of the San Francisco 49ers threw the ball to where the receiver was supposed to be, but wasn't. The ball was intercepted, and the 49ers lost the game. Afterward, an interviewer pointed out to Young that it appeared his receiver had run the wrong route and asked him if this was so. In truth, the receiver had run the wrong route, and it must have been tempting for Young to agree with the interviewer and avoid being unfairly blamed for the interception. But as I recall, Young replied, "I threw an interception. It was my responsibility. I'm the quarterback of this team, and I came up short." As a result, fans and commentators were tough on Young. But the coaches and others players (who knew that the interception had been the receiver's fault) responded to Young's stepping up and taking the blame with a huge increase in loyalty and trust.

> *A good leader takes more than their fair share of the blame and gives more than their share of the credit.*
>
> —Arnold Glasnow

Another great example is Scott Waddle, former commander of the USS *Greeneville*—the 6,900-ton nuclear sub that crashed into a Japanese fishing vessel off the Hawaiian coast, killing nine people. During the investigation, it became clear that there were many people in the chain of command, and many mistakes had been made by junior officers and crewmembers in not relaying information properly to Waddle. But Commander Waddle stepped up and—at great personal cost—took full and sole responsibility as leader of the crew. Against the strong advice of his legal counsel, Waddle testified on his own behalf in the inquiry. He said:

> *For my entire career, including the day 9 February, 2001, I have done my duty to the best of my ability. . . . If I made a mistake or mistakes, those mistakes were honest and well intentioned. I'm truly sorry for this accident. It has been a tragedy for the families of those lost, for the crew of the USS Greeneville, for their families, for the submarine force, for me, and for my family. I understand by speaking now I may be forfeiting my ability to successfully defend myself at a court-martial. . . . This court and the families need to hear from me despite the personal legal prejudice to me . . . and because it is the right thing to do.*

Waddle was stripped of his command and he resigned from the navy. He traveled to Japan to offer his personal apologies to the family members of the victims of the incident. Even though this ended his military career, the way he took personal responsibility and handled this entire process gained Waddle enormous credibility, respect, and trust—both in and out of the military and within society at large.

Contrast these examples with the behavior of Michael Brown, former director of the Federal Emergency Management Agency (FEMA), with regard to accusations surrounding the U.S. federal government's response to Hurricane Katrina. After he testified before Congress, the front-page headline in *USA Today* captured its perception of Brown's testimony with the following headline: "Ex-FEMA Chief Blames Locals." The article begins:

> *In a combative hearing pitting an unapologetic Michael Brown against frustrated members of Congress, the former FEMA director defended his handling of Hurricane Katrina and laid the blame for evacuation failures on Louisiana Gov. Kathleen Blanco and New Orleans Mayor Ray Nagin.*

CNN.com's headline was similar: "Brown Puts Blame on Louisiana Officials." While accepting some responsibility, Brown essentially said, "It wasn't my fault. It was the fault of the local government." Many felt that he not only failed to deliver, he also pointed the finger, attempting to shift the blame to others.

One reason why taking responsibility and holding ourselves accountable is challenging is that we live in an increasingly victimized society. To Practice Accountability is essentially a 180-degree turn from this basic, overwhelming cultural phenomenon of victimization. As the Russian proverb says, "Success has many fathers while failure is an orphan."

On the other hand, this is also a reason why taking responsibility is so powerful in building trust. While victimization creates dependency and distrust, accountability creates independency and trust. And the geometric effect is powerful. When people—particularly leaders—hold themselves accountable, it encourages others to do the same. When a leader says, "I could have done that better—and I should have!" it encourages others to respond, "Well, no, I was really the one who should have noticed that. I could have supported you more."

This is also true in a marriage or a family. When someone says, "I'm sorry I spent that money impulsively. That wasn't in harmony with our agreement," or "I shouldn't have yelled at you. That didn't show respect," or, on the other hand, "I committed to you that I'd be there, and I was," that acknowledgment of accountability encourages others to be accountable for their own behavior. It also creates an environment of openness and trust.

HOLD OTHERS ACCOUNTABLE

In addition to holding yourself accountable, it's important to hold others accountable, both at work and at home. In truth, people respond to accountability—particularly the performers. They *want* to be held accountable. They feel trust grow with bosses, leaders, team members, peers, and other stakeholders as they are given the opportunity to account for performing well. They also feel the increase of their own self trust and self-confidence as they repeatedly make and keep performance commitments.

In addition, performers also want others to be held accountable. They thrive in an environment where they know that everyone is expected to step up and be responsible, where they can trust that slackers and poor performers won't just slip by.

> *Get good people and expect them to perform. Terminate*
> *them quickly and fairly if you make the wrong choice.*
>
> —J. WILLARD MARRIOTT JR., CHAIRMAN AND CEO,
> MARRIOTT INTERNATIONAL

Accountability builds extraordinary trust in the culture when people feel secure in the knowledge that everyone will be held to certain standards. When leaders don't hold people accountable, the opposite is true. People feel it's unfair: "Well, look what he did . . . and he got off scot-free!" It creates a sense of disappointment, inequity, and insecurity. You see this a lot in families where discipline is inconsistent, where a parent will hold one child accountable and not another, or will hold a child accountable in one situation and not another.

With my son's permission, I'd like to share a personal story about this behavior. When Stephen turned 16, he got his driver's license. Jeri and I sat down with him and said, "Okay, if you want to drive, there are certain rules and responsibilities that we need to talk about." We wrote up a one-page contract containing all the rules you might expect— things such as "drive safely," "use seat belts," and "obey the laws." We also said that in order to maintain driving privileges, he needed to do other things, including fulfilling his responsibilities at home and maintaining good grades.

Less than a month after Stephen began driving, his football team was eliminated in the play-offs. Everyone was discouraged. Stephen and a couple of his friends went out in the car. About midnight, I got a call from the police. Stephen had been pulled over for driving fast—really fast. There was no drinking or anything like that involved, but the infraction was sufficient that the police had given me a call. I told the officer that I would come and pick him up. Jeri came with me to bring the other car home.

Jeri and I had been clear with Stephen on expectations: "If you don't obey the law, you will lose the privilege to drive." Now it was a question of holding him accountable. And, as any parent who has ever had a teenager knows, it isn't easy. We realized that life had become a lot simpler now that he had been providing his own transportation and sometimes helping out with errands and other family needs. If we stuck to our agreement, we were going to lose all that. Besides, I felt a little sorry for him. He was only 16. The fine was huge. How was he ever going to pay it? What was this going to do to his reputation and relationship with his friends? And what was it going to do to his relationship with us?

I realized that we really had no choice. Stephen needed to be held accountable. And we needed to hold him accountable. If we didn't, how was he going to feel he could trust us? And how could the other kids trust us? Clearly this was an issue that impacted not only Stephen, but the whole family culture, as well.

In the end, Stephen paid the ticket. It cost him $555, which took almost all his savings from his summer job. While law enforcement officials did not suspend his license, we did—not forever, but for the several months we had designated in our agreement. It was very, very hard on him. But he learned a lesson, and he's been a model driver ever since. In fact, he gained the reputation as the safe driver among his friends. It actually became a joke with his friends that whenever they were all going somewhere and their parents told them to be careful and safe, the kids would reply, "Don't worry—we're going with Covey!" That clearly meant they would be going the speed limit, wearing seat belts, and obeying the law.

A great example of holding people accountable on the job is Ursula Burns, president of Business Group Operations at Xerox. Burns has been an indispensable part of CEO Anne Mulcahy's team and Xerox's improvement. In operations reviews, her style has been to call on people who missed their goals. As Mulcahy reported in *Fortune*, "She'd say, 'Jim, you blew it; tell us what happened.'" Burns wasn't mean about it, but she was relentless. Betsy Morris described the effect of Burns' style in the same magazine, noting that, "Pretty soon people got the message: If they met their goals, they got to sit back and watch the others squirm."

It's not always easy to hold others accountable. In fact, sometimes it's really hard. But the benefits in terms of trust are incredible. There is a definite and direct connection to speed and cost.

TRUST TIPS

On the bell curve for this behavior, the peak clearly reflects the power of the 4 Cores. On the left side of the curve, you have underowning. This comes from failure to appropriately accept full responsibility or follow through with accountability . . . or failure to create an effective system of accountability in an organization or family. To move to the "sweet spot" often necessitates strengthening character (Integrity and Intent), particularly in holding ourselves accountable. But it always necessitates strengthening Competence—improving your ability to consistently define and meet personal expectations and also to create accountability in a culture, whether at home or at work.

On the right side of the curve is overowning. It's the person who takes the blame for everything in a broken marriage, including detestable things done by his/her spouse. It's the child who takes responsibility for his/her parents' bad relationship or divorce. It's parents who do everything possible to appropriately raise a child and then feel guilty and responsible when that child uses his/her agency to make bad choices. It's managers who use accountability with the wrong intent—to punish, to validate their poor opinion of someone instead of to help them produce results and to improve. It's businesspeople who take responsibility for the effects of things they can't control, like currency fluctuations or interest rates. Moving back to the "sweet spot" requires both character and competence, and the judgment created by all 4 Cores.

As you work to Practice Accountability, you might try one of the following:

- Listen to your language and to your thoughts. When things go wrong and you find yourself blaming or accusing others, stop. Draw back and ask yourself, How can I close the window and focus on the mirror? In your mind, compare the difference in establishing trust between an approach of blaming and pointing fingers versus an approach of taking personal responsibility.

- At work, Practice Accountability by holding your direct reports accountable for their actions. Always clarify expectations first so that everyone knows what they're accountable for and by when. When people account to you, allow them to evaluate themselves first against the results you've agreed upon (most people will be tougher on themselves than you'll be); then follow through with the agreed-upon or natural consequences of people performing (or not). Remember, the people you rely upon most in your company—the performers—like to be held accountable and want others to be held accountable, too.

• Look for ways to create an environment of accountability in your home. Set up trust talks with your partner on matters you've agreed to work together on, such as finances. Create agreements with your children concerning their responsibilities at home, and include consequences—both natural and logical, both good and bad. Follow through on your agreements. Give family members a person—and a culture—they can trust.

SUMMARY: BEHAVIOR #10— PRACTICE ACCOUNTABILITY

Hold yourself accountable. Hold others accountable. Take responsibility for results. Be clear on how you'll communicate how you're doing—and how others are doing. Don't avoid or shirk responsibility. Don't blame others or point fingers when things go wrong.

BEHAVIOR #11: LISTEN FIRST

> *If there is any great secret of success in life, it lies in the ability to put yourself in the other person's place and to see things from his point of view—as well as your own.*
>
> —HENRY FORD

As we look now at Behavior #11—Listen First—we move into the final three behaviors, which require an almost equal blend of character and competence.

To Listen First means not only to really *listen* (to genuinely seek to understand another person's thoughts, feelings, experience, and point of view), but to do it *first* (before you try to diagnose, influence, or prescribe).

I learned a little about the value of listening first years ago when I was in high school. I decided to join the debate team, and I was excited to debate my first case. As I was making my presentation, I noticed that at certain times, the judge would lift his hand and move it in quick, circular motions. I thought he was trying to tell me to elaborate on the point I'd just made, so I came back at it from another angle. This happened repeatedly, so I kept coming back to my points in different ways time and time again. I remember thinking that I must not be doing a very good job making my points.

After the debate was over, however, I discovered that what the judge was actually trying to communicate to me was the exact opposite of what I had thought. He was saying, "Right. I got the point. Move on!" What an embarrassment it was to me (and a loss to our team) that I had not understood!

Years later, I ran into a similar situation when I was doing a presentation for a group from a large corporation. I was facilitating a discussion about the company culture, bringing up all kinds of jugular issues. People were really involved and participating. Suddenly things got very quiet and nobody seemed to want to talk about the tough issues anymore. Unbeknownst to me, the plant manager (whom nobody trusted) had walked into the room and sat down in the group. Sensing my confusion, someone behind this man finally pointed to him, trying to communicate, "He's here. He's the reason why we're all being quiet." But I interpreted his pointing to mean, "Ask him. Call on him." So—to the dismay of both my colleagues and the entire group of participants—I did just that. (Let me just say that it was *not* one of my better experiences in presenting!)

I'm sure you get the point. It's vital to listen, to understand *first*. Otherwise you may be acting on assumptions that are totally incorrect—acting in ways that turn out to be embarrassing and counterproductive.

The *principles* behind Listen First include understanding, respect, and mutual benefit. The *opposite* is to speak first and listen last—or not to listen at all. It's focusing on getting out your agenda without considering whether others may have information, ideas, or perspectives that could influence what you have to say. It's ignoring other people's need to be understood—often before they're ready to listen to anyone else. It's self-focused, ego-driven behavior, and it does not build trust.

> *We've all heard the criticism "he talks too much." When was the last time you heard someone criticized for listening too much?*
>
> —NORM AUGUSTINE, FORMER CHAIRMAN,
> LOCKHEED MARTIN

The *counterfeit* is pretend listening. It's spending "listening" time thinking about your reply and just waiting for your turn to speak. Or it's listening without understanding. In either case, you're not influenced by what others have to say, and usually those you "listen" to don't feel understood, even though you've given them the time.

Interestingly, when I have interviews or when people come up to me with questions after a program or presentation, I find that, by far, Listen First is the behavior I recommend most. It's the starting point in almost any situation. So often, the problems people have, both at work and at home, come because they don't really Listen First.

THE IMPACT ON SPEED AND COST

Some people say that to Listen First is inefficient, that it takes too much time. I couldn't disagree more. I am firmly convinced that this behavior is highly pragmatic—that it has an almost unparalleled positive impact in establishing trust, and on speed and cost.

In an article published and then reprinted in *Harvard Business Review*, management authority Peter Drucker lists eight practices of effective executives. At the end, he concludes:

> *We just reviewed eight practices of effective executives. I'm going to throw in one final bonus practice. This one is so important that I will elevate it to a rule: <u>Listen first, speak last</u>"* [emphasis added].

Why would he elevate it to a rule? Because when you Listen First, you get insight and understanding you wouldn't have had. You make better decisions. Also you show respect. You give people psychological air. And the impact on trust is amazing.

Smart organizations recognize the power of Listen First, particularly as it pertains to customers and other external stakeholders. If companies don't do market research to determine the needs and preferences of consumers *before* they produce products, they don't make money. Sometimes they have to invest tremendous time and money in order to redesign and relaunch the product. Sometimes they end up out of business.

Smart leaders recognize the power of Listen First, particularly as it relates to coworkers and internal customers. If they don't, they cheat themselves and the company out of the information, feedback, innovation, collaboration, and partnering inherent in a high-trust environment and vital to success in today's global economy.

> *Leadership has less to do with walking in front and leading the way than it does with listening to the needs of the people of the company and meeting them.*
>
> —CHARLES M. CAWLEY, CHAIRMAN AND CEO,
> MBNA AMERICA

When Mike Garrett became president of Georgia Power, I asked him what his plans were in his new role. He said, "I'm going to go in and basically just listen for the first couple of months. I'm going to see what's happening. If I were to go in and start to lay out a vision and a plan without listening, I wouldn't have near the effectiveness, near the trust to do what I want to do. I always go in listening first."

The wisdom of this approach was enormously helpful to me when I came in as CEO of the Covey Leadership Center. At the time, we had eight legal disputes on the docket. These disputes had dragged on for months—in one case, even years. They were consuming enormous time and energy, and I was frustrated because I felt we should be focusing our efforts elsewhere. In addition, I was disappointed that we had those kinds of disagreements in the first place. So I determined that we would have them resolved within two months.

My basic approach was to listen to the other parties first. In seven out of the eight cases, listening created the openness, trust, and understanding needed to come up with solutions (which were often synergistic) that worked for everyone. In the last case, the person involved did not have mutual benefit intent and simply tried to manipulate the situation, so we ended up with a compromise. I think the end result would have been the same had we not listened and simply gone down the legal path, but I still feel better about having attempted to listen first. And, except for the final case, which took a few months longer, we did meet our two-month goal.

> *I have found that the two best qualities a CEO can have are the ability to listen and to assume the best motives in others.*
>
> —JACK M. GREENBERG, CHAIRMAN
> AND CEO, McDONALD'S

In another situation at the Leadership Center, we felt we needed to sever our relationship with an affiliate who had not been performing. I knew he felt like there were a number of variables involved in his lack of performance, so when I met with him, I said, "I want to just listen. Let me hear your perspective." After I spent about two hours listening, he sat back and said, "I feel so understood, I don't even care what you decide anymore. Now I feel like you understand all the things I thought you might not be aware of or appreciate, and I believe you will take those things into consideration in making your decision." We ended up terminating this relationship, but this man left in a good place. If he hadn't felt understood, the whole situation might well have ended up in another legal dispute, costing us far more and taking a lot longer than the time I spent listening.

MAKING DEPOSITS

One of the huge benefits of Listen First is that it helps you learn *how* to build trust. It helps you understand which behaviors make deposits in a particular Trust Account and which do not. Acting on this understanding results in greater speed because you're speaking—and behaving— in the same language as the person with whom you're trying to build the account.

In Gary Chapman's book on relationships, *The Five Love Languages*, he makes the interesting argument that while there are infinite expressions of love, there are only five emotional love languages. He says: "Your emotional love language and the language of your spouse may be as different as Chinese from English. . . . We must be willing to learn our spouse's primary love language if we are to be effective communicators of love." While Chapman applies this language of love to personal relationships, the same concept also applies in our professional relationships. By learning and speaking the same native tongue as our customers, investors, suppliers, distributors, and coworkers, we are able to understand and communicate with them better. As Heinrich Pierer, CEO of Siemens AG, has said, "Leadership ultimately means understanding people."

In relationships it's important to keep in mind that sometimes words communicate only a little of what a person really thinks, feels, or means. In fact, sometimes words do not communicate at all. Research shows that face-to-face communication regarding attitudes and feelings is 7 percent what people say, 38 percent how they say it, and 55 percent body language. So Listen First means to listen with more than your ears; it means to also listen with your eyes and your heart. This becomes more of a challenge in today's companies where so much communication is done remotely and with people whom you've never met face-to-face. This actually puts more—not less—of a premium on listening. Barnes & Noble CEO Leonard Riggio says, "I try to hear things through the ears of others, and see things through their eyes."

Listen First means to listen *for* as well as to listen *to*. When you listen *to* customers, you're listening *for* what matters most to them. When you listen *to* investors, you're listening *for* what's most important on their agenda. When you listen *to* coworkers, you're listening *for* what would engage their interest and creativity. An observer listening *to* conversations at the watercooler would listen *for* discussions about how people behave—which would tell him more about the company's culture than their mission or values statement.

Finally, and perhaps most importantly, Listen First means to listen to yourself, to your gut feelings, your own inner voice, before you decide, before you act. I remember one time I had to make a tough business decision about downsizing that would have huge implications for the company and for many people whose lives would be impacted by my decision. I listened to many who gave me advice on this matter—people I really trusted and saw as credible, ranging from board members to outside consultants to other coworkers and my direct reports. Everyone's advice was so contradictory. It was like a scattergram—all over the board. I was confused and overwhelmed, and I felt the weight of so many lives hanging on my decision.

Perplexed, I came to the conclusion that I was listening too much to other people. I needed to just listen to myself instead—to my instincts, my gut—and that would lead me to the best decision. As I did this, I became clear on what to do, and the decision was implemented with success. Through it all, I learned that when you have a foundation of Self Trust, sometimes the best voice to listen to is your own inner voice.

TRUST TIPS

Obviously, the "sweet spot" on the bell curve is to Listen First with Integrity, Intent, Capabilities, and Results. If you're on the left—either not listening or not listening first—you may need to focus on humility (Integrity), a mutual benefit agenda (Intent), empathic listening skills (Capabilities), or ensuring that the other person feels understood (Results). Here are two keys that may be helpful to you in working on Results:

1. Generally, as long as a person is communicating with high emotion, he or she does not yet feel understood.
2. A person will usually not ask for your advice until he or she feels understood. To offer advice too early will usually only stir up more emotion—or cause someone to simply ignore what you say.

If you're on the right side of the curve—spending all your time listening and never bringing the conversation to the point of decisionmaking, counseling, or influencing—you may want to focus on courage (Integrity), *acting* in the person's best interest (Intent), developing decision-making and collaboration skills (Capabilities), or simply getting things done (Results).

As you work to Listen First, you may find the following ideas helpful to increase trust.

- Think back over your interactions with others during the past week, both at work and at home. Think of a time when you did or didn't Listen First. What were the results? What would have been the results if you had behaved differently?

- The next time you're in a conversation, stop and ask yourself, Have I really listened to this other person? Do I really understand how he or she feels? If not, simply stop and do it. Set your own agenda aside and really focus on understanding the other person's point of view before you share your own.

- In your company, take proactive steps to understand your stakeholders—both internal and external. Don't get caught up in the illusion that you know everything or have all the right answers. Consider what you can do to ensure others that you are listening to them and making an effort to meet their concerns and needs.

SUMMARY: BEHAVIOR #11—LISTEN FIRST

Listen before you speak. Understand. Diagnose. Listen with your ears—and your eyes and heart. Find out what the most important behaviors are to the people you're working with. Don't assume you know what matters most to others. Don't presume you have all the answers—or all the questions.

BEHAVIOR #12: KEEP COMMITMENTS

Stand up for what's right, in small matters and large ones, and always do what you promise.

—REUBEN MARK, CHAIRMAN AND CEO,
COLGATE-PALMOLIVE

Behavior #12—Keep Commitments—is the "Big Kahuna" of all behaviors. It's the quickest way to build trust in any relationship—be it with an employee, a boss, a team member, a customer, a supplier, a spouse, a child, or the public in general. Its *opposite*—to break commitments or violate promises—is, without question, the quickest way to destroy trust.

Obviously, this behavior involves making commitments as well as keeping them. To paraphrase my friend Roger Merrill, when you make a commitment, you build hope; when you keep it, you build trust. Given the impact of violating commitments, it's vital to be careful with the commitments you make.

However, the *counterfeit* of this behavior is to make commitments that are so vague or elusive that nobody can pin you down, or, even worse, to be so afraid of breaking commitments that you don't even make any in the first place. That's following Napoleon Bonaparte's line of reasoning: "The best way to keep one's word is not to give it." But this kind of approach clearly lacks courage and promise, and it certainly won't work in today's global economy, where companies sometimes need to make and follow through on remarkable promises to even get noticed in the clutter of so many companies offering the same products and solutions.

In addition, this approach didn't really work for Napoleon, and I can guarantee, it won't build trust for you, either.

> [I]t is a leader's responsibility to demonstrate what it means to keep your word and earn a reputation for trustworthiness.
>
> —HANK PAULSON, CHAIRMAN AND CEO, GOLDMAN SACHS

Recently I did an interview in which I shared how making and keeping commitments was the number one behavior to either build or destroy trust. When I finished, the interviewer excitedly said, "Do you want further validation?" He told me how he'd recently purchased a multi-million-dollar company. This was the third time the company had been sold in the last four years, and the managers and employees were very skeptical because they had seen other buyers make a lot of promises that were never kept. However, this new leader brought everyone together and just listened as people expressed their frustrations and concerns. After asking for and listening to their suggestions, this man made 14 commitments to the employees concerning improvements he would make and attached deadlines to each. Everyone was extremely skeptical. But within a week, this leader delivered on every commitment he had made. He came back to his people and said, "I told you I would do this, and I've done it. Now, what else needs to be done?" His credibility instantly skyrocketed. Almost overnight, he created an environment of trust, transforming the long-standing tax into a dividend. And results quickly followed. After several years of stagnant or negative growth, revenues doubled in the first year, and profits increased even faster.

> [A]lways deliver what you say you will. [N]ever make a promise that you can't follow through on. [T]he way you really build trust, in a sense, is through crucibles. You have to show that you will do your part, even if it is difficult.
>
> —DENNIS ROSS, FORMER U.S. AMBASSADOR

Keep Commitments is based on the *principles* of integrity, performance, courage, and humility. It's closely tied to other behaviors, including Talk Straight and Deliver Results. It's the perfect balance of character and competence. Particularly, it involves integrity (character) and your ability to do what you say you're going to do (competence).

THE IMPACT ON TRUST

In almost any discussion of trust, keeping commitments comes up as the number one influencing behavior. In the AMA/HRI 2005 study on business ethics, "keeping promises" was ranked as the number one behavior in creating an ethical culture. On the other hand, a 2002 survey on leaders for the World Economic Forum identified "not doing what they say" as the number one trust breaker.

Although Keep Commitments is one of those behaviors that seem obvious and is just plain common sense, as the expression goes, "Common sense is not always common practice." And the impact on trust is devastating.

I worked with one leader who was bright, talented, and extremely capable, but he couldn't keep things confidential. Because people assumed a commitment of confidentiality, it created huge withdrawals and literally changed the nature of their discussions with him because they felt they couldn't trust him. As a result, he did not get the information that could really have been of help to him in leading and decision making.

In another circumstance, I read of a leader who, after taking his company public, told his senior team to not sell their stock in order to help stabilize the stock price. But then he turned around and sold some of his own stock. He justified it by saying that as a percentage of the total amount of stock he owned, it was minuscule. But in the eyes of the senior team members, his instructions to them to not sell their stock had included an implicit commitment from him to not sell his, and he paid a massive trust tax as a result.

In a third situation, a company had built up a database and the company leadership had explicitly promised they wouldn't sell or rent their list. But a few years later, a new decision maker came in and decided to rent the list. Within a short time, one customer recognized that the direct mail solicitations he had begun to receive from new companies had the same, unique, and distinguishing errors on the address label he had seen on labels from the company that had promised not to rent their list. He thought this was beyond coincidence and called the company on it. The company acknowledged their behavior and apologized, but the customer said he could no longer trust a company that would make an explicit commitment and then break it, so he quit doing business with them.

> There are three signs of a hypocrite: when he speaks he
> speaks lies, when he makes a promise he breaks it, and
> when he is trusted he betrays his trust.

—MUHAMMAD

As these examples clearly show, there are implicit as well as explicit commitments, and the violation of either creates huge withdrawals of trust. Many people assume that most businesses have commitments to honesty, integrity, and quality. When entities such as Enron, World-Com, Parmalat, or the City of San Diego (nicknamed "Enron by the Sea" for fiscal improprieties) behave in ways that violate those implicit commitments, it creates enormous withdrawals and immediate distrust. And the same is true in relationships. For example, most people who get married assume that their spouse is fully committed to the marriage relationship and to the welfare of any children born into that relationship. When a spouse violates those commitments, it creates a serious breach of trust.

Whether commitments are explicit or implicit, they will have an impact on speed and cost. To violate them causes doubt, suspicion, cynicism, and distrust that rust the wheels of progress. To keep them generates the hope, enthusiasm, confidence, and trust that increase momentum and lubricate the accomplishment of results.

CULTURAL INTELLIGENCE

In the new global economy, it's vital to understand that sometimes different cultures view commitments differently. And understanding the difference is a key to making deposits and avoiding withdrawals.

And I'm not just talking about ethnic or geographic cultures. I've been in many company cultures, for example, where when you set up a meeting at two, everyone is expected to be there promptly at two ready to go. I've been in other cultures where the nature of commitment is best reflected by a clock a friend told me about that shows the hours as "one-ish," "two-ish," "three-ish," and so on; it depends on what people consider most important at the time. This difference is reflected in the Greek words *chronos* and *kairos*. *Chronos* means chronological time and *kairos* means quality time, or the value you get out of whatever time you have.

I well remember the first meeting we held after the announcement of the FranklinCovey merger. The Franklin people were there in the formal boardroom all dressed nicely in suits and right on time. Those of us from the Covey group arrived in khakis 10 minutes late. The Franklin people came from a company culture of "manage your time"; we came from a company culture that emphasized "lead your life." I know people from both companies were thinking, What have we done?

The point here is that by being sensitive to the nature of commitments—both explicit and implicit—in different cultures, you will be able to build trust much more quickly than if you're insensitive or clueless.

THE MOST IMPORTANT COMMITMENTS OF ALL

When it comes to dealing with a commitment to a client, people tend to be more rigid. But when it comes to a family commitment, they tend to be more flexible—sometimes simply because they're trying to provide for their families and they tend to justify breaking those commitments more easily. But I affirm that commitments to people at home are every bit as important—or even more important—than commitments to people at work.

Some time ago, my daughter McKinlee had the lead role in her high school musical, and I made a commitment to her that I would be there. I was scheduled to be on the road, but I planned to fly back in time to see her in the play. To me, I hadn't made an "I will be there at all costs" commitment; it was more of an "Oh, yeah. I think I can make it." But to her, it was a commitment and it was important.

As I was talking to the client representatives several weeks in advance of my road trip, they said, "Stephen, we really need you to stay longer." I went to my daughter to see if I could renegotiate. However, I quickly realized that even trying was a big withdrawal. So I tried to lower expectations with the client. They were not happy with the request and really pushed me to stay.

So I had a dilemma. I decided to apply what my colleague Blaine Lee calls the 10-Year Rule. I asked myself, Ten years from now, what will I be glad I did? I clearly concluded that ten years from now, I'd be glad I kept what my daughter viewed as a commitment. So I told the client I wouldn't be able to stay. As a result, I lost some economic opportunity, but the client survived and I was happy. My daughter was thrilled. The night she performed, I was there on the front row with a dozen roses in my arms.

Because keeping commitments has such an impact on trust—and because trust is so vital to a thriving family culture—it's wise to keep in mind that commitments to family members are often the most important commitments of all. Also—as we discussed in the chapter on Integrity—making and keeping commitments to yourself is the key to success in making and keeping commitments to others. That's where it all starts, and that's what gives you the power and the confidence—the Self Trust—that enables you to build trust with others.

TRUST TIPS

If you're on the left end of the bell curve in this behavior—you're not making enough commitments or not following through very well—you may need to focus on increasing your Integrity, strengthening your mutual benefit Intent, developing the Capability to repeatedly perform this behavior and turn it into a habit, or become more aware of the trust-building Results.

If you're on the right end—maybe overextending yourself by making too many commitments or keeping commitments at all costs, even when the situation changes and makes it impractical or unwise—you may need to focus on building the judgment that comes from strengthening all 4 Cores. You may want to especially focus on Integrity and consider the Results of making commitments that you can't or shouldn't keep.

As you work to Keep Commitments, you may want to do one of the following:

- In establishing a new relationship where you want to build trust fast, follow this process: Find a value-added reason to make a commitment and keep it . . . and do it again . . . and again . . . and again. As you implement this "Make-Keep-Repeat" cycle, notice how quickly the Trust Account grows.

- The next time you make a commitment to someone at work, be sure the commitment is realistic. Even if you have to disappoint someone, it's far better to do it up front than to overpromise and under deliver. Make sure you follow through with what you've committed to do. If you have to miss a deadline, attempt to renegotiate expectations as early as possible; don't just ignore it and be late.

• Pay attention to your language at home. Realize that when you say you will do something, the members of your family see that as a commitment. Treat what you say you will do seriously and follow through. Recognize that the trust you build at home is likely the most important trust of all.

**SUMMARY: BEHAVIOR #12—
KEEP COMMITMENTS**

Say what you're going to do, then do what you say you're going to do. Make commitments carefully and keep them. Make keeping commitments the symbol of your honor. Don't break confidences. Don't attempt to "PR" your way out of a commitment you've broken.

BEHAVIOR #13:
EXTEND TRUST

*Trust men and they will be true to you; treat them
greatly and they will show themselves great.*

—RALPH WALDO EMERSON

One season when I coached Little League flag football, I had a
very courageous player on my team named Anna Humphries.
She was the only girl on our team. In fact, as I recall, there
were only one or two other girls in the whole league. Anna wasn't a bad
player, but she didn't have the same level of experience and skill as
some of the others.

According to the Little League rules, I was required to play every
player about half of each game. That assumed I would have fourteen
players to fill the seven player positions. However, that season I only
had ten players. Considering Anna's limited experience and skill, I
could have played her for half of each game and then pulled her out,
but I felt that she was being courageous to compete with these boys and
I wanted to encourage her, so I decided to keep the playing time fairly
equal.

Everything went great until we came down to the big game. It was
the end of the season, and both teams were undefeated. On the last play
of the game, the other team ran toward Anna's side and scored a touch-
down. They were now only one point behind. With one play remaining, they were going for two points for the win.

I had a choice. I could take Anna out and put another person in her
place, or I could leave her in. She had competed hard all year, and

based on my earlier decision to play everyone equally, it was still her turn to play. With our team goal of winning it all on the line, I decided to leave her in, and I told her that if they ran to her side again, she could make the play and stop them.

Anna felt that extension of trust and rose to the occasion. Sure enough, the other team ran toward her side, but Anna made the play, pulling the runner's flag and stopping him just inches short of the goal line. This was only the second flag she had pulled the whole year, and she pulled it on the most crucial play of the year.

We won the game and the unofficial league championship. To this day, every time I see Anna, I feel happy that I believed in her and extended trust to her. I tell her, "You are my hero! You made it happen!"

FROM TRUSTED PERSON TO TRUSTING LEADER

Behavior #13—Extend Trust—is different in kind from the rest of the behaviors. It's about shifting from "trust" as a noun to "trust" as a verb. While the other behaviors help you become a more trusted person or manager, this behavior will help you become a more trusting leader. Not only does it build trust, it leverages trust. It creates reciprocity; when you trust people, other people tend to trust you in return. Additionally (and ironically), extending trust is one of the best ways to create trust when it's not there.

> *Leadership without mutual trust is a contradiction in terms.*
>
> WARREN BENNIS, AUTHOR OF *ON BECOMING A LEADER*

Consider Warren Buffett's acquisition of McLane Distribution. That deal could happen with such speed and low cost only because Warren Buffett was willing to extend trust. A similar example is the way in which A. G. Lafley, CEO of Procter & Gamble, and Jim Kilts, CEO of Gillette, extended trust to each other in the process of merging their companies. In *Fortune* magazine, Lafley describes this remarkable approach as follows:

> *I decided that we were going to be collaborative in the negotiations. We had a friendly deal here, and there was absolutely no reason not to have the cards on the table. I called on a person Jim trusted and I trusted,*

> *Rajat Gupta, the head of McKinsey, who urged Jim to give me an open-book look at the cost synergies and a look at Gillette's technology into the future. We did collaborate—and without all the typical advisors. At one point Jim said to me, "Aren't you bringing any bankers?" I said, "We don't need any bankers." He said, "Aren't you bringing any lawyers?" I said, "We don't need any lawyers." . . . That was a very important signal that we trusted each other.*

This last illustration is an example of *transference* of trust, wherein Rajat Gupta of McKinsey acted as what I call a "trust bridge" between the two parties. Because both parties independently had trust in the same individual, and that individual expressed his trust in each party to the other, the two parties were able to then transfer his trust to each other.

I'm certainly not suggesting that the way Warren Buffett or A. G. Lafley handled these mergers is the way everyone should do deals. You could easily meet someone, shake hands on a deal, and do no "due diligence" only to discover you bought a warehouse that doesn't even exist! In fact, during a break in one of my programs, a woman came up to me and told me that she had had a terrible experience in extending trust. She said, "Some time ago, I bought a company. During the negotiations, when I started talking about needing an employment agreement, the CEO whose company I was buying told me he didn't want to do one. He said, 'Look, you're buying my company. You've got to trust me. If you don't trust me, why buy my company?' It seemed to be a very logical argument, so I said, 'Okay, I trust you.'" According to this woman, however, after the deal went down, this CEO (whose expertise and relationships she desperately needed) caused all kinds of havoc, threatening to leave if he didn't get more money. Not having an employment agreement in place nearly turned the entire deal into an absolute disaster. In the end, she said, it made her never want to extend trust again.

Clearly, you don't want to be gullible. You don't want to be a Pollyanna. You don't want to extend trust indiscriminately or unwisely. You'll get taken to the cleaners. You'll get burned. But neither do you want to withhold trust when extending it could bring such enormous benefits.

The last section of this book is all about Inspiring Trust. In that section, we'll talk in depth about when and how to extend "Smart Trust" so that you can minimize your risk and you don't get caught up in situations like this woman did. But in this chapter, I simply want to point out that most of the time, extending trust will have an extraordinary impact on building trust in relationships and in the culture. Clearly it is one of the best and fastest ways to establish and grow trust, and this is the aspect of it we will focus on now.

WHAT HAPPENS WHEN YOU EXTEND TRUST

Extend Trust is based on the *principles* of empowerment, reciprocity, and a fundamental belief that most people are capable of being trusted, want to be trusted, and will run with trust when it is extended to them.

The *opposite* of Extend Trust is to withhold trust, which creates an enormous cost everywhere, especially in organizations.

When you think about it, why is it that such a low percentage of employees trust their senior leaders? There are undoubtedly many reasons, but I contend that a principal reason is that senior leaders don't trust their people, and this distrust gets reciprocated. Thus, senior leaders are actually complicit in helping to produce their employees' distrust. It becomes a vicious downward cycle: People tend to not trust people who don't trust them.

As an example of this distrust, many companies do not allow overtime, after hours, or weekend work unless a supervisor is present. Why? Because fundamentally, they don't trust employees to do their jobs. As an employee in one such company said, "They think we're just going to sit around eating donuts and racking up overtime!"

Now contrast that kind of behavior to the approach of Ritz-Carlton Hotels, where management gives every employee—including the maids—the ability to resolve a customer's concerns and comp up to $2,000 without approval. Or to the retailer Nordstrom, where employees have only one rule governing the way they provide customer service: "Use good judgment in all situations."

Or contrast it to the approach of JetBlue, widely recognized for its quality service. JetBlue doesn't have a reservation center—instead, people work out of their homes. In the vast majority of cases, these reservationists are mothers who want to balance work and family and don't want to leave their homes. JetBlue managers set them up on terminals and trust them to be at their task when they're supposed to be. A less trusting company might be worried that they'd be off task attending to their kids or other matters. But these reservationists are known for being superbly responsible and incredibly courteous, kind, pleasant, and engaging on the phone—partly because they reflect back to the customer the way they are treated, the trust extended to them, and how they feel about their company and their job.

Interestingly, other airlines have attempted to copy the JetBlue (and Southwest) discount airline model, including Ted (run by United) and Song (run by Delta). At this point, however, they have been able to copy the strategy, but they haven't been able to implement it nearly as effectively as JetBlue because they can't copy a culture of trust. When asked how JetBlue was different from other "legacy" airlines, Vice President of People Vincent Stabile responded, "We treat our people the way we want them to treat the customers."

> Companies should trust people to work at home more. Commuting kills so much time and energy that could be spent creating.
>
> —Sir Richard Branson, founder and Chairman, the Virgin Group

Best Buy extends trust to its employees in a similar way. In 2002, following a sharp rise in employee turnover and stress-related health claims, the company decided to allow employees to work whenever and wherever they liked as long as they got the job done. On a recent *60 Minutes* program, one of their managers, Chap Achen, said, "I have trust that my team is going to get the work done in this environment, and . . . the ironic thing about it is that it's that trust factor that actually makes them work harder for you." It's obviously working—productivity has gone up by 35 percent.

Gordon Forward, former president and CEO of Chaparral Steel, has said:

> *We don't have policies. What we started with essentially were some very basic ideas. First, we decided that such things as trust and honesty were going to play a big role in what we were doing. We felt that a lot of the procedures in many organizations were designed to catch the 3 percent who were trying to cheat in one way or another. We decided to design our rules for the 97 percent we can trust. The others would stand out like sore thumbs, we figured, and they'd eventually leave. That's exactly what happened.*

One of the biggest restraining forces against working at home is that at the end of the day, employers really don't know whether or not they can trust their people, so they make the choice to treat the 97 percent that can be trusted like the 3 percent that can't, instead of the other way around.

Some might argue that 3 percent is unrealistically low—that it's more like 10 percent who can't be trusted. But even if that is true, what about the 90 percent you *can* trust? Are we letting the "few" define the "many"? And if we are, what's the impact on speed and cost?

I contend that the impact is devastating! It literally kills the potential enthusiasm, engagement, collaboration, and the reciprocal trust that could catapult the organization miles ahead, as examples such as JetBlue and Best Buy clearly show.

The *counterfeit* of Extend Trust takes two forms. The first is extending "false trust." It's giving people the responsibility, but not the authority or resources, to get a task done. The second is extending "fake trust"—acting like you trust someone when you really don't. In other words, you entrust someone with a job, but at the end of the day, you "snoopervise," hover over or "big brother" the person, or perhaps even do his job for him.

A simple example of someone who extends fake trust is the faculty advisor to the student council at a junior high school. One of my colleague's sons, who serves on this council, was recently assigned by this advisor to call a local university about borrowing a game for an upcoming activity. When he did so, he discovered that the faculty advisor had already made the call and arranged to borrow the game. Evidently, this is a typical experience for members of the council.

And what is the impact on initiative and on trust?

A POWERFUL MOTIVATOR

As I learned when my father gave me the responsibility to make our yard "green and clean," there is nothing that motivates, or inspires, people like having trust extended to them. When it is, people don't need to be managed or supervised; they manage themselves.

In fact, when people are asked to think of the person who has been most influential in their lives and to describe why that person was so influential, they will usually say, "She believed in me when no one else did," or "He saw something in me that no one else saw." What they are basically saying is that that person trusted them, and that they were powerfully influenced by and responded to that trust.

> *People ask me how I've had the interest and zeal to hang in there and do what I've done. I say, "Because my father treated me with very stern discipline: he trusted me." I'm stuck, I've got to see the trust through. He trusted me. I trust other people. And they did the job.*
>
> —ROBERT GALVIN JR., FORMER CEO, MOTOROLA

By extending trust, you empower people. You leverage your leadership. You create a high-trust culture that brings out the best in people, creates high-level synergy, and maximizes the ability of any organization—whether it be a business, a school, an NPO, or a family—to accomplish what it sets out to do.

TRUST TIPS

To Extend Trust clearly takes strength in Integrity, Intent, Capabilities, and Results. If you're on the left side of the bell curve, you're likely not extending enough trust or not extending it effectively. You may want to particularly focus on increasing courage (Integrity) or enhancing your propensity to trust (Intent), or on improving your ability to clarify expectations, hold others accountable, or extend Smart Trust in more actionable ways (Capabilities).

If you're on the right side, you're probably extending too much trust and getting burned. You need the judgment that comes from development of the 4 Cores. In the last section of this book, I'll give you more specifics that will help you move to the "sweet spot" of extending "Smart Trust."

As you work on this behavior, you might want to consider the following application ideas:

- Think about a relationship where you feel someone doesn't trust you. Ask yourself, Could this person's lack of trust in me, at least in part, be a reflection of my own lack of trust in him or her? If you're caught in a downward spiral, try to reverse it. Start behaving in ways that extend trust, and notice the results.

- On a scale of one to ten, determine where you think you are in terms of extending trust to others, either at work or at home. Imagine the result of moving your performance point to the left (extending less trust) . . . and then to the right (extending more trust). If you rated yourself a five or less, identify one or two steps you could take to extend more trust.

- If you're a parent, pay attention to the ways in which you interact with your children. Do you tend to be suspicious, hover over them, or micromanage? Or do you tend to treat them as responsible people who are worthy of your trust? In the section on Inspiring Trust, we'll talk about how to extend "Smart Trust" to children, but at this point, you might at least want to consider your tendencies and what message they are communicating to family members . . . and what are the results.

SUMMARY: BEHAVIOR #13—EXTEND TRUST

Demonstrate a propensity to trust. Extend trust abundantly to those who have earned your trust. Extend conditionally to those who are earning your trust. Learn how to appropriately extend trust to others based on the situation, risk, and credibility (character and competence) of the people involved. But have a propensity to trust. Don't withhold trust because there is risk involved.

CREATING AN
ACTION PLAN

In the beginning of this 13 Behaviors section, I issued a personal challenge for you to make this material highly relevant and action-able by identifying two relationships—one professional and one personal—in which you wanted to build trust. I said that at the end of the section, I would give you the opportunity to look back, determine which two or three behaviors would make the greatest difference, and create an action plan to create change.

Well, here we are. If you didn't do it before, I encourage you to do it now. This is where you can make decisions that will build trust, that will transform taxes into dividends, that will improve your relationships with two people, and—geometrically—with many others, as well.

Many people find it helpful to use a chart such as the one on the fol-lowing page. If this approach works for you, I suggest you start with one relationship. Go over the behaviors. Mark on the continuum where you think you are now with regard to each one. Then go back and circle the two or three behaviors that you feel will make the great-est positive difference.

Identify one or two next steps for each of those behaviors to create change. You may want to use one of the Trust Tips at the end of each chapter, or you may come up with something that will work better in your situation. The key is to make the steps actionable and to make and keep a commitment to yourself to do them.

Then go back and do the same for the second relationship you chose.

As you create your plan, keep in mind that the quickest way to make a withdrawal is to violate a behavior of *character*; the quickest way to make a deposit is to demonstrate a behavior of *competence*. This may help you in determining how to most quickly build trust in your situation.

If you prefer to use a different approach to implementation, that's fine. However, you may still want to look at the chart. It will give you an overview of all 13 Behaviors, including their opposites and counterfeits. It's a good way to capture a vision of the way high-trust leaders interact with others.*

	BEHAVIOR	CURRENT PERFORMANCE	OPPOSITE/ COUNTERFEIT
C	Talk Straight	└─┴─┴─┴─┴─┘	Lie, spin, tell half-truths, double-talk, flatter.
H A R	Demonstrate Respect	└─┴─┴─┴─┴─┘	Don't care or don't show you care; show disrespect or show respect only to those who can do something for you.
A C	Create Transparency	└─┴─┴─┴─┴─┘	Withhold information; keep secrets; create illusions; pretend.
T	Right Wrongs	└─┴─┴─┴─┴─┘	Don't admit or repair mistakes; cover up mistakes.
E R	Show Loyalty	└─┴─┴─┴─┴─┘	Sell others out; take the credit yourself; sweet-talk people to their faces and bad-mouth them behind their backs.

(chart continued on next page)

---

* Do you practice the 13 Behaviors or their more common counterfeits? To find out, go to www.speedoftrust.com.

	BEHAVIOR	CURRENT PERFORMANCE	OPPOSITE/ COUNTERFEIT
C	Deliver Results	└─┴─┴─┴─┴─┘	Fail to deliver; deliver on activities, not results.
O **M** **P**	Get Better	└─┴─┴─┴─┴─┘	Deteriorate; don't invest in improve-ment; force every problem into your one solution.
E **T**	Confront Reality	└─┴─┴─┴─┴─┘	Bury your head in the sand; focus on busywork while skirting the real issues.
E **N**	Clarify Expectations	└─┴─┴─┴─┴─┘	Assume expecta-tions or don't disclose them; create vague and shifting expectations.
C **E**	Practice Accountability	└─┴─┴─┴─┴─┘	Don't take respon-sibility: "It's not my fault!"; don't hold others accountable.
B	Listen First	└─┴─┴─┴─┴─┘	Don't listen; speak first, listen last; pretend listen; listen without understanding.
O **T**	Keep Commitments	└─┴─┴─┴─┴─┘	Break commitments; violate promises; make vague and elusive commitments or don't make any commitments.
H	Extend Trust	└─┴─┴─┴─┴─┘	Withhold trust; fake trust and then snoopervise; give responsibility without authority.

THE THIRD, FOURTH, AND FIFTH WAVES— STAKEHOLDER TRUST

You now have the trust-building tools—the 4 Cores of Credibility and the 13 Behaviors. In this section, we will focus on the context in which you can use these tools to increase speed, lower cost, create value, establish trust, and maximize your influence and the influence of your organization.

In the Third Wave—Organizational Trust—we will deal with establishing trust with *internal* stakeholders. The focus will be on creating *alignment* that will eliminate taxes and increase dividends inside the organization.

In the Fourth Wave—Market Trust—we will deal with establishing trust with *external* stakeholders. The focus will be on building a *reputation* or brand that inspires trust in the marketplace.

In the Fifth Wave—Societal Trust—we will talk about building trust within society based on the principles of *contribution* and global citizenship that are rapidly becoming recognized as an economic, as well as a social, necessity.

As we move into this section, I encourage you to make a choice now that will affect how you read these next three chapters and the impact they will have on your ability to build Stakeholder Trust. This choice involves defining "organization" on the level, or within the context, that is most actionable for you.

If you are a president and/or CEO of an organization, you may want to define organization on the "macro" or broadest contextual level. The glasses through which you look at this material would be your organization as a whole, so your internal stakeholders would be all who work within the organization. All other stakeholders—including customers, suppliers, distributors, and investors—would be considered external.

If you are the manager of a department or unit

within an organization, you would want to define organization on a more "micro" level. Your organization would be your department. Your internal stakeholders would be those who work in your department. In this context, your external stakeholders would include all those outside of your immediate department, including other departments within the company, customers outside the company, or even so-called internal customers you might serve within the company.

If you are a school district superintendent, your organization would be your school district. If you are a school principal, your organization would be your school. If you are a teacher, your organization would be your class. If you are a student, your organization would also be your class. If you work on a team, your organization would be the team. If you have a family, your organization would be the family. In each case, internal stakeholders would be considered in the chapter on Organizational Trust, and external stakeholders in the chapters on Market and Societal Trust.

Whatever your role, I strongly believe you will get the most out of this section if you define your organization on the most actionable level—in other words, in the most relevant context in which you have stewardship—and you use that as the lens through which you read and engage with this content. Once you complete this section, however, you may want to go through it a second time at the most macro level, defining your organization as the entire company, in order to open up a whole new level of insight and application.

THE THIRD WAVE— ORGANIZATIONAL TRUST
THE PRINCIPLE OF ALIGNMENT

Organizations are no longer built on force, but on trust.
—PETER DRUCKER

In our work with clients—before we even talk about the 4 Cores or the 13 Behaviors—we often ask four questions which I'd like to ask you now. If you will take a few minutes to answer these questions in your own mind before reading further, it will make a big difference in your ability to engage in and apply the ideas in this chapter.

How would you describe a low-trust organization?

How would you describe a high-trust organization?

Which description best represents your organization?

What are the results?

In our workshops and presentations, participants typically say that in a low-trust organization, they see cultural behaviors such as the following:

- People manipulate or distort facts
- People withhold and hoard information
- Getting the credit is very important
- People spin the truth to their advantage
- New ideas are openly resisted and stifled
- Mistakes are covered up or covered over
- Most people are involved in a blame game, bad-mouthing others
- There is an abundance of watercooler talk
- There are numerous "meetings after the meetings"
- There are many "undiscussables"
- People tend to overpromise and underdeliver
- There are a lot of violated expectations, for which people try to make excuses
- People pretend bad things aren't happening or are in denial
- The energy level is low
- People often feel unproductive tension—sometimes even fear

Participants say that in a high-trust organization, they typically see different behaviors, such as these:

- Information is shared openly
- Mistakes are tolerated and encouraged as a way of learning
- The culture is innovative and creative
- People are loyal to those who are absent
- People talk straight and confront real issues
- There is real communication and real collaboration
- People share credit abundantly
- There are few "meetings after the meetings"
- Transparency is a practiced value
- People are candid and authentic
- There is a high degree of accountability
- There is palpable vitality and energy—people can feel the positive momentum

Before we can even ask participants which list best represents the company they work for, most are already looking at that first list, laughing, and saying, "That is *our* company. That's exactly what happens in the organization I work in."

Then we ask them questions about the results of these behaviors, such as:

- What is it like to work in your company?
- What percentage of your time is focused on the real work?
- What is your ability to partner—internally? Externally?
- How are "sacred cows" dealt with?
- How collaborative is your culture?
- What is innovation like?
- Are coworkers engaged?
- How well are people able to execute the strategy?
- Do people know what the organization's priorities are?
- Do the decision makers get the data they need—unfiltered?
- What are meetings like?
- What about ethics . . . is it a matter of compliance or of doing the right thing?
- What is the span of control?
- What kinds of systems and processes are in place?
- What is the impact on speed?
- What is the impact on cost?

It's interesting that the biggest "aha!" in this exercise does not come when people see the effects of low trust in their organizations. This is their world. It's what most of them deal with every day.

The biggest "aha!" comes when they realize that it's happening as a result of violating principles—not only individually, but also organizationally. It's not just violating the 4 Cores and 13 Behaviors; it's also violating the principles of organizational design that create *alignment* with the cores and behaviors. And it happens when people—particularly leaders—blame the behaviors of people in the organization on a low-trust environment without understanding their own responsibility to create, deploy, and maintain systems that promote an environment of high trust.

Organizational design expert Arthur W. Jones has said, "All organizations are perfectly aligned to get the results they get." I would add: "All organizations are perfectly aligned to get the level of *trust* they get." So if you don't have the level of trust and the high-trust dividends you want in your organization, it's time to look at the principle of alignment. It's time to look at the structures and systems that communicate—far more eloquently than words—the underlying paradigms affecting cultural trust.

> *An enterprise that is at war with itself [misaligned] will not have the strength or focus to survive and thrive in today's competitive environment.*
>
> —PROFESSOR JOHN O. WHITNEY,
> COLUMBIA BUSINESS SCHOOL

Earlier I said that trust is the hidden variable that affects everything. The reason it's hidden in organizations is that leaders aren't looking for it in the systems, structures, processes, policies, and frameworks that all the day-to-day behaviors hang on. They're focused on the symptoms—on the glare of the sun on top of the water. They don't put on the glasses that allow them to see the "fish" moving below. As a leader, you can be successful at the Self Trust and Relationship Trust levels so that people trust you as a person, but then fail at the Organizational Trust level by not designing and aligning systems that promote trust.

SYMBOLS: MANIFESTATIONS OF ALIGNMENT (OR LACK OF IT)

At one of our workshops, a participant said that her husband recently left the company he was working for and went into academia because he felt that was where his interest really lay. But after four days at the university, he went back to his former company. With all the university's bureaucratic policies and procedures, he'd had to fill out a requisition with three levels of approval to even get a pen! He basically said, "I don't want to deal with this. I don't like what it does to me. I don't like how it makes me feel." Clearly the policies at this university were a *symbol* of distrust.

> *[T]rust is the most significant predictor of individuals' satisfaction within their organizations.*
>
> JIM KOUZES AND BARRY POSNER, BUSINESS AUTHORS

I saw similar misalignment in a large consulting company. The company had begun to struggle financially, and in an effort to manage costs, the new financial officers put a highly detailed and cumbersome expense reimbursement policy in place. It contained extremely nitpicky requirements such as, "If you arrive at the airport to turn in your rental car and you didn't fill it with gas, you have to pay for it personally at the higher cost." Consultants who were out rushing from client to client to client in different cities and scrambling to barely make their flights were being treated as though they were lazy and irresponsible. Another requirement was that unless people were at the partner level, the company wouldn't reimburse them for their cell phone calls while on the road. Again, the assumption being communicated was that these consultants would use up cell time making personal calls rather than using it for work purposes.

The whole policy became a huge symbol of distrust. But fortunately, this company had some highly credible consultants who pushed back. They said, "We don't like this. You're treating us like children. You're showing zero trust in us." As a result, the policies were eventually changed and brought into alignment with the larger company values of respect and trust.

> [G]ood leaders should trust those around them.
>
> —Sir Richard Branson, founder and
> Chairman, the Virgin Group

Both of these examples show the impact when structures and systems are not aligned with the principles that promote trust. They also demonstrate the power of organizational *symbols*—those things that represent and communicate underlying paradigms to everyone in the organization.

Truly, symbols are powerful. They carry disproportionate value. They always override rhetoric. They communicate paradigms far more clearly than words. And they do so with geometric influence. It's been said that "a picture is worth a thousand words" and the same can be said of a symbol. It communicates so much, so fast, to so many.

Symbols can be either positive or negative, and they can take many forms, including tangible objects, systems or processes, consistently applied behaviors, or legendary stories. Symbols include everything from 500-page policy manuals to top managers who park their expensive cars in reserved executive parking spaces, to newly appointed CEOs who refuse to accept a pay raise because it might send the wrong message to workers, to legends such as Howard Shultz responding in a caring way when the Starbucks employees were murdered. They include expensive art that's been purchased for a boardroom while people are being laid off and the CEO who reads all 10,000 customer feedback forms because he really cares what customers think. They also include organizational legend and lore that get told and retold throughout a company, such as the time JetBlue's CEO David Neeleman drove to JFK Airport and checked passengers in on his personal computer during a blackout in New York.

During one season of my life, I worked for a large real-estate development company that had three primary company values—to work hard, work smart, and have fun. At one point, a broker approached us, representing a client who wanted to do a huge project. He had decided to get bids from the top 10 developers in town. We were excited about the opportunity, but as negotiations progressed, we discovered that this broker was so difficult to work with and so adversarial in his demands that our meetings with him became arduous, one-sided, and actually painful. As we were sitting in the tenth meeting on this project, the senior partner in charge turned to me and said, "Stephen, I have one question: Are you having any fun working on this deal?" I had to admit that I was not. "Well," he said, "I'm not having any fun, either. Having fun is one of our values. We're not having any, so we're backing out of the bidding." Our withdrawal from such a big potential opportunity was shocking to the broker and his client, but was in complete alignment with company values, and it sent a dramatic message throughout the culture that we were serious about those values. That decision became a symbol of our values, and was told and retold as a meaningful part of company lore.

Whatever form they take, symbols become disproportionately valued as representations, icons, and images of what is right or wrong in an organization.

> *A trusted leader can only exist over the long term in a*
> *large organization if there are good myths about him,*
> *and particularly about his consistency.*
>
> —HENK BROEDERS, HEAD OF CAP GEMINI,
> E&Y FOR THE NETHERLANDS

Here are a few examples of symbols that communicate and build high trust.

1. Some years after starting Hewlett-Packard, cofounder Bill Hewlett stopped off one weekend at a company storeroom to pick up a tool, only to find that there was a lock on the tool bin. This was contrary to the explicit practice the company had established from the beginning to keep all parts bins and storerooms open so that HP employees would have free access to any tools they might need. The decision to keep the bins open had been made consciously to demonstrate trust in HP employees. It grew out of cofounder David Packard's experience years earlier working for a company that had overzealously guarded its tool and parts bins "to make sure employees didn't steal anything."

Disgusted by the lock on the storeroom, Hewlett broke it open, threw it away, and put up a sign where the lock had been. The sign read: HP TRUSTS ITS EMPLOYEES. From that day forward, the open bins truly did become a symbol of trust—a symbol that inspired loyalty and creativity. More eloquently than anything else could have, it affirmed that the company "placed great faith and trust in HP people." As Packard later said: "The open bins and storerooms were a symbol of trust, a trust that is central to the way HP does business."

2. In a time when many company employee handbooks and policy manuals are hundreds of pages long, as I mentioned earlier, the Nordstrom policy manual consists of only one card. The front of the card reads:

EMPLOYEE HANDBOOK
Welcome to Nordstrom
WE'RE GLAD TO HAVE YOU WITH OUR COMPANY.
Our number one goal is to provide outstanding customer service.
Set both your personal and professional goals high.
We have great confidence in your ability to achieve them.
So our employee handbook is very simple.
We have only one rule . . .

The other side of the card says:

ONE RULE
Use good judgment in all situations.
Please feel free to ask your Department Manager, Store Manager,
or Human Resource office any question at any time.

According to David Sirota, Louis A. Mischkind, and Michael Irwin Meltzer in their book, *The Enthusiastic Employee*:

> *This one page handbook speaks volumes about the company, yet highlights Nordstrom's focus on customer satisfaction, its deliberately nonbureaucratic culture and the trust it places in the capabilities and character of its employees. The statement is the epitome in words of a welcoming and respectful organization.*

Nordstrom's "employee handbook" is a symbol of trust, and it is completely aligned with their stated value of providing outstanding customer service through people exercising good judgment.

3. If you walk into the offices of Michael Dell—chairman—and Kevin Rollins—president and CEO—of Dell Inc., you will discover that these two leaders have arranged their working area so that there is only a clear glass wall between them, and their desks face each other. They even took the doors off the hinges so that they could freely talk at all times. This has become a great symbol to the entire Dell culture of their trust—a symbol that these two leaders are completely open with each other and that they're not talking behind each other's back.

What symbols exist in your own organization? What do they communicate to your internal stakeholders? Are the symbols aligned with the principles that create high trust? What are the results?

HOW TO EFFECT ORGANIZATIONAL CHANGE

If the symbols in your organization communicate and cultivate distrust—or less trust than you would like to have—go back to the 4 Cores with your organizational hat on. Ask yourself:

- Does my organization have Integrity? Do we know what we stand for? Do our structures and systems reflect a basic paradigm of respect and trust? Do we have a culture of honesty? Of humility? Do we listen to one another's ideas? Can we make and admit mistakes? Do we have the courage to engage the tough issues? Do our systems and structure encourage ethical behavior?
- Does my organization have good Intent? Do we have a culture of caring—for one another? For our work? For our customers? Do we genuinely want everyone to win? Are the systems set up to

reward competition or cooperation? Does the system encourage people to share ideas and information freely—or does it encourage people to withhold?

- What are the Capabilities of my organization? Do we have the means to deliver value? Do we attract and retain the Talents, Attitudes, Skills, Knowledge, and Style (TASKS) we need to compete in today's market? Do we have the right people in the right seats on the bus? Are we continuously improving and innovating? Do we reinvent ourselves, if needed?

- Does my organization get Results? Do we deliver what we promise? Can people rely on us to create value and fulfill commitments? Do we have a track record that promotes confidence? Do clients recommend us to others? Do we deliver results in a way that inspires trust?

If you find your organization lacking in any of these areas, this is the place to begin to create alignment and build Organizational Trust.* Even if you are not the formal leader of the organization, there are things you can do to influence. And if you can't influence, your first step is to return to the 4 Cores as an individual and increase your own credibility so that you can.

Some of the same 4 Cores application ideas that work on the individual level will help create alignment on the organizational level, as well. For example:

To increase organizational Integrity, you can create or improve your organizational mission or values statement, engaging everyone in the process to ensure that it's more than just some platitude hanging on the wall. You can also work on creating a culture of making and keeping commitments within the organization. This is particularly important for leaders, and it's especially important in the small things. I've known of situations where leaders did not take seemingly small commitments seriously, and it spread to the extent that before long, everyone was treating internal commitments lightly.

To improve organizational Intent, you can ensure that your mission and values reflect motives and principles that build trust. You can also

---

* For a free executive briefing on how to measure trust and its impact on your organization, along with a sample Organizational Trust Audit, go to www.speedoftrust.com.

set an example of caring. Remember the impact in an organization when even one person—particularly a leader—demonstrates respect or shows concern. In addition, you can work to create systems that carry out a mutual benefit agenda—systems that use stewardship accountability agreements, reward cooperation instead of competition, and demonstrate trust.

To increase organizational Capabilities, you can take steps to ensure that the structures and systems in your organization (including recruiting/hiring and compensation systems) are designed to attract and retain the talent you need to be competitive in today's market. You can provide ongoing training and mentoring (development systems) to ensure relevancy and the satisfaction that comes from growth. You can make sure that information and decision-making systems are aligned with efforts to meet organizational and customer needs.

To improve organizational Results, you can help people create shared vision concerning desired results through a system that includes cascading goals and getting everyone on the same page. You can also create a "balanced scorecard," in which results reflect meeting the needs of all stakeholders, not just owners. In addition, you can create a culture in which people have the opportunity to account for results—not activities—on a regular basis.

I guarantee that if you will put on your trust glasses and see the impact of strengthening these 4 Cores in your organization at whatever level you define it, you will be amazed. And if you actually *do* the things necessary to strengthen the cores, the positive results in terms of alignment—and the dividends of trust that flow from it—will be remarkable.

After you address the 4 Cores organizationally, consider the degree to which your organizational culture manifests and encourages the 13 Behaviors. Look at the following chart again, this time wearing your organizational hat. Which side of the chart more accurately describes the culture in your "organization," however you're defining it?

	BEHAVIOR	CURRENT PERFORMANCE	OPPOSITE/ COUNTERFEIT
C	Talk Straight	└─┴─┴─┴─┴─┘	Lie, spin, tell half-truths, double-talk, flatter.
H A R A	Demonstrate Respect	└─┴─┴─┴─┴─┘	Don't care or don't show you care; show disrespect or show respect only to those who can do something for you.
C T	Create Transparency	└─┴─┴─┴─┴─┘	Withhold information; keep secrets; create illusions; pretend.
E	Right Wrongs	└─┴─┴─┴─┴─┘	Don't admit or repair mistakes; cover up mistakes.
R	Show Loyalty	└─┴─┴─┴─┴─┘	Sell others out; take the credit yourself; sweet-talk people to their faces and bad-mouth them behind their backs.

(chart continued on next page)

	BEHAVIOR	CURRENT PERFORMANCE	OPPOSITE/ COUNTERFEIT
C	Deliver Results	⌊_I_I_I_I_⌋	Fail to deliver; deliver on activities, not results.
O **M** **P**	Get Better	⌊_I_I_I_I_⌋	Deteriorate; don't invest in improvement; force every problem into your one solution.
E **T**	Confront Reality	⌊_I_I_I_I_⌋	Bury your head in the sand; focus on busywork while skirting the real issues.
E **N** **C**	Clarify Expectations	⌊_I_I_I_I_⌋	Assume expectations or don't disclose them; create vague and shifting expectations.
E	Practice Accountability	⌊_I_I_I_I_⌋	Don't take responsibility: "It's not my fault!"; don't hold others accountable.
B	Listen First	⌊_I_I_I_I_⌋	Don't listen; speak first, listen last; pretend listen; listen without understanding.
O **T**	Keep Commitments	⌊_I_I_I_I_⌋	Break commitments; violate promises; make vague and elusive commitments or don't make any commitments.
H	Extend Trust	⌊_I_I_I_I_⌋	Withhold trust; fake trust and then snoopervise; give responsibility without authority.

Now, if your organizational culture is best described on the right side of the chart in one or more of these behaviors, ask yourself why. What is it in the systems and structures of the organization that's rewarding—either formally or informally—low-trust behavior?

> The core of the matter is always changing the behavior of people.
>
> —PROFESSOR JOHN KOTTER, HARVARD BUSINESS SCHOOL

A few weeks ago, a friend of mine returned an unopened stereo he had received as a gift to the customer service department of a large retailer. He had his receipt with him, and it was obvious that the box had never been opened. After he had waited in line for several minutes, a customer service representative told him, "I'm sorry, but I can't refund this until we get someone from our electronics department to come here and check out this box." Frustrated, my friend pointed out that he was in a hurry and it was obvious that the box had never been opened. The customer service representative completely agreed with my friend that the box had never been opened, but said it was the policy of the company to have Electronics check it out, and she had to follow it. It took more than 10 minutes for someone from electronics to arrive. When he did, he simply looked at the box, declared that it was obvious it had never been opened, and said that no inspection was needed. My friend walked out of the store determined to never return, and he recounted this story to many others.

As you can see, this company's policy was internally focused, and it was clearly not aligned with the principles of customer service and extending trust to its own employees to exercise good judgment. And this absolutely impacts the bottom line.

A careful analysis of all your structures and systems—including information, communication, decision making, and compensation—will pinpoint areas of misalignment. It will show you where you're being taxed, where you're losing speed and increasing cost, and where you're throwing away the dividends that could come from high trust.

Ultimately you'll want to make sure that leadership paradigms are aligned with the principles that create trust. When leaders fundamentally don't believe people can be trusted, they create systems and structures that reflect that belief, such as hierarchy, multiple layers of management, and cumbersome processes. In turn, these systems and structures ultimately help produce the distrusting behaviors that validate the leaders' perceptions that people can't be trusted in the first place. It becomes a vicious, downward cycle.

> [T]he surest way to make [a man] untrustworthy is to distrust him and show your distrust.
>
> —HENRY STIMSON, FORMER U.S. SECRETARY OF STATE

David Packard validates the reality of this cycle from his experience in working for that company that zealously guarded its storerooms and tool bins. He said:

> *I learned, early in my career, of some of the problems that can be caused by a company's lack of trust in its people. . . . Faced with this obvious display of distrust* [the locks on the bins], *many employees set out to prove it justified, walking off with tools or parts whenever they could.*

By contrast, when leaders such as David Packard, Blake Nordstrom, and David Neeleman fundamentally believe that people can be trusted, they create systems and structures that reflect that belief, such as open storage bins, one-page employee manuals, and home reservationists. These systems and structures reinforce and ultimately help produce the trusting behaviors that validate the leaders' perceptions that people can be trusted to begin with. Thus, the paradigms and the behaviors work together to create a virtuous, upward cycle.

The 4 Cores and 13 Behaviors are your tools. They are the keys to creating organizational alignment and trust. They empower you to create significant shifts on all three levels—to help your internal stakeholders to *see* how trust affects every relationship and outcome in your organization, to *speak* about trust in a way that promotes understanding, dialogue, and problem solving, and to *behave* in ways that build trust. They enable you, as a leader, to create a high-trust organization—and both the symbols and the bottom line of your organization will reflect it.

FROM TAXES TO DIVIDENDS

If you don't yet have enough incentive to work on increasing trust in your organization, here's one more piece of information which I believe will be the "clincher."

I've said that if you don't have a high-trust organization, you are paying a tax, and it's a wasted tax. While these taxes may not conveniently show up on the income statement as "trust taxes," they're still there, disguised as other problems. So I invite you to put on your trust glasses so that you can see what's happening below the surface. I want to show you the hidden taxes in your organization. Then I'll show you the extraordinary dividends that can come from high trust.

THE 7 LOW-TRUST ORGANIZATIONAL TAXES

1. Redundancy

Redundancy is unnecessary duplication. Of course, redundant mission-critical systems and data management are necessary. But a redundancy tax is paid in excessive organizational hierarchy, layers of management, and overlapping structures all designed to ensure control. For the most part, it grows out of the paradigm that unless people are tightly supervised, they can't be trusted. And it is very costly.

My father shared with me an experience he had once when he did a presentation for a gaming organization in Las Vegas. The management showed him the gambling floor of the casino. They pointed out that because of the low-trust environment, coupled with the high risk of theft, the gambling floor has four to five levels of management. Thus, they have people watching people watching people watching people. In a high-trust scenario, however, two levels of management would have sufficed.

In some circumstances, rework and redesign might also be considered costs of redundancy that's triggered by low-trust behavior. In software development, as much as 30 to 50 percent of expenditures can be on rework. In manufacturing, rework costs can often exceed the original cost of producing the product.

2. Bureaucracy

Bureaucracy includes complex and cumbersome rules, regulations, policies, procedures, and processes. It's reflected in excessive paperwork, red tape, controls, multiple approval layers, and government regulations. Rather than focusing on continuous improvement and getting better, bureaucracy merely adds complexity and inefficiency—and costs—to the status quo. And as management theorist Laurence Peter has said, "Bureaucracy defends the status quo, long past the time when the quo has lost its status."

The costs of bureaucracy in all types of organizations—including government, health care, education, nonprofits, and business—are extraordinary. In 2004, one estimate put the cost of complying with federal rules and regulations alone in the U.S. at $1.1 trillion, which is more than 10 percent of the gross domestic product. In Germany, Chancellor Angela Merkel states that 4 to 6 percent of sales revenues for midsize businesses are spent on bureaucratic compliance. In 2003, the cost of health care bureaucracy in the U.S. was $399 billion—far more than it would cost to provide health care to all of the uninsured!

Low trust breeds bureaucracy, and bureaucracy breeds low trust. In low-trust organizations, bureaucracy is everywhere.

3. Politics

In an organization, "politics" is defined as the use of tactics and strategy to gain power. Office politics divide a culture against itself by creating conflict with what author Lawrence MacGregor Serven calls the "enemy within" instead of the enemy without.

Office politics generate behaviors such as withholding information, infighting, trying to "read the tea leaves," operating with hidden agendas, interdepartmental rivalries, backbiting, and meetings after meetings. These behaviors result in all kinds of wasted time, talent, energy, and money. In addition, they poison company cultures, derail strategies, and sabotage initiatives, relationships, and careers. The indirect costs related to office politics are estimated at $100 billion per year; some observers put them substantially higher.

Office politics thrive in low-trust environments. In fact, in many ways, "politics" is an antonym for trust.

4. Disengagement

Disengagement is what happens when people continue to work at a company, but have effectively quit (commonly referred to as "quit and stay"). They put in what effort they must to get their paycheck and not get fired, but they're not giving their talent, creativity, energy, or passion. Their bodies are there, but not their hearts or their minds. There are many reasons for disengagement, but one of the biggest reasons is that people simply don't feel trusted.

The Gallup organization put a conservative price tag of $250 to $300 billion a year on the cost of disengagement in America alone. Their research estimates that only 28 percent of U.S. employees are engaged, and in many other countries, the figure is even lower. With regard to trust, Gallup's research shows that 96 percent of engaged employees—but only 46 percent of actively disengaged employees—trust management. As the age-old question goes, Which came first, the chicken (distrust) or the egg (disengagement)? It's a self-perpetuating cycle that gradually grinds the organization to a crippled pace, or even to a halt.

5. Turnover

Employee turnover represents a huge cost for organizations, and in low-trust cultures, turnover is in excess of the industry or market standard. I'm not talking about the desirable turnover of nonperformers, but the undesirable turnover of performers. Low trust creates disengagement, which leads to turnover—particularly of the people you least want to lose. Performers like to be trusted and they like to work in high-trust environments. When they're not trusted, it's insulting to them, and a significant number will ultimately seek employment where they're trusted. This turnover also flows from the first two taxes. People just don't want to deal with all the bureaucracy and politics of a low-trust environment, so they leave. Or, as Gallup's research suggests, their relationship with their boss is so poor (i.e., has such low trust) that they leave.

Unwanted turnover is expensive. On average, it costs companies one and a half to two times the annual salary to replace an exiting worker.

> If your workplace culture isn't open and honest, it won't create employee satisfaction, and you'll experience turnover and a lack of productivity that will cost you money, ideas and time. On the other hand, if the work environment is ethical, productive and positive, people will stay—and stay committed. They'll drive your company forward.
>
> —KENT MURDOCH, PRESIDENT AND CEO,
> O.C. TANNER COMPANY

6. Churn

Churn is the turnover of stakeholders other than employees. When trust inside an organization is low, it gets perpetuated in interaction in the marketplace, causing greater turnover among customers, suppliers, distributors, and investors. This is becoming increasingly an issue as new technologies such as blogs continue to develop, effectively empowering employees to communicate their experience to the world.

When employees aren't trusted, they tend to pass that lack of trust on to their customers, and customers ultimately leave. My sister told me about a restaurant she went to recently where she asked the waiter what he recommended from the menu. The waiter's response? "I recommend going to another restaurant."

Now, I don't know the context of this waiter's comment, but I do know that employees tend to treat customers the way they're treated by management. That's why Southwest Airlines President and COO Colleen Barrett says, "Because we approach customer service exactly the same way—whether it's internal or external—I place the same degree of importance on the word 'trust' talking about employees or passengers."

Studies of customer defection indicate the financial impact of having to acquire a new customer versus keeping an existing one is significant; some say by as much as 500 percent!

7. Fraud

Fraud is flat-out dishonesty, sabotage, obstruction, deception, and disruption—and the cost is enormous. In fact, most of the first six organizational taxes are actually a result of management's response to this "fraud tax"—particularly the taxes of redundancy and bureaucracy. So in addition to all the individual taxes, there is a circular tax at play—the "fraud tax" giving rise to multiple low-trust taxes intended to deal with the fraud, but creating their own drain of time and money in the process.

In a 2004 study done by the Association of Certified Fraud Examiners, it was estimated that the average American company lost 6 percent of its annual revenue to some sort of fraudulent activity. In Enron's case, the fraud tax was ultimately 100 percent, which sank the company.

Fraud is almost exclusively an issue of character—a lack of Integrity coupled with self-centered Intent. If our only approach to this character challenge is to tighten the reins and put more controls in place, we will reduce the fraud tax only slightly, and in so doing, trigger the other six taxes, which are cumulatively far greater—maybe even *five to ten times greater*—than the original fraud tax.

Common sense suggests that we need to draw back and approach this problem differently. We need to utilize the 4 Cores of Credibility. We need to hire for character as well as competence. We need to focus our training and development to help people increase Integrity and improve Intent. We need to build and rely on an ethical culture to become the primary enforcer of cultural mores and values. As sociologist Émile Durkheim has said, "When mores [cultural values] are sufficient, laws are unnecessary; when mores are insufficient, laws are unenforceable." The key is to strengthen the cultural mores or values; without them, there are not enough means to enforce compliance everywhere.

> *Rules cannot substitute for character.*
>
> —ALAN GREENSPAN, FORMER CHAIRMAN,
> U.S. FEDERAL RESERVE

When you add up the cost of all these taxes that are being imposed on low-trust organizations, is there any doubt that there is a significant, direct, and indisputable connection between low trust, low speed, and high cost?

THE 7 HIGH-TRUST ORGANIZATIONAL DIVIDENDS

Now consider the dividends of high trust. Obviously the opposites of the 7 Low-Trust Organizational Taxes we've just discussed are dividends. To lower or eliminate redundancy, bureaucracy, disengagement, politics, turnover, churn, and fraud will certainly make a huge positive difference in the Trust Accounts and results in any organization.

But there are additional high-trust dividends—dividends that clearly show how trust always impacts speed and cost . . . and also a third measure: value.

1. Increased Value

High trust increases value in two dimensions.

The first dimension is shareholder value—and the data is compelling. As I noted earlier, in a Watson Wyatt 2002 study, high-trust organizations outperformed low-trust organizations in total return to shareholders (stock price plus dividends) by 286 percent. Additionally, according to a 2005 study by Russell Investment Group, *Fortune* magazine's "100 Best Companies to Work for in America" (in which trust constitutes 60 percent of the criteria) earned over four times the returns of the broader market over the prior seven years. As *Fortune* declared, "Employees treasure the freedom to do their job as they think best, and great employers trust them."

The second dimension is customer value. As a result of the last five dividends described below, high-trust organizations are consistently able to create and deliver more value to their customers. This customer value, in turn, creates more value for other key stakeholders.

2. Accelerated Growth

High-trust companies outperform low-trust companies, not only in shareholder value, but also in sales and profits. Research clearly shows that customers buy more, buy more frequently, refer more, and stay longer with companies and people they trust. Plus, these companies actually outperform with less cost. It's "Jim," the donut and coffee guy writ large. The net result is not just accelerated growth, but accelerated profitable growth. As Vanguard Investments CEO John Brennan said, "Trust is our number one asset. . . . As customers learn to trust us, they generate a surprising amount of growth."

3. Enhanced Innovation

High-trust companies are innovative in the products and services they offer customers, and they have strong cultures of innovation, which only thrive in an environment of high trust. Innovation and creativity demand a number of important conditions to flourish, including information sharing, an absence of caring about who gets the credit, a willingness to take risks, the safety to make mistakes, and the ability to collaborate. And all of these conditions are the fruits of high trust.

The benefits of innovation are clear: opportunity, revenue growth, and market share. Apple Computer—nearly "dead" a few years ago—completely rejuvenated itself through innovation in the development of the iPod and the iTunes Music Store. Recently *BusinessWeek* and The Boston Consulting Group ranked Apple as the most innovative company in the world.

As John Marchica notes in *The Accountable Organization:*

Many heralded Apple's service as a savior of the music industry. . . . With the introduction of iTunes, it appeared that . . . [Apple CEO Steve] Jobs . . . finally got it right. "Consumers don't want to be treated like criminals, and artists don't want their valuable work stolen," he remarked. "The iTunes Music Store offers a ground-breaking solution for both."

4. Improved Collaboration

High-trust company environments foster the collaboration and teamwork required for success in the new global economy. Different than the traditional approaches of *coordination* and *cooperation*, real *collaboration* creates the key opportunity model of today's world. In the words of business consultant Dr. Michael Hammer, "Reengineering was just a warm-up act for the collaborative economy." And this collaboration isn't just internal to an organization—it's also with external customers and suppliers. *Forbes* highlighted this "collaboration as opportunity" trend in 2006, pointing out what they call the "bedrock" of collaboration: trust. Without trust, collaboration is merely cooperation, which fails to achieve the benefits and possibilities available to true collaborators in the knowledge worker age.

5. Stronger Partnering

The Warwick Business School study I mentioned earlier confirmed that partnering relationships (such as outsourcing deals) that are based on trust experienced a high-trust dividend of up to 40 percent of the value of the contract. Those that rely on the contract language, and not on a relationship of trust, fare far worse. The report reads: "We found that contracts with well-managed relationships based on trust—rather than stringent SLAs [service-level agreements] and penalties—are more likely to lead to a 'trust dividend' for both parties. Real trust is not naïve. It . . . is earned from performance."

6. Better Execution

High-trust companies are better able than low-trust companies to execute their organization's strategy. The importance of execution was made clear to me on my first day at Harvard Business School. At the end of a four-hour case study, my professor said something I will never forget: "If you only remember one thing in your two years at Harvard

Business School, let it be this: It is better to have grade-B strategy and grade-A execution than the other way around."

Voted the number one enduring idea by *Strategy+Business* magazine readers, execution is appropriately a huge focus in organizations today, and execution is significantly enhanced by trust. FranklinCovey's execution quotient tool—"xQ"—has consistently shown a strong correlation between higher levels of organizational execution and higher levels of trust. In a 2006 study on grocery stores, top executing stores had significantly higher trust levels than lower executing stores in every dimension measured.

7. Heightened Loyalty

High-trust companies elicit far greater loyalty from their primary stakeholders—coworkers, customers, suppliers, distributors, and investors—than low-trust companies. The evidence for every one of these relationships is clear:

- Employees stay longer with high-trust companies.
- Customers remain customers of high-trust companies.
- Suppliers and distributors stay partnered longer with high-trust companies.
- Investors hold their investment longer with high-trust companies.

Dr. Larry Ponemon, chairman and founder of Ponemon Institute, a leader in measuring trust in privacy and security, put it clearly: "Trust is becoming the vital component in customer loyalty and brand strength."

When you add up all the dividends of high trust—and you put those on top of the fact that high trust decreases or eliminates all the taxes we've just discussed—is there any doubt that there is a significant, direct, measurable, and indisputable connection between high trust, high speed, low cost, and increased value?

> [Business executives need to] recreate a trust agenda. Nothing good happens without trust. With it you can overcome all sorts of obstacles. You can build companies that everyone can be proud of.
>
> —JIM BURKE, FORMER CHAIRMAN AND CEO,
> JOHNSON & JOHNSON

As I've said: Nothing is as fast as the speed of trust. Nothing is as profitable as the economics of trust. Nothing is as relevant as the pervasive impact of trust. And if you have on glasses to see, these realities become unarguable when it comes to building trust with the internal stakeholders in your organization.

Thus, I again affirm on the organizational level: The ability to establish, grow, extend, and restore trust truly is *the* key leadership competency of the new global economy.

FAMILIES ARE ORGANIZATIONS, TOO

I would not want to leave this section without pointing out that families are organizations, too, and everything we've talked about in this chapter applies just as powerfully to the family as it does to any other organization.

Families have greater trust when they are aligned, when they have structures and systems that recognize values and reward high-trust behavior, when they have symbols that communicate the paradigms that create high-trust relationships.

Recently one of my associates told me about a conversation he had with a friend. When my associate asked his friend if his son was going to play basketball, the man said, "Well, his grades were not what they needed to be, so he will not be playing ball this year." After a brief exchange, he concluded by saying, "I'm trying to raise a boy, not a basketball player."

Think about it! Suppose you want to encourage your son to get better grades, but the structures and systems in your family are not aligned. Suppose they're as follows:

The rewards system: When he wins a game, you have a huge celebration and take him out to dinner. When he brings home an A, you merely say, "Good job!"

The communication system: Every week you ask him excitedly, "When's the next game?" You talk about his grades only once a quarter when report cards come out.

The decision-making system: Everything you do as a family is based on the next game, the next event. Grades are never a part of the decision.

The structure: Your son makes his own decisions relative to when he goes to bed, how much television he watches, and how much time he spends with his friends—regardless of his grades.

The family is perfectly aligned to get the results it's getting: a sports-focused kid who doesn't care a lot about his academic performance in school.

If people really take family seriously, they need to ask the same questions people do with regard to any organization:

- Does our family have Integrity? Are the values clear, and do the rules and guidelines (structures and systems), and the behavior of the parents support those values? Is there an environment of honesty and humility? Do family members have the courage to express their ideas and opinions freely, and do they do so with respect?
- Does our family have good Intent? Have we structured a culture of respect and caring? Is the agenda mutual benefit, or is it just the adults, or children, who win? Do our systems reward cooperation?
- What are our family's Capabilities? Does the structure provide for and encourage development and growth? Is it safe to learn by making mistakes? Are systems in place to help children develop the life skills they will need to succeed as adults?
- What Results does our family produce? Are systems in place to create joy in shared accomplishment? Is there an abundance of rich interaction, support, and love? Are family members achieving important goals, both individually and as a family?

Do we *behave* in high-trust ways? Do we Talk Straight? Do we Demonstrate Respect? Do we Show Loyalty? Do we Keep Commitments? If not, what structures and systems are rewarding low-trust behavior? And what can we do to create change?

What are the symbols in our family? Are they aligned with the values we believe in and want to promote?

The most powerful way I can build trust as a leader in my home is by modeling the 4 Cores and 13 Behaviors and by creating alignment in the family so that the structures and systems support the values I'm trying to help family members understand and live. And in doing so, I create that geometric multiplier. In our own home, for example, because our son tested us and we held him accountable on his driving, our daughter knows how she needs to drive. We didn't have to spend the same amount of time training her, and she doesn't constantly test us on whether or not we will follow through. She can trust that we will. It's the "discipline one, teach a whole family" dividend. But it has to be consistent. It has to be in the structure and systems to create a culture of trust.

Whatever your organization—be it a business, a not-for-profit, a department or team within a larger organization, or a family—it's vital to realize that designing or aligning it in a way that establishes trust may well be your greatest influence. In doing so, you positively affect everything else within the organization.

THE FOURTH WAVE— MARKET TRUST

THE PRINCIPLE OF REPUTATION

In the end, all you have is your reputation.

—OPRAH WINFREY

I invite you to take a look at the logos on the following page, and as you do, examine your reaction. What do you feel as you look at each one? Do you feel the same about all of them? If not, why?

If your experience is like most, when you look at some of these logos, you have positive feelings. Maybe you know the company. Maybe you've had experience with their products and services, or you have close friends or relatives who have. Maybe you've heard positive comments on their financials, their leadership, or their sense of social responsibility, or

you've read other good things about them in the press. As a result, you might buy or recommend a product or service from one of these companies just because their name is behind it.

When you look at other logos, perhaps you have negative feelings. Maybe you, or an acquaintance, have had an unsatisfactory personal experience with a product or service offered by these companies or heard disturbing things about them in the media. For whatever reason, the feeling is different, and likely you would not purchase a product or service from these companies—nor would you recommend it to others.

Market Trust is all about brand or reputation. It's about the feeling you have that makes you want to buy products or services or invest your money or time—and/or recommend such action to others. This is the level where most people clearly see the relationship between trust, speed, and cost.

In fact, you could say that a "brand" is trust with the customer, trust with the marketplace, or even more boldly, "trust monetized." Most people understand this at least intuitively, if not also measurably. As a result, companies invest all kinds of money in creating a brand that inspires trust. Some brand-building companies actually have formulas that attempt to quantify the economic value of a brand. PR firm Golin/Harris describes their brand-building work as nothing less than "building trust worldwide."

> *Trust is a key building block in the creation of a company's reputation, and as a direct result, its shareholder value.*
>
> —ROBERT ECKERT, CEO, MATTEL

The direct connection between brand, trust, speed, and cost is evident on every level. At one presentation I did for the Sales & Marketing Executives International conference, an executive from a hundred-year-old, multibillion-dollar company came up to me and said, "We have an extremely trusted brand, and it pays enormous dividends. Our renewal rate for our services is an amazingly high 90 percent. That's the best indicator of our brand's value. We work constantly to protect the integrity of this trust relationship, which is our most valuable asset. Many businesses want to partner with our brand; however, our partner selection criteria are very stringent in order to protect the trust relationship we have with our customers."

> *When customers are loyal to your brand [have trust], they are more apt to listen to your message, read information from your organization more carefully and be more willing to accept calls marketing new products and services.*
>
> —CHARLES GIORDANO, BELL CANADA INTERNATIONAL

"BRAND" MATTERS ON EVERY LEVEL

Obviously corporate brand is important to companies with products and services to sell. But it's also important to all organizational entities, including governments, school districts, charities, hospitals, cities, and states. When families move, for example, many will investigate the various schools in the area to find out which ones have the best reputation before deciding where to look for a home. This has a significant impact on the amount of tax money available to the school, their priority in the district in terms of new building or remodeling, and their ability to attract and hire administrators and teachers.

Cities have reputations, which are reflected in published lists of best places to visit or best places to live . . . which translate into tax dollars, tourist dollars, businesses attracted, and home value appreciation. Local governments, state governments, and national governments all have reputations, which affect their ability to transact business, as well as attract business. On a more micro level, the reputation of a particular team or division within an organization has significant impact on factors such as resource allocation and budget planning. Often a manager will think his department is far more deserving of funds because of the importance of that department's work, only to find his budget request trumped by other departments that have a better reputation for delivering results. In other situations, the reputation of one division in an organization will impact the way the people in other divisions interact with it.

For instance, I remember being in one circumstance in which the division I managed had to depend on another division to get materials produced and products shipped. This other division didn't have a good reputation—their inventory system was bad and their execution was poor. Our division knew that customers wouldn't stay with us if we didn't serve them well, so we took the easy but expensive way out and did it ourselves. We stockpiled materials in our closets. We created our own distribution and shipping processes to make sure things got out on time. In effect, we created our own redundant systems, and the whole organization was taxed for it in terms of the time and effort we had to put into something that should have been done by somebody else.

On the most micro level, every individual has his or her own brand or reputation, and that reputation affects trust, speed, and cost. It comes across in your résumé and in the comments of your references when you're applying for a job. It translates into the way people interact with you at work or in social situations. It affects whether someone will go out with you, how seriously your child listens to you, how much influence you have in any situation.

It also determines whether or not you are given the benefit of the doubt. In the chapter on the 4 Cores of Credibility, I gave the example of how Warren Buffett's personal brand was so strong that it gave him the benefit of the doubt from the very outset in the governmental investigation of the AIG Insurance transaction with General Re. Anne Mulcahy, chairman and CEO of Xerox, has said of Buffett: "I respect him and believe his integrity is unmatched. This is a man whose values permeate every decision he makes, every interaction with people and every piece of counsel he shares." That kind of reputation pays enormous dividends.

The importance of personal brand was brought home clearly to me one time when I needed to evaluate and run numbers on some sensitive financial data involved in a significant business opportunity. The financial officer at the time was clearly capable, but he had earned a reputation of not being able to keep confidences. As a result, I bypassed him completely and went to someone I trusted instead.

Even a child's reputation is important. If you're a parent, you probably find it a lot easier (as I do) to extend privileges to a child who has earned the reputation of being responsible than to one who has not. With one child, you may not even think twice about saying, "Sure!"; with another, it might be, "Did you get your homework done? Did you finish your piano practice? What time will you be back? Who can I call to verify this?"

On every level, in every relationship, your brand, your reputation makes a difference. That difference is quantifiable—and it is directly related to trust, speed, and cost.

THE COMPELLING EVIDENCE

As we take a look at some of the compelling evidence in the area of Market Trust, I again urge you to look through the glasses of your own actionably defined "organization," be it a company, school district, government agency, team or division within a larger organization, or a family. Remember that Market Trust deals with *external* stakeholders. While those might well include suppliers, distributors, and investors as well as customers, it would probably be simpler at this point for you to look at them all as your "customers." As you go through the following material, notice the direct connection between reputation and trust.

Fortune magazine's annual list of the World's Most Admired Companies is what *Fortune* calls "the definitive report card on corporate reputations," drawing an obvious correlation between reputation and esteem.

In research conducted by the Hay Group, 8,645 executives, directors, and securities analysts in 23 countries ranked 351 companies in 30 industries. Companies are measured globally against nine attributes or "areas of leadership" that make up reputation, including social responsibility (Integrity), people management (Intent), innovation (Capabilities), and financial soundness and long-term investment (Results). For the sixth time in eight years, General Electric was recognized as the World's Most Admired Company. Toyota was second on the list (the best ranking ever for a non-U.S. company), largely because of their results. They made more profits than the next twelve car manufacturers on the list combined.

Why do these things matter? Because another term for "reputation" is "brand," and another term for "brand" is "trust with the marketplace." And trust affects people's behavior. According to a Golin/Harris poll in 2003:

- 39 percent of individuals say they would start or increase their business with a company specifically because of the trust or trustworthiness of that company.
- 53 percent say they would stop, reduce, or switch their business to a competitor because they have concerns about a company's trust or trustworthiness.
- 83 percent say they are more likely to give a company they trust the benefit of the doubt and listen to their side of the story before asking a judgment about corporate behavior.

In addition, the 2006 Annual Edelman Trust Barometer points out that "trust is more than a bonus; it is a tangible asset that must be created, sustained, and built upon. . . . Just as trust benefits companies, mistrust or lost trust has costs. At least 64 percent of opinion leaders in every country surveyed said they had refused to buy the products or services of a company they did not trust." Most also criticized them to others (bad word of mouth), refused to do business with them, and refused to invest in them. About half refused to be employed by them.

> [W]e've got a business principle that says, "Our assets are our people, our capital and our reputation." And if any of those are diminished, the last one is the hardest one to regain.
>
> —HANK PAULSON, CHAIRMAN AND CEO, GOLDMAN SACHS

THE COUNTRY TAX
AND THE INDUSTRY TAX

One interesting dimension of today's global marketplace is that many brands are now being taxed (or receiving dividends) based on people's perception of and trust in the country of origin of the brand. For example, whether a company is based in China, France, India, or the U.S. will often affect people's perception of whether the company can be trusted to do what is right. A variety of factors create perceptions of trust, including history, culture, and current governmental policies. But regardless of the reasons, the country tax or dividend is very real.

In today's global market, this tax is hitting United States–based brands hard. U.S. brands that receive dividends in the U.S. and Asia are being taxed heavily in parts of Europe and in other markets. The Edelman Trust Barometer, which highlights these trust taxes and dividends, notes that in a survey of 750 opinion leaders in eleven countries, U.S. brands were discounted or taxed significantly in Canada, the United Kingdom, France, and Germany, while they were not taxed in Asia and received a dividend in Japan. More specifically with regard to U.S. brands, trust in UPS was 84% in the U.S. and 53% in Europe; trust in Procter & Gamble was 70% in the U.S. and 44% in Europe; trust in Coca-Cola was 65% in the U.S. and 41% in Europe; and trust in McDonald's was 51% in the U.S. and 30% in Europe.

However, this country tax is generally not reciprocated—UK- and Germany-based companies experienced no significant tax anywhere, and neither did France (except in the U.S.). Interestingly, the most significant tax across the board was for companies based in China, where the discount was substantial everywhere.

Similarly, the Edelman Trust Barometer identifies what I refer to as an "industry tax or dividend," in which the overall industry influences the perception of whether or not a company can be trusted. For example, in most countries, energy and media industries are generally taxed. In contrast, retail and technology sectors typically receive dividends. For companies operating in industries that are taxed, it's important to create an individual reputation that outpaces the industry reputation— much like Johnson & Johnson has done in the pharmaceutical industry, an industry that is significantly taxed in the U.S.

THE SPEED OF TRUST IN BUILDING (OR DESTROYING) REPUTATION

Another interesting dimension of the new global marketplace is evident in the Annual Reputation Quotient (RQ) 2005 study conducted by Harris Interactive and published in the *Wall Street Journal*. This study ranks the 60 most visible companies in America based on their reputation. In 2005, number one (for the seventh straight year) was Johnson & Johnson. This company has a long-established track record of trust. They've been in business for 120 years.

Most fascinating to me, however, is the fact that number three on the list is Google—which has only been in business for seven years! To me, this is irrefutable evidence that especially in today's global, high-tech economy trust can be built fast.

When Pierre Omidyar, founder of eBay, was asked what was the most significant lesson learned from eBay, he replied, "The remarkable fact that 135 million people have learned they can trust a complete stranger. That's had an incredible impact. People have more in common than they think."

Going back to Harris Interactive's Annual Reputation Quotient, guess who was at the very bottom of the list? WorldCom (now MCI) was number 59; Enron was number 60. Obviously, even though it's possible to build trust fast, it's much easier to destroy it even faster. Remember what Warren Buffett said: "It takes twenty years to build a reputation and five minutes to ruin it." As I've pointed out, in our new global economy, it doesn't necessarily take 20 years to build a reputation. But Buffett's point remains the same—you can destroy a reputation almost instantaneously.

> Smart companies will amass trust assets that can be called upon to protect the brand in tough times. Without these deposits in its Trust Bank, a single breach of trust can devastate a company because you have no track record of trust enhancing behavior to call upon.
>
> —ELLEN RYAN MARDIKS, CMO, GOLIN/HARRIS

HOW TO BUILD YOUR BRAND

So how do you build your brand? And how do you avoid destroying it? By now, I'm sure you won't be surprised by my answer: "The 4 Cores and the 13 Behaviors," applied at the organizational and marketplace levels.

But you may be surprised by this: I strongly contend that if your organization (however you define it) strengthens its 4 Cores and demonstrates the 13 Behaviors with its stakeholders, you will be able to *measurably* increase the value of your organization's brand. These cores and behaviors are the keys to building credibility and trust in the marketplace.

Put on your trust glasses again, and this time, look through the lens of your own "organization" in terms of Market Trust. Consider the perspective of your "customers." Ask yourself:

- Does my brand have Integrity? Do we have a reputation for honesty? Do we have values people believe in and can trust? Do we have a reputation in the market for courageously addressing tough issues quickly and for honestly admitting and repairing mistakes?
- Does my brand demonstrate good Intent? Are we perceived as simply "out to make a profit," or do people feel that we genuinely care, that we want to help others win?
- Does my brand demonstrate Capabilities? Do people associate our name with quality, excellence, continuous improvement, and the ability to change to maintain relevance in a global economy age? Are we recognized as having the ability to accomplish our objectives in ways that build trust?
- Is my brand associated with Results? Do people feel we deliver what we promise? Is a good track record associated with our name? Are people willing to answer "yes!" to what Bain consultant Frederick Reichheld calls the ultimate question: Would you recommend this business to a friend?

If you don't have the brand or reputation you desire, the 4 Cores provide a great diagnostic tool to help you pinpoint the reason why and the area where investment will bring the greatest returns. Once you determine whether the problem is one of character (Integrity or Intent) or competence (Capabilities or Results), you can zero in on the area where improvement will have the greatest positive effect.

> *A brand for a company is like a reputation for a person.*
> *You earn reputation by trying to do hard things well.*
>
> —JEFF BEZOS, FOUNDER AND CEO, AMAZON.COM

You can maximize your efforts even further by analyzing your organization's performance with regard to the 13 Behaviors. Just as applying these behaviors builds trust at the relationship level, applying them in interactions with external stakeholders—customers, suppliers, distributors, investors, communities—builds trust at the marketplace level.

Consider a few examples:

Talk Straight. Johnson & Johnson has created "Direct to Consumer" education ad campaigns on prescription drugs, in which they communicate candidly and treat consumers as educated adults. Challenging other industry players to step up with similar straight talk, CEO William Weldon has said:

> *I believe we should start by recognizing that the framework we call "DTC [Direct to Consumer] advertising" may inadvertently minimize the importance and power of medicines and their risks. Our communication with patients should really be thought of as Direct to Consumer education* [emphasis added].

This kind of straight talk is one reason why Johnson & Johnson remains the highest-rated brand on the Reputation Quotient list.

Create Transparency. eBay CEO Meg Whitman and her team lead what she describes as a "dynamic self-regulating economy" in the complete openness of the worldwide web. Whitman recognizes her company's distinctiveness: "We have a unique partner—millions of people." According to *BusinessWeek* OnLine, rather than controlling or hoarding information, eBay has chosen to let their citizens have full access to "every trend, every sale, every new regulation in the eBay world. The system is utterly transparent."

Listen First. Superquinn—a grocery chain and shopping mall operator in Ireland—has built an empire based on what they call a multi-channel "listening system." This system includes regular customer panels, customer-comment forms, formal market research, a service desk in every store, and personal calls to participants in their loyalty program. Through listening, Superquinn has gained insights that have led to its being a pioneer in food safety and providing innovative customer services. The organization dominates the market, even in competition against much bigger rivals.

Superquinn's CEO, Feargal Quinn (known as Ireland's "Pope of Customer Service"), has said, "Genuine listening ability is one of the few true forms of competitive advantage. . . . Listening is not an activity you can delegate—no matter who you are."

The experience of companies like J&J, eBay, and Superquinn clearly shows the value of the 13 Behaviors in increasing Market Trust and receiving the abundant dividends that flow from it.

> *Without customers' trust, the rest doesn't matter.*
>
> —RAM CHARAN, BUSINESS AUTHOR

WALKING TAX OR WALKING DIVIDEND?

As I've said, it's at this Fourth Wave—Marketplace Trust—that most people already see the connection between trust and reputation to bottom-line economics. That's because most understand the value of a brand.

What most don't see as clearly, however, is that the same principle that produces dividends to a trusted company at the level of Market Trust also operates at the Self Trust, Relationship Trust, and Organizational Trust levels.

So in addition to whatever trust issues we might address with regard to our companies, schools, not-for-profits, families, or other organizations we represent, we need to ask, first and foremost, what is my reputation? What is my brand? Am I a walking tax or a walking dividend?

> *Employees with integrity are the ones who build a company's reputation.*
>
> —ROBERTO GOIZUETA, FORMER CEO, COCA-COLA

Keep in mind: Whatever trust we are able to create in our organizations and in the marketplace is a result of the credibility we first create in ourselves.

THE FIFTH WAVE—
SOCIETAL TRUST
THE PRINCIPLE OF CONTRIBUTION

Executives tempted to take shortcuts should remember the dictum of Confucius that good government needs weapons, food and trust. If the ruler cannot hold onto all three, he should give up weapons first and food next. Trust should be guarded to the end, because "without trust, we cannot stand."

—*FINANCIAL TIMES* EDITORIAL

In late April of 1992, the Rodney King trial sparked riots that resulted in the burning and looting of entire city blocks in Los Angeles, California. The devastation was immense; the loss to businesses was in the billions.

Amazingly, all the McDonald's restaurants within that devastated area were untouched. They stood as unscathed beacons in the midst of the blackened ruins.

Obviously the question arose: Why would the McDonald's buildings be left standing when nearly everything around them was destroyed? The responses of local residents carried a common thread: "McDonald's cares about our community. They support literacy efforts and sports programs. Young people know they can always get a job at 'Mickey D's.' No one would want to destroy something that does so much good for us all."

McDonald's sense of social responsibility created societal trust, and that trust produced clearly observable and measurable results.

> *Every kind of peaceful cooperation among men is primarily based on mutual trust and only secondarily on institutions such as courts of justice and police.*
>
> —ALBERT EINSTEIN

FISH DISCOVER WATER LAST

Perhaps you've heard the French proverb "Fish discover water last." But have you ever really thought about what it means?

For fish, water simply *is*. It's their environment. It surrounds them. They are so immersed in its presence, they're unaware of its existence—until it becomes polluted or nonexistent. Then, the immediate and dramatic consequence makes it quickly apparent that quality water is absolutely essential for their well-being. Without it, the fish will die.

In a similar way, we as human beings discover trust last. Trust is an integral part of the fabric of our society. We depend on it. We take it for granted—unless it becomes polluted or destroyed. Then we come to the stark realization that trust may well be as vital to our own well-being as water is to a fish. Without trust, society closes down and will ultimately self-destruct.

> *[C]ommerce dies the moment, and is sick in the degree in which men cannot trust each other.*
>
> —HENRY WARD BEECHER, NINETEENTH-CENTURY AMERICAN AUTHOR

This pervasive nature of trust is why, as I said in the very beginning, it is the one thing that changes everything.

Just consider a small example. When we drive our cars, we trust that other drivers on the road are competent and that they will follow the rules, that they aren't out to do us harm. But what happens if you live in a society where every time you go out to get in your car, you have to worry about whether the car has been wired with a bomb, or whether other cars on the road might explode or other drivers might purposefully crash into you? Or what happens if—as was the case recently in the Washington, D.C., area—you have to worry about a simple act such as getting out of your car at a gas station, fearing that doing so might put you in the scope of a deadly sniper?

It's hard to even imagine a world without trust. As Thomas Friedman contends in *The World Is Flat*, trust is essential to a flat or open society. And the principal aim of terrorists is to destroy that trust. It's to make us fearful of doing the things we do every day. While a flat, open global economy thrives on behaviors such as talking straight, creating transparency, righting wrongs, practicing accountability, keeping commitments, and extending trust, a closed, terroristic society thrives on counterfeits and opposites—on deception, hidden agendas, justifying wrongs, disregarding commitments, blaming others, and trusting none except those in an elite "inner circle." Even then, trust is fragile and is subject to the whims of those in charge.

> To beat back the threat of openness, [terrorists] . . . have, quite deliberately, chosen to attack the very thing that keeps open societies open, innovating, and flattening, and that is trust.
>
> —THOMAS FRIEDMAN, AUTHOR OF *THE WORLD IS FLAT*

Just think about the taxes imposed in a closed, low-trust society. Then think about all dividends—such as shared knowledge, medical breakthroughs, technological advances, economic partnerships, and cultural exchanges—that are not available to a closed society.

In a high-trust society, there's more for everyone. We have more options and opportunities. We interact with less friction, resulting in greater speed and lower cost. This is why our opportunity to build a high-trust society is so meaningful. There is nothing we could do that would so dramatically impact not only speed and cost, but also quality of life for everyone on the planet.

THE PRINCIPLE OF CONTRIBUTION

The overriding principle of societal trust is *contribution*. It's the intent to create value instead of destroy it, to give back instead of take. And more and more, people are realizing how important contribution—and the causes it inspires—are to a healthy society.

Just consider all that is taking place, from individuals seeking to make a difference in their own sphere of influence, to corporations accepting the responsibility to serve all stakeholders (not just shareholders), to entrepreneurial organizations whose primary purpose is to serve societal ends.

In 2005, for example, Microsoft guru Bill Gates; his wife, Melinda; and U2 lead singer Bono were recognized by *Time* magazine as "Persons of the Year," not for their talent, technical skill, innovation, productivity, or massive wealth, but for the enormous investment they have made in both time and money to improve the health, education, and welfare of impoverished or less fortunate people around the globe. The Gateses set up the Bill and Melinda Gates Foundation for this purpose, and in June 2006, Bill Gates announced an upcoming "reprioritization" that will enable him to shift his major focus from day-to-day involvement in Microsoft to the work of the foundation. Within two weeks, Warren Buffett announced that he would give $37 billion (84 percent of his net worth) to charity, $30.7 billion of which would go to the Gates Foundation.

In 1998, Oprah Winfrey created her "Angel Network" to inspire individuals to create opportunities that help underserved people rise to their own potential. Since that time, the network has supported numerous humanitarian projects, including building rural schools in eleven different countries worldwide, raising $50 million for the Christmas-Kindness South Africa initiative, raising $10 million for the victims of Hurricane Katrina, and "supporting groups that help women in post-conflict areas become productive and regain their dignity."

One great contributor to society who has made a deep impression on me personally is Buckminster Fuller, inventor and architect of the geodesic dome. One of his protégés, Marshall Thurber, told me that when Fuller would receive his royalty checks (one of which was for $1.2 million), he would pay the bills for his company and then give the rest of the money away. In fact, Thurber said, Fuller would frequently write his checkbook down to zero. Fuller maintained, "If you devote your time and attention to the highest advantage of others, the Universe will support you, always and only in the nick of time."

Though these are examples of high-profile individuals, the great bulk of contribution that is woven through the fabric of society is made by individuals contributing in communities throughout the world. Thousands of doctors and nurses donate their time and means to perform medical surgeries to correct physical deformities in children and adults in developing countries. Many donate to help victims of disasters, such as the recent Indian Ocean tsunami, Hurricane Katrina, and earthquakes, mudslides, and other calamities worldwide. In local communities, people volunteer their time and energy to further causes such as literacy, health, education, and social welfare, including helping the homeless and victims of spouse and child abuse.

Just think of how diminished our society would be without contributions such as these! And think of the impact contributions such as these have on societal trust!

My purpose in this chapter is not to present an impractical, utopian, or political view of the world. It is simply to focus on the pragmatic benefits that flow and the trust that emerges from the principles of contribution and responsibility at the societal level.

THE PRINCIPLE OF CONTRIBUTION IN BUSINESS

Today more and more businesses, as well as individuals, are recognizing the value of contribution. Many businesses are structured to contribute to others on a regular basis, such as Newman's Own products (established by actor Paul Newman), which has generated profits in excess of $200 million, all of which has been donated to charities. *Business Ethics* magazine annually publishes its "100 Best Corporate Citizens," which recognizes companies that serve all stakeholders with excellence and integrity. In 2006, corporate giants such as Intel, Wells Fargo, Texas Instruments, and General Mills were all in the top 20. *Fast Company* and Monitor Group have created the "Social Capitalist" awards, which they give annually to 25 socially responsible, entrepreneurial companies. One such social capitalist, PATH, partners with corporations, governments, and other nonprofits to bring technological innovation in medicine to communities that could otherwise never afford it.

While many meaningful contributions still come in the form of the industrial age notion of *philanthropy*—of earning profits and then donating money to worthwhile causes—the trend today is turning toward the more comprehensive knowledge worker age paradigm of *global citizenship* (also called social consciousness, corporate citizenship, and most recently, corporate social responsibility or CSR). This approach includes traditional philanthropy, but it also integrates the social and ethical agenda into the very fabric of the business. Doing good is no longer seen as something in addition to business; it is a part of business itself.

> There has been a tendency in the business world to confuse citizenship with philanthropy. They're not the same thing. Enron was a great philanthropist, and clearly, it was not a good corporate citizen. The heart of global citizenship is about ethics and conduct. It begins with the way a company thinks about its role in the world. Does it simply exist to make as much money as possible?
>
> —DEBORAH DUNN, SENIOR VICE PRESIDENT,
> HEWLETT-PACKARD

Many developments have signaled this shift to global citizenship. One such example is the rise of microfinancing, powerfully modeled by Muhammad Yunus, founder of the Grameen Bank in Bangladesh. This bank was set up to make small loans (usually $50 to $200) to poverty-stricken individuals, 96 percent of whom are women, to help them establish themselves and their skills profitably in the market. Yunus began doing this in the 1970s, and his efforts and the similar efforts of others have had such success that the United Nations declared 2005 as the International Year of Microcredit. According to eBay founder Pierre Omidyar, microfinance can have the same kind of social impact that eBay has had on society through hundreds of millions of people learning that they can trust complete strangers.

The microfinancing trend is now beginning to expand into microfranchising, in which social entrepreneurs are providing education and financing to help others create scalable businesses so they can leverage their efforts, hire others, and make meaningful profits.

"INTENTIONAL VIRTUE" AND "CONSCIOUS CAPITALISM"

While we enthusiastically applaud these wonderful emerging efforts, we need to understand that the idea of corporate social responsibility is not new. In fact, it was originally the conceptual framework behind the whole idea of the free enterprise system. Adam Smith, the father of free enterprise and author of *The Theory of Moral Sentiments* and *The Wealth of Nations*, taught that "intentional virtue" was foundational to a prosperous economy, and that when a critical mass of people competed for their own best interests *within the framework of intentional virtue*, there was an "unseen hand" that would guide society in a way that would create prosperity and wealth for all.

During the last part of the twentieth century, however, the "intentional virtue" part somehow got left out, and the message was fatally diluted: "If you simply compete in the marketplace, the 'unseen hand' will guide the creation of wealth." This dilution led to a massive violation of the 4 Cores and 13 Behaviors—to greed, materialism, fraud, falsification, duplicity, and skyrocketing low-trust taxes.

> Falsification and fraud are highly destructive to free-market capitalism and, more broadly, to the underpinnings of our society . . . our market system depends critically on trust—trust in the word of our colleagues and trust in the word of those with whom we do business.
>
> —ALAN GREENSPAN, FORMER CHAIRMAN,
> U.S. FEDERAL RESERVE

As a result—as I said in the first chapter of this book—generally today, low trust is everywhere. But here's the intriguing paradox: In the midst of this pervasive low trust, a backlash response is creating a virtual global renaissance of trust. More and more, people are coming to recognize the cost of low trust and are making efforts to establish and restore trust. It's the "fish discover water last" syndrome in action; as trust has begun to disappear, we're finally recognizing how vital it is to our survival.

Some are even making efforts to replace the fundamental materialistic paradigm with the more sustainable paradigm of contribution. The Acton Institute, for example, has taken on the media representation of business as money grabbing and socially irresponsible, and seeks to bridge the chasm of distrust between business and religious leaders by helping them merge values and resources in ways that build society. Paul Dolan, CEO of Fetzer Vineyards, urges all businesses to commit to the "triple bottom line," a measure of corporate success that takes into account not only financials but also social and environmental impact.

GLOBAL CITIZENSHIP: AN ECONOMIC NECESSITY

Forbes magazine's James Surowiecki has said:

> *The evolution of capitalism has been in the direction of more trust and transparency, and less self-serving behavior; not coincidentally, this evolution has brought with it greater productivity and economic growth. That evolution, of course, has not taken place because capitalists are naturally good people. Instead, it's taken place because the benefits of trust—that is, of being trusting and of being trustworthy—are potentially immense and because a successful market system teaches people to recognize those benefits.*

In *Megatrends 2010,* Patricia Aburdene notes the rise of "conscious capitalism" and its direct connection to the bottom line. She points out that during the period between 1984 and 1999, "stakeholder superstars"—companies that excel in relationships with all stakeholders (as opposed to merely shareholders), including investors, customers, employees, suppliers, and communities—outperformed the S&P 500 by 126 percent. Interestingly, six of the seven megatrends Aburdene highlights in her book have to do with the principles of contribution, value, meaning, purpose, and responsibility that are inherent—both individually and organizationally—in the Fifth Wave of Societal Trust.

A 2002 study by DePaul University showed that overall financial performance of *Business Ethics'* 100 Best Corporate Citizens was also "significantly better" than the S&P 500. In fact, financial performance is now one of the criteria of their corporate citizenship. This is becoming an excellent illustration, at the societal level, of how leadership is "getting results in a way that inspires trust" with all stakeholders.

> People talk about businesses needing to be responsible as if it's something new we need to do on top of everything else. But the whole essence of business should be responsibility. My philosophy is "We don't run companies to earn profits, we earn profits to run companies." Our companies need meaning and purpose if they're to fit into the world, or why should they live at all?
>
> —TACHI KIUCHI, FORMER MANAGING DIRECTOR, MITSUBISHI ELECTRONICS

The Mercer Investment Consulting Group in the UK suggests that organizations may initially participate in global citizenship mostly because they want to avoid the consequences—and taxes—of being branded as socially irresponsible. Orin Smith, president and CEO of Starbucks (a 100 Best Corporate Citizens company) says, "Only a small proportion of customers buy a company's products because it is socially responsible. But if they think for a moment that you aren't responsible, a much larger percentage will have a negative response."

> [C]ustomers get impressions about products from hundreds of sources, but when they believe a company is a good citizen, they feel more positively about a brand.
>
> —SHELLEY LAZARUS, CHAIRMAN AND CEO,
> OGILVY & MATHER

Though fear of pain might initially motivate global citizenship, I am persuaded that, over time, the dividends and abundance created by contribution will become primary drivers for both individuals and organizations.

I am also personally convinced that ultimately global citizenship will be demanded as good business. Over time, it will become a price of entry. Even today, more and more consumers are voting with their wallets to support companies that demonstrate Integrity and Intent as well as Capabilities and Results. And I believe this inspiring trend will eventually become an economic necessity

In the early days of the Covey Leadership Center, we developed what we described as the "universal mission statement," because it applies to every individual and every organization simply because all are a part of society. It consisted of only 12 words: *To increase the economic well-being and quality of life of all stakeholders.*

I like to think that this universal mission statement was an early attempt to describe global citizenship (and a balanced scorecard) in at least two key respects: first, in recognizing the importance of *all* stakeholders (not just owners); and second, in understanding the importance of quality of life (not just financial profit). Trust has always been the universal currency, and ultimate catalyst, for this universal mission statement to take root.

GLOBAL CITIZENSHIP: AN INDIVIDUAL CHOICE

At the heart of organizational global citizenship is individual global citizenship. It's you and me making the conscious decision to value and invest in the well-being of others. It's you and me carrying out that decision in every dimension of our lives.

As Gandhi said, "One man cannot do right in one department of life whilst he is occupied in doing wrong in another department. Life is one indivisible whole." So we don't urge our employees to give incredible service to our "paying" customers, toss a few corporate dollars to charity, and ignore an "unpaying" neighbor in need. When we do that, we compartmentalize our lives. And the message that comes across to employees and family members alike is that contribution is token or for show and if the time comes that they don't have what we want or need, they—like our neighbor—can become irrelevant. In addition, our inconsistent behavior—acting one way in one situation and a different way in another—comes across as hypocrisy and creates a huge tax.

Instead, we focus on developing true global citizenship in all dimensions of our lives from the inside out. We come back to the 4 Cores, and we start with self: Am I credible? Do I have Intent to do good, to contribute, to give back? Do I give to society a person they can trust?

Then we move to family. We ask: Do I exercise the leadership in my family that inspires and helps family members to become good global citizens? Do I set the example? Am I a good citizen within my own family as well as in the world? Do I align family structures and systems in a way that supports citizenship in the family and in the world? I am personally convinced that our opportunity to model citizenship in our families and to teach our children to be global citizens is one of the greatest opportunities we have to build societal trust.

Then we move to our organizations. We ask: Is our organization credible? Do we have integrity, and do we model it in our behavior? Do we demonstrate Intent to do good, to contribute, to give back? Do we have the Capabilities to make a difference? Do we produce Results, not only for shareholders but for all stakeholders? Do we give to society an organization they can trust? We also ask: Do I exercise the leadership that inspires the people in my organization to become good global citizens? Have I aligned the structures and systems of the organization, or my team, in a way that promotes citizenship within the organization and also in the world?

> *The success of big business and the well-being of the
> world have never been more closely linked. Global issues
> cannot be removed from the business world because
> business has only one world in which to operate.
> Businesses cannot succeed in societies that fail.*
>
> —JORMA OLLILA, CHAIRMAN AND CEO, NOKIA

We look at the 13 Behaviors. We ask: Do I (or does my organization or my family):

- Talk Straight?
- Demonstrate Respect?
- Create Transparency?
- Right Wrongs?
- Show Loyalty?
- Deliver Results?
- Get Better?
- Confront Reality?
- Clarify Expectations?
- Practice Accountability?
- Listen First?
- Keep Commitments?
- Extend Trust?

If we have on our glasses to see, we realize that it is at this societal level that the words of psychologist Carl Rogers become clear: "That which is most personal is most general." We see that trust at the Fifth Wave is a direct result of trustworthiness that begins in the First Wave and flows outward in our relationships, in our organizations, and in the marketplace to fill society as a whole.

Truly, global citizenship is an individual choice and a whole-life choice. And as we make that choice in our own lives, we influence those with whom we work and live to make a similar positive choice in theirs. Together, we build organizations and families that contribute to the well-being of the world.

> *The true and solid peace of nations consists not in
> equality of arms, but in mutual trust alone.*
>
> —POPE JOHN XXIII

A SUMMARY AND A CHALLENGE

Now that we've gone through this section on Stakeholder Trust, I'd like to recap the essential messages:

1. The 4 Cores and the 13 Behaviors are the tools that establish or restore trust in every context—in organizations (including the family), in the marketplace, and in society.
2. The main principle of establishing Organizational Trust is *alignment*—ensuring that all structures and systems within the organization are in harmony with the cores and behaviors. This is what builds trust with *internal* stakeholders.
3. The main principle of establishing Market Trust is *reputation* or brand. It's using the cores and behaviors to create the credibility and behavior that inspires the trust of *external* stakeholders to the extent that they will buy, invest in, and/or recommend your products and services to others.
4. The main principle of establishing Societal Trust is *contribution*. It's demonstrating the intent to give back, to be a responsible global citizen, and it is becoming both a social and an economic necessity in our knowledge worker age.

Having said that, I would also like to say that until you are actually in a frontline situation where you are dealing with these cores and behaviors in the context of your organization, your market, and your society, you will not even begin to see the full power of these things on speed, cost, and trust. (In other words, I hope you've gotten some idea of the power of the cores and behaviors through this book, but "baby, you ain't seen nothin' yet!")

For this reason, in our workshops we often play a simulation game. We give each person at a table a set of cards—4 Cores cards and 13 Behavior cards. We then have them draw additional cards containing possible scenarios.

For example, if you were playing, you might draw a card that says:

You're in a corporate culture. You're following a corporate script you've been told to follow, but it's coming across as spinning the truth and is creating distrust. What do you do?

You would always play one or more 4 Cores cards (the "Start with Self" cards) first. You might say, "If I'm going to have a confronting talk with my boss, I need to first ask: What's my credibility? If I'm not credible, she's going to care less about what I say. She won't see my input as helpful constructive criticism; she'll see it as whining. But if I'm producing results, if I'm hitting my numbers, she'll probably be much more likely to listen." So you would play your "Core 4: Results" card.

Then the person next to you might play a Behavior card, such as "Confront Reality" or "Talk Straight." It quickly becomes apparent that the Behaviors cards will only work well when you've played one or more of your 4 Cores cards first.

There are no right or wrong answers in these role plays; the object is to create awareness and choice around how to solve the problems in these scenarios in the best possible way. In fulfilling this objective, the game not only inspires stimulating, thought-provoking discussion, it also brings people up short when they realize that understanding on a conceptual level and understanding on an experiential level—where you're actually on the front lines making decisions with consequence—are two entirely different things. By playing the game, participants relearn the content on a deeper level and gain good preparation for real-life application.

So I encourage you, as a reader, to get into this material on an experiential level as quickly as possible. Look for ways to immediately apply it. Find opportunities to teach it to others. As you do, I believe you will literally be astonished at the results. Not only will you better understand and realize the power of the cores and behaviors; you will also be amazed how quickly great things can happen with all stakeholders when you operate at the speed of trust.

A Summary of the 5 Waves of Trust

INSPIRING TRUST

By now I hope you're convinced that, as I've said, nothing is as fast as the speed of trust. Nothing is as profitable as the economics of trust. Nothing is as relevant as the pervasive impact of trust. And the dividends of trust can significantly enhance the quality of every relationship on every level of your life.

BUT . . . you may still be hesitant or fearful when it comes to actually extending trust to others. Maybe, deep down, you really feel that other people can't be trusted. Maybe you grew up in a low-trust environment. Maybe you've been burned in the past. Maybe no one has ever extended trust meaningfully to you.

In this final section, I want to show you that, whatever your situation, you can learn how to extend "Smart Trust." You can develop the competence to extend trust in ways that avoid the pitfalls and ensure the greatest dividends for all concerned. You can also learn how to restore trust when it has been lost, and how to develop the propensity to trust that is absolutely vital to effective leadership and life.

Aside from being personally worthy of trust and knowing how to build trusting relationships on all levels, your ability to appropriately extend trust to others is the single most impactful factor in creating a high-trust environment, both at work and at home. In fact, you may recall that "Extend Trust" was included as the last of the 13 Behaviors because of its impact in building trust. In this section, we'll explore it in much greater depth.

The first job of a leader is to inspire trust. The ability to do so, in fact, is a prime differentiator between a manager and a leader. To inspire trust is to create the foundation upon which all truly successful enterprises—and relationships—stand.

EXTENDING "SMART TRUST"

It is equally an error to trust all men or no man.

—LATIN PROVERB

Have you ever failed to trust someone and missed significant opportunities—either personally or professionally—as a result? How did that make you feel?

When you get right down to it, the practical issues with regard to extending trust are these: How do you know when to trust somebody? And how can you extend trust to people in ways that create rich, high-trust dividends without taking inordinate risk?

When you're dealing with trust, it seems there are two extremes. On one end of the spectrum, people don't trust enough. They're suspicious. They hold things close to the vest. Often the only people they really trust are themselves. On the other end, people are too trusting. They're totally gullible. They believe anyone, trust everyone. They have a simplistic, naïve view of the world, and they don't even really think (except superficially) about the need to protect their interests.

Extending trust can bring great dividends. It also creates the possibility of significant risk. So how do you hit the "sweet spot"? How do you extend "Smart Trust" in a way that maximizes the dividends and minimizes the risk?

I'm aware of a situation in one company in which there had been an apparently high-trust relationship between the chairman and the president. However, one day the chairman learned that the president had, in effect, organized a mini "coup" in the organization. He had rallied a number of the company leaders in an effort to take the company in a different direction than what the chairman (who was also the founder) and the board had desired. As a result, trust was totally destroyed. This was particularly painful to this chairman because he felt he had been betrayed. The president was let go, and the company was restructured. Professionally, the president and the chairman parted ways.

However, because of the friendship these two men had developed in prior years, they made efforts to restore trust in their personal relationship. There were months of discussions, sincere apologies, even tears. Finally, there was forgiveness, and these men reached a point where they were able to feel good about their relationship once again.

One day, the former president approached the chairman with another business proposition. Before any serious discussion took place, the chairman said thoughtfully, "I appreciate your interest. I would work with you on a personal or family endeavor. I would serve with you on a civic committee. I would be a chairman if you were a committee member; I would be a committee member if you were the chairman. However, I choose not to go into business with you."

In the end, this chairman exercised "Smart Trust." He wasn't reactive. He didn't continue to harbor ill feelings. He forgave and did all he could do to restore what trust it was possible to restore with his former business associate and friend. But he didn't ignore the lessons of his experience. At the point at which he felt he could not fully trust, he drew the line.

THE "SMART TRUST" MATRIX

Life is filled with risk. However, as noted historian and law professor Stephen Carter has observed: "Civility has two parts: generosity when it is costly, and trust, even when there is risk."

The objective, then, is not to avoid risk. In the first place, you can't; and in the second place, you wouldn't want to because risk-taking is an essential part of life. Instead, the objective is to manage risk wisely—to extend trust in a way that will avoid the taxes and create the greatest dividends over time.

Learning how to extend "Smart Trust" is a function of two factors—propensity to trust and analysis—which are juxtaposed on the matrix on page 290.

"Propensity to Trust" is primarily a matter of the heart. It's the tendency, inclination, or predisposition to believe that people are worthy of trust and a desire to extend it to them freely. The degree to which you have this tendency may be due to your inherent personality, to the way important people in your life have (or have not) trusted you, or to your own experience (good or bad) in trusting others—or, most likely, to a combination of these factors.

"Analysis" is primarily a matter of the mind. It's the ability to analyze, evaluate, theorize, consider implications and possibilities, and come up with logical decisions and solutions. Again, the degree to which you have "strong analysis" may be due to a variety or combination of factors, including your natural gifts or abilities, your education and the way you think, your style, and/or your life experience.

An experience with my sons, Christian and Britain, clearly demonstrates both of these factors. One day I took them fishing. We had a great time, and afterward we went to get something to eat. Britain (who was five and had a high propensity to trust at the time) thanked me profusely. He said, "Dad, thank you. Thank you SO MUCH! You're the BEST dad in the WHOLE WORLD!" Christian (who, at nine, had become more analytical) said, "Britain, you can't just say that he is the best dad in the world. You don't know that, and there are a lot of nice dads out there." Then, suddenly realizing he didn't want to offend me, he added, "I'll bet he's the . . . *ninth* best dad in the world!"

As you think about these two factors—propensity to trust and analysis—how would you rate yourself on each? Do you typically tend to trust people easily, or do you tend to be suspicious and hold things close? Do you tend to analyze, theorize, and ponder over things—or do you give problems your cursory attention and then move on?

To what degree do you think your present tendencies add to or reduce your ability to extend "Smart Trust?" Take a look at the matrix. You may be surprised!

Zone 1 (High Propensity to Trust; Low Analysis) is the "Blind Trust" zone of *gullibility*. It's the Pollyanna approach where people blissfully trust everyone. This is where we find those "suckers who are

Smart Trust™ Matrix

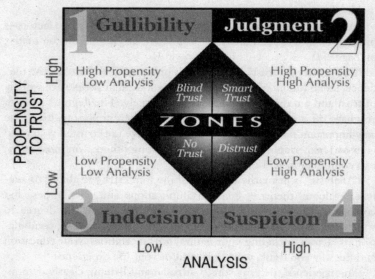

born every minute"—those people who are a sure bet to fall for Internet, marketing, investment, and other scams.

Zone 2 (High Propensity to Trust; High Analysis) is the "Smart Trust" zone of *judgment*. This is where you combine the propensity to trust with the analysis to manage risk wisely. This is where you get both good business judgment and good people judgment—including enhanced instinct and intuition. If you have a propensity to *not* trust, instinct and intuition will disproportionately tell you to not extend trust to others. On the other hand, without analysis, you might well mistake a propensity to trust alone for instinct and intuition. Thus, a significant dimension of combining high analysis with high propensity to trust is the synergy that elevates instinct and intuition to the realm of good judgment.

Smart Trust doesn't mean that you extend trust to everyone. Based on the circumstances, your judgment may be to not extend trust or to extend only a limited measure of trust—like the chairman did with the former president in the example I used before.

> *Trust, but verify.*
>
> —RONALD REAGAN

Zone 3 (Low Propensity to Trust; Low Analysis) is the "No Trust" zone of *indecision*. People here tend to not trust anyone. Because their own analysis is low, they tend to not even trust themselves. This zone is characterized by indecision, insecurity, protectiveness, apprehension, tentativeness, and immobilization.

Zone 4 (Low Propensity to Trust; High Analysis) is the "Distrust" zone of *suspicion*. This is where you find people who extend trust very cautiously or not at all. In fact, some are so suspicious that they do not trust anyone *but* themselves. People in this zone tend to rely almost exclusively on analysis (usually their own) for all evaluation, decision making, and execution.

Now, here's what may surprise you. In terms of extending trust, where do you think the greatest risk lies?

Obviously, there's enormous risk in Zone 1 (Gullibility). If you unquestioningly trust everyone, sooner or later, you're going to get burned.

Zone 3 (Indecision) is clearly a wipeout. With poor analysis and a low propensity to trust, you're going to get the worst of both worlds. It's low return for high risk.

The biggest surprise for most people comes in Zone 4 (Suspicion). Many tend to think that this is the lowest risk zone of all. This is where you analyze and calculate and consider issues carefully. You're suspicious and guarded, so you don't readily extend trust to others. You hold things close; you try to keep everything within your direct control.

While it may sound low risk, this is actually one of the highest risk zones of all. When you're highly suspicious, you tend to try to validate everything, to analyze everything to death—which ends up decreasing speed and increasing cost. In addition, you miss opportunities. You cut off collaboration and synergy. The only analysis you really have is your own, which—believe it or not—may well be limited or skewed; but you may not even realize it because you cut yourself off from access to the valuable thoughts, ideas, wisdom, and perspectives of others.

Ultimately micromanagers who trust only themselves can take their companies only as far as they themselves can take them. They're unable to leverage themselves. In addition, they're demoralizing to work with. They run the high risk of driving away their best and most talented people who simply won't work in a restrictive environment of control.

I once knew a business owner who was so suspicious that his employees might be stealing from him that he would literally interrogate them almost daily. He would even do occasional spot "frisk checks" when they left the office. This man was convinced that people were trying to steal from him. In reality, no one was, but his suspicious actions drove away his most talented people, who wouldn't tolerate working in such a distrustful environment or for such a suspicious boss.

Managers and leaders in Zone 4 also incur many of the low-trust taxes we talked about in Organizational Trust—including bureaucracy, politics, disengagement, and turnover—and they lose high-trust dividends such as innovation, collaboration, partnering, and loyalty. Sadly, their suspicion sometimes even helps produce the very behaviors they fear, which further validates their suspicion. By treating people as if they can't be trusted, they help to create the collusive, downward cycle of distrust David Packard talked about with regard to the distrustful behavior of his former employer in locking the tool bins. As he said, "[M]any employees set out to prove [the company's obvious display of distrust] justified."

> *There is no rule more invariable than that we are paid for our suspicions by finding what we expected.*
>
> —HENRY DAVID THOREAU

The risk of being in Zone 4—particularly as a leader—is extremely high. It's the risk of having limited perspective, lack of collaboration, alienation of talent, and lost opportunity. It's the risk of paying high taxes and forfeiting dividends. And this is one reason why—in this "flat world" global economy—*not* trusting people is often the greatest risk of all.

> *There is no point in hiring people with specialist knowledge if you are going to monitor their every move. That is where trust comes in. People not only have to be trusted to do their jobs. They have to be able to trust each other. Successful knowledge work requires collaboration.*
>
> —MICHAEL SKAPINKER, MANAGEMENT EDITOR,
> *FINANCIAL TIMES*

So why do people get into Zone 4? For some, it may be a fundamental issue of style—an inclination toward extremely high attention to detail, perfectionism, or even micromanagement. For others, it may be a deep-rooted, fundamental paradigm that has to do with their lack of belief in people. Maybe they genuinely think they're better or smarter than everyone else. Maybe they trust only themselves. Maybe they've been burned in the past, and it's made them overly suspicious. Or maybe no one has ever extended trust to them. Whatever the case, they seem to have the fundamental paradigm that others can't be trusted. And unless they take the steps necessary to change that paradigm, they will be stuck forever in high-risk, slow-speed, high-cost Zone 4.

> *You may be deceived if you trust too much, but you will live in torment if you don't trust enough.*
>
> FRANK CRANE, AUTHOR AND COLUMNIST

By far, the lowest risk and highest return is in Smart Trust Zone 2 (Judgment). There the risk, while real, can be wisely moderated and managed. Not only do you have the personal analysis to carefully evaluate and consider issues, you also have that propensity to trust that releases, encourages, and generates synergy with the creativity and judgment of others. Thus, in Zone 2, "judgment" is geometrically multiplied. The propensity to trust is also geometrically multiplied, as your own propensity to trust becomes the catalyst in creating that same propensity in others. And they want to live up to that trust.

In other words, Zone 2 is literally effervescent. High analysis and high propensity to trust not only create strong judgment, they create a dynamic synergy that produces ongoing and endless possibility.

Remember: Smart Trust doesn't necessarily mean you extend trust to someone. You may decide to extend limited trust or no trust at all—just as you might do in Zone 4. But while your decision may appear to be the same, beginning in Zone 2 makes all the difference because the approach itself will almost always build trust.

DEFINING THE FACTORS

The Smart Trust Matrix can be extremely helpful as both a diagnostic and a prescriptive tool.

With regard to analysis, it's helpful to consider three vital variables, which you can do by asking these questions:

1. What is the *opportunity* (the situation or task at hand)?
2. What is the *risk* involved?
    * What are the possible outcomes?
    * What is the likelihood of the outcomes?
    * What is the importance and visibility of the outcomes?
3. What is the *credibility* (character/competence) of the people involved?

Let's see how these questions would help determine Smart Trust in a real-life situation. Remember my experience with Anna Humphries, the young girl on my Little League flag football team?? If we used the analysis questions, we would ask:

"What is the *opportunity*?" The championship was at stake, it was the last play of the game, Anna was less skillful and less experienced than the other players, and I had played her for the amount of time required by the Little League rules so I could easily call someone else in.

"What is the *risk*?" We could win or we could lose. The entire team could be enormously thrilled—or hugely disappointed. Anna could feel like a winner, or she could feel like the reason for the team's defeat—or she could feel like, when push came to shove, I didn't have faith in her that she could do what needed to be done. I could have been branded as a hero . . . or a fool. And though the outcome of a community Little League game may not seem like the end of the world to most people, it would have been highly visible and important to Anna, the other team members, and everyone else involved.

"What is the *credibility* of the people involved?" All of the team members were great kids, and they had worked hard to develop their skills to make it to this championship game. Anna's character was manifest not only in the way she behaved, but also in the way she showed courage in deciding to compete with these boys in the first place. Her competence, however, was not as great as that of others on the team.

Based on the answers to these three questions—in other words, on intellectual analysis alone—many coaches would have made the decision to bring in a different player for the last minute of the game with the championship hanging in the balance.

But then the second factor—propensity to trust—comes into play. And that involves a dimension that is different from intellectual analysis; it involves visceral feelings ranging from *suspicious* to *guarded* to *abundant* (see the expanded Smart Trust Matrix on page 295).

I was not *suspicious* of Anna's motives or her intent (which, combined

Smart Trust™ Matrix

PROPENSITY TO TRUST

Abundant	
Guarded	
Suspicious	

1 Gullibility
High Propensity
Low Analysis

Blind Trust

Judgment 2
High Propensity
High Analysis

Smart Trust

ZONES

No Trust

Distrust

Low Propensity
Low Analysis

Low Propensity
High Analysis

3 Indecision

Suspicion 4

ANALYSIS
- Opportunity
- Risk
- Credibility (Character/Competence) of those involved

with my analysis, would have put me in Zone 4). Clearly, I trusted her character.

I was *guarded* in my confidence in her capabilities and in her ability to deliver results (in other words, in her competence), which would have put me either in the upper part of Zone 4, or in the lower part of Zone 2.

I was, however, *abundant* in my general Propensity to Trust. I believed in the principle of inspiring people through extending trust, and I believed in Anna. I knew that this could be a defining moment in her life.

Though I didn't have time to consciously go through all of these factors on the field that day, they all came into play as I quickly determined to make a moment of decision a moment of trust. And I believe that the choice I made was clearly in Smart Trust Zone 2. Based at least in part on that choice, we won the game, everyone on the team felt great, and Anna had a significant positive experience in her life.

Would I still believe that my decision was an exercise of Smart Trust if we had lost the game? Yes, I would. I believe it sent a message not only to Anna, but to every member of the team, that I believed in them and would support them, regardless of what was on the line. Winning the game was not the only issue involved. What was at stake, as much as anything, was the way these kids felt about their efforts, and the way their overall experience in being part of a team would impact their confidence and their ability to feel trusted and to extend trust throughout their lives.

In extending trust, the general guideline is to extend trust conditionally to those who are earning it and abundantly to those who have already done so. Keep in mind that even when you extend trust abundantly, there should still always be accountability because that is a principle that actually enhances trust.

MANAGING RISK

The decision to extend or not extend trust is always an issue of managing risk. In order to get an even better idea of how this plays out, let's take a look at some of the other examples I introduced earlier and look at them through the matrix lens.

First, let's look at Warren Buffett's acquisition of McLane Distribution from Wal-Mart. The opportunity was a potential acquisition. To *not* do due diligence seems extremely risky, and for most people, it would probably have been. But in this circumstance, the risk was not as great as it might normally have been. Wal-Mart was a public company, subject to rules and regulations and public scrutiny. In addition, the credibility (character and competence) of the people at Wal-Mart were high. Besides, Buffett's own reputation and influence were extremely high, and—let's get real here—no one's going to try to swindle Warren Buffett in a public deal. So Buffett decided to extend trust abundantly and do the deal on a handshake with no due diligence, which dramatically increased speed and lowered cost. Smart trust? Absolutely. That's Zone 2.

Now let's take another example: the woman I mentioned in the 13 Behaviors chapter on "Extending Trust." As you may remember, the CEO of the company she had decided to buy didn't want to do an employment agreement. "You're buying my company," he said. "You've got to trust me." She did—and it turned into an absolute disaster. Smart Trust? No. In this case, she didn't have Warren Buffett's clout and he didn't have the credibility or public accountability of Wal-Mart. So to extend trust abundantly without doing "due diligence" probably didn't show the best judgment. This was in Zone 1—a high propensity to trust, low analysis, "gullible" transaction.

Take another example—me extending trust to my son Stephen by letting him drive the family car. There was obviously significant risk. (After all, he was a teenager!) However, the risk was somewhat mitigated by the fact that he was generally well intended, and he'd taken a driver's training class and passed the exams necessary to get his license. In addition, we had an agreement in place that provided clear consequences for misbehavior or bad choices. Well, Stephen made a bad choice and drove too fast. And with the agreement in place, he was the one who primarily had to deal with the consequences of his choice. Was this Smart Trust? I think so. It was certainly smarter than the alternatives of extending trust unconditionally (Zone 1) or not extending trust at all.

In parenting, you're always dealing with issues of extending trust with children, and sometimes it can be a real roller-coaster experience as they go through the maturing process. I've found it especially helpful as a parent to make a conscious effort to stay in Zone 2—to have a high propensity to trust, but also to do the analysis so that you extend trust in a way that encourages and helps a child take trust seriously and grow in the ability to handle a stewardship responsibly.

Obviously there's room for variety in approach even in Zone 2. Depending on the situation, Smart Trust judgment could involve anything from extending complete trust to extending no trust at all, or from extending trust in some core dimensions (Integrity, Intent, and Capabilities, for example), but not in others (i.e., Results). It takes into consideration the general dividends of high-trust relationships, as well as the specific situation, risk, and character and competence of those involved. It combines the propensity to trust with analysis in a way that truly maximizes dividends and minimizes risk.

> *The obsession with measurement is the problem. There is something we can use instead of measurement: judgment. Some of the most important things in the world cannot be measured.*
>
> —HENRY MINTZBERG, AUTHOR AND PROFESSOR

WHY MANY TRUSTED MANAGERS NEVER BECOME LEADERS

Throughout this book, I have said that "leadership" is getting results in a way that inspires trust. Many trusted managers—credible people who have high character and technical competence—never become "leaders" because they don't know how to extend Smart Trust. They essentially operate in Zone 4, the zone of suspicion. They may *delegate*, or assign tasks to others with parameters for their accomplishment. They may *extend fake trust*—in other words, give "lip service" to extending trust, but micromanage the activities. But they don't fully *entrust*. They don't give to others the *stewardships* (responsibilities with a trust) that engage genuine ownership and accountability, bring out people's greatest resourcefulness, and create the environment that generates high-trust dividends.

While delegation is intellectual, entrusting is visceral—it's something you feel. When people don't learn to extend trust, they don't become "leaders" in the full sense of the word—either at work or at home.

At the end of one program, a man who was retiring as general counsel of a company came up to me and said, "My legal training and experience have given me a propensity to not trust. At times, this has served me well, but much of the time it has created huge problems. It's gotten me bogged down in expensive and time-consuming legal relationships, and it has hurt me enormously in personal relationships as I have extended my professional mind-set into my personal life. Now I'm beginning a new career, and I'm inspired by this idea of starting with a propensity to trust. I don't know what the results will be, but I am convinced that this is the front edge. It's a better place to start."

I certainly agree—it *is* a better place to start.

The number one job of any leader is to inspire trust. It's to release the creativity and capacity of individuals to give their best and to create a high-trust environment in which they can effectively work with others. And this is true both at work and at home.

> The first thing for any leader is to inspire trust.
>
> DOUG CONANT, CEO, CAMPBELL SOUP COMPANY

So how do you inspire trust? By doing the things we've been talking about throughout this book. First, you inspire trust by starting with yourself and your own credibility (the 4 Cores). Second, you inspire trust by consistently behaving in trust-building ways with other people (the 13 Behaviors), including purposefully and wisely extending trust to others (Smart Trust). In your larger leadership role, you use the 4 Cores and 13 Behaviors to create the alignment in your "organization" (your business, department, team, or family), reputation in the marketplace, and contribution in the world. As you do those things, you will get results in a way that inspires confidence and trust.

Some leaders have detail-oriented styles that—while they're not really micromanagement—may nevertheless be seen as not trusting. Considering the taxes of low trust, it's wise for all leaders to think about the way their style is perceived, and for those who are more detail-oriented to make an extra effort to communicate and practice a fundamental propensity to trust.

Once again, I affirm that especially in our "flat world" economy, the ability to establish, grow, extend, and restore trust is *the* key professional and personal competency of our time. And the ability to exercise Smart Trust is a vital part of that competency. It will enable you to create a powerful balance and synergy between analysis and the propensity to trust, which, in turn, will produce the judgment that enables you to effectively leverage yourself and to inspire the talent, creativity, synergy, and highest contribution of others.

RESTORING TRUST WHEN IT HAS BEEN LOST

Men build too many walls and not enough bridges.
—Sir Isaac Newton

I recently read an article by a leading business author who wrote:

> *The truth is, you can't regain trust. Period. You doubt? Think hard about the times you've been betrayed. Did the villain ever find their way back into your heart? If you're like the thousands I've asked, the answer is never. Trust can be gained once and lost once. Once lost, it's lost forever.*

Perhaps you've had experiences that seem to validate this position. Maybe you've broken trust in a professional or personal relationship, and you've tried to restore it, but failed. Or maybe someone has broken trust with you, and you vowed you would never again trust that person—no matter what! Or perhaps you vowed that you would never trust *anyone* again.

Obviously broken trust creates pain, disappointment, and loss. It wreaks havoc with relationships, partnerships, plans, dreams, and enterprises of all kinds.

I am the first to admit that there are situations in which trust cannot be restored. The violation has been too severe, the betrayal too deep, the pain too great. Trust has been shattered, and there is no way to put the pieces back together in a viable whole. In fact, there may not even be an opportunity to *try* to restore it. Thus, I heartily agree with those who say that the best approach, by far, is to never violate trust in the first place. Trust is not something to be taken for granted; it is something to be built up, valued, cherished, protected, and carefully preserved.

However, the nature of life is such that all of us will undoubtedly have to deal with broken trust at some time—maybe a number of times—during our lives. Sometimes we do something stupid. We make a mistake in a personal or professional relationship, and we're brought up short by a severely depleted or even overdrawn Trust Account. Suddenly suspicion replaces synergy. An association is severed. Business is taken elsewhere. A family is torn apart. Retribution is sought.

At other times, we may make an honest mistake or demonstrate some failure of competence, only to discover our behavior is being interpreted as a violation of character—which is much harder to restore.

"Look at what you did!"

"But I didn't mean to . . ."

"But I was only trying to . . ."

As we discussed earlier in the chapter introducing the 13 Behaviors, it's not just how we behave that affects trust. It's also the interpretations people make of those behaviors and the conclusions people draw from them that affect trust. Again, as Nietzsche said, "There are no facts, only interpretations." Remember, people tend to judge others based on behavior and judge themselves based on intent. Thus, poor but well-intended behavior can lead others to assume bad intent, which significantly increases the withdrawal and the difficulty of restoring trust.

On the other side of the coin, there may be times when others break trust with us and we're faced with the decision of how to deal with it. Maybe a business partner misuses funds, a team member doesn't come through on a responsibility, a supplier bad-mouths us to others in the industry, a spouse independently and impulsively uses the credit card, a child repeatedly breaks curfew. How we handle these violations of trust may well influence business relationships and opportunities, civic associations, our personal happiness and that of our families—even for generations to come.

So what do we do?

Is it really possible to restore trust?

Is it wise—or foolish—to even try?

THE CHALLENGE *IS* THE OPPORTUNITY

As I said in Chapter 1, the idea that trust cannot be restored once it is lost is a myth. Though it may be difficult, in most cases, lost trust *can* be restored—and often even enhanced!

For example, that night I got called by the police at midnight to pick up my son for excessive speeding, my trust in him took a nosedive. Jeri and I had gone to great lengths to spell out the conditions on which Stephen would be allowed to drive the family car. And he had agreed to those stipulations. Then he'd consciously gone out and violated one of the most important ones—to abide by the law.

However, the trust we were willing to extend to Stephen before his infraction has not only been restored, it has actually increased. I can honestly say that my trust in Stephen is infinitely stronger today than it was before this experience, and a good part of the reason is a result of of what happened as we worked through the process.

As Stephen admitted his violation, apologized, and spent months working through the challenges of paying the fine and suffering the consequences of his actions, he grew in understanding, maturity, and resolve to never be in that position again. His personal credibility increased. He strengthened his Integrity and improved his Intent. He increased his Capabilities by finding more mature ways to handle disappointment in his life. He produced Results—better attitudes, better habits, better driving, even to the point that he became the acknowledged "safe" driver among his peers. Unknowingly he also implemented some of the 13 Behaviors. He worked to Confront Reality, Right Wrongs, Deliver Results, Keep Commitments, and Get Better. In doing so, he strengthened his own core and also his relationship with us.

Because I've seen Stephen go through this process—because he has been tested and our relationship has been tested, and Stephen came through—I truly feel that our Trust Account is much higher than it's ever been. Painful though it was, the situation provided the opportunity for him and for us to learn, get better, and build trust.

One of the greatest obstacles to building and restoring trust is the superficial, two-dimensional paradigm that the ideal life is challenge-free. It's not. We are going to have challenges. We are going to make mistakes. And others are going to make mistakes that affect us. That's life. The issue is how we respond to those things—whether or not we choose to prioritize the enormous long-term dividends of trust over whatever temporary satisfaction we may get from doing things that break trust, trying to justify low-trust behavior, holding grudges, or failing to forgive.

I am absolutely convinced that in most cases, prioritizing trust—actively seeking to establish it, grow it, restore it, and wisely extend it—will bring personal and organizational dividends that far exceed any other path. So while trying to restore trust may be difficult, it is definitely worth it. Even if trust is not restored in the particular relationship you're working on, your efforts to restore it will increase your ability to build trust in other relationships.

As in almost every other aspect of life, breakdowns can create breakthroughs. Challenges and mistakes can become some of our greatest opportunities to learn, grow, and improve. With that in mind, let's look now at what we can do to restore trust—first, when we have broken trust with others, and second, when others have broken trust with us. In both cases, the key is in the 4 Cores and 13 Behaviors. Not only do they help us establish trust, they also enable us to restore it.

WHEN YOU HAVE LOST THE TRUST OF OTHERS

Whether you lose the trust of others through a conscious act of betrayal, poor judgment, an honest mistake, a failure of competence, or a simple misunderstanding, the path to restoration is the same—to increase your personal credibility and behave in ways that inspire trust.

However, understanding how trust was lost in the first place is an important key to understanding how to apply the Cores and Behaviors in attempting to restore it. Generally speaking, a loss of trust created by a violation of character (Integrity or Intent) is far more difficult to restore than a loss of trust created by a violation of competence (Capabilities or Results). Violations of Integrity are the most difficult of all to restore in all relationships, whether they are personal, family, professional, organizational, or in the marketplace.

Keep in mind that when you talk about restoring trust, you're talking about changing someone else's feelings about you and confidence in you. And that's not something you can control. You can't force people to trust you. You can't make them have confidence in you. They may be dealing with other issues in their own lives that make the challenge more difficult for them. Or they may have interpreted a breach of competence on your part as a breach of character, which significantly complicates the issue. The point is that you can only do what you can do. But that's a lot. And even if you're unable to restore trust in a particular situation or relationship, by strengthening your Cores and making habits of the Behaviors, you will increase your ability to establish or restore trust in other situations and relationships throughout your life.

So keep in mind that we're not talking here about "fixing" someone else. You can't do that. But you can give to others someone who is credible and worthy of trust and behaves in ways that inspire trust. And experience shows that this kind of example over time will do more than anything else you could do to restore trust.

RESTORING TRUST ON ALL LEVELS

Now let's look at some examples in each of the 5 Waves and see how credibility and behavior can help you restore trust on every level. Notice how, in many of the situations, going through the challenge of dealing with broken trust provides the foundation for even greater trust.

Societal Trust

Restoring trust on the societal level means rebuilding trust in countries, institutions, industries, professions, and in other people generally. It includes counteracting suspicion and cynicism and replacing it with contribution, value creation, and ethical behavior.

There are many data points that indicate trust can be improved in society. Shortly following the Enron and WorldCom scandals, a 2002 Watson Wyatt study showed employee trust in management at only 44 percent. A second Watson Wyatt study done just a few years later showed the number had increased to 51 percent. Some countries, such as Japan, Denmark, and the Netherlands, have grown trust in their societies at large over the past two decades.

In the Republic of Ireland, leaders over the past 30 years have changed the nation's focus from inward to outward. They have moved the nation from economic independence to interdependence. They have overhauled a once archaic educational system to make Ireland one of the world's undisputed education leaders. They have improved labor harmony through purposeful collaboration, wooed back expatriates, and helped Ireland become a major technology player, ultimately attracting foreign investment—in fact, drawing nearly 25 percent of U.S. investment in Europe, with only 1 percent of the European population.

As Ireland's Prime Minister Bertie Ahern commented: "Technology is clearly the driving force for us. It has given a whole new generation of Irish people confidence. It has helped create employment and stem the huge tide of emigration by giving our people a future."

The leadership of the Republic of Ireland has done all of this through a conscious and collaborative effort that included behaviors such as Confront Reality, Get Better, and Deliver Results. In consequence, they have built up their global credibility and trust as a nation.

Market Trust

With regard to Market Trust, it's true that in many cases, if you violate a customer's trust, you're not going to get a second chance. Ultimately that decision is up to the customer, who may simply choose to not play anymore and go his/her own way. As I said before, this is especially true if the violation has been one of character—particularly of Integrity.

However, in some cases, experience shows that the 4 Cores and 13 Behaviors make it possible to restore—and even enhance—Market Trust. In *Tales of Knock Your Socks Off Service*, business authors Kristen Anderson and Ron Zemke share the following:

> *Good friends of ours were celebrating their 25th wedding anniversary. We called to congratulate them, and to check on the flowers we'd ordered for their big day—and for the big party they were having that evening. To our chagrin, what had arrived was hardly the large pair of festive arrangements we had envisioned—it was, instead, a puny potted plant, an itsy-bitsy, teeny thing that, at best, might brighten some little corner of the half bath off their family room.*
>
> *It was after 6 P.M. and their party was set for 7:30. We called and caught Jerry on his way out the door and explained the foul-up. "Don't say another word. I'll fix this right now." At 7:10 P.M. our friends called back to tell us a truck had just delivered two magnificent arrangements and a centerpiece for their buffet table. Oh—and did I mention? Our friends live in North Carolina—and we, and our florist, live in Minneapolis, one time zone and half a continent away.*
>
> *When the bill arrived it was for the cost of our original order only, and was hand delivered by Jerry the florist with hat—and a small arrangement—in hand. He apologized again for the problem, and assured it would not happen again. No excuses. No passing the blame to the fulfilling florist in Charlotte. No "You can't believe the kind of help I have to deal with today." No nothing; just—"Once again, I'm sorry for the problem. I hope you will think of us again when you think of flowers." And you can bet we will. And have.*

In this situation—as in many situations involving service recovery—the problem itself became the catalyst for the creation of even greater trust as the companies took the issues head-on and worked through the difficult problem in a way that restored confidence. This kind of service recovery can win you a customer for life.

For another example, in the 1990s, Nike was criticized heavily by activists for not being socially responsible, based on the conditions in some of the plants of their foreign manufacturing partners. Chairman Phil Knight took steps to Right Wrongs. He acknowledged the problem as "a bumpy original response, an error for which yours truly was responsible." By Nike's actions and behavior over the ensuing years, they have demonstrated tangible results and a strong commitment to elevate the conditions of the entire industry and to be a leading corporate citizen. In 2006, they were listed as #13 on the "Best Corporate Citizens" list. Trust that may have been lost has been restored as they have behaved themselves out of this problem with transparency. There are still critics out there, but as Nike brand presidents Mark Parker and Charlie Denson say in their Corporate Responsibility Report, "We want to build trust and enable stakeholders to judge us not on perception, but fact. Transparency is an essential tool in this process."

Organizational Trust

Restoring trust within an organization may seem difficult, particularly if the focus is almost exclusively on producing and is not balanced by the need to maintain the capacity to produce in the future. However, the fact that high-trust organizations outperform low-trust organizations by three times provides a strong incentive to make the effort. High trust not only creates a great working environment, it also provides a powerful competitive edge.

I had a personal experience in losing and then restoring organizational trust during my first weeks as CEO at the Covey Leadership Center. As I went into this position, I deeply questioned the wisdom of continuing to sponsor our education division. I sincerely valued the mission and potential impact of this division, but because we had significantly reduced our pricing to the education marketplace to make it more accessible, the widespread belief and perception was that the division was not contributing profit to the organization. And unfortunately, we didn't have good enough financial data at the time to know otherwise.

Although I'd had a good relationship with the employees of the education division in the past, I now found myself facing the director of the group across the table in meetings and challenging the division's very existence. In addition, I'm sorry to say that I violated some of the 13 Behaviors by talking about it with others behind his back in ways I wouldn't have had he been present. Obviously these things had a significant negative impact on the balance in the Trust Accounts I had both with the leader and with the entire division.

Finally we got our company's financial house in order, developed accurate financial reporting systems, and applied activity-based costing and activity-based management techniques to give us a full picture of the real profitability of all our divisions. As it turned out, in spite of discounted pricing, the education division was not only profitable, the margins were almost as high as our top income-producing divisions.

The day the numbers came out, I walked into the director's office, and I said, "I'm sorry. I was wrong, and I apologize to you and to your whole group. I'm going to make it up to you and your team. I'm going to become the chief advocate for the education division." And I did. I became the champion of the division. I went out of my way to make sure that everyone knew that education was a profitable business and a well-run operation.

As a result, my Trust Account with the director and with the entire division skyrocketed. Though I had no idea of the impact at the time, the director later told me that my apology was a significant moment for him personally, as well as for the entire group, and that it set the tone for the significant success of the division over the next decade.

All I know is that trust was not only restored, it was enhanced, with both the director and the team. Looking back, I can see how this experience validated the importance of showing loyalty and righting wrongs, the value of restoring trust in the organization, and the impact of trust on speed and cost.

Relationship Trust

As I indicated earlier, if you're a customer of a company that violated your trust, you may not give them a chance to restore it. That's a transactional thing, and you may not consider it a big deal. But if a family member violates your trust, it's not transactional. Because family relationships are significantly more important and have more far-reaching implications, you would hope that the willingness and openness to restore trust would be much greater.

An associate of mine shared this story:

A reputable doctor in a nearby community held a respected position in his church, contributed his time to patients in need in third-world countries, was a friend to many in his neighborhood and community, and was a loving father and husband . . . until he got mixed up in an affair with another woman. His secret life and embarrassing behavior, which was contrary to the values he had taught in his church and in his family, was discovered, and instantaneously his world turned upside down. His marriage was in turmoil, his children so hurt that most of them would not speak to him, his position in the church terminated, and his reputation seriously damaged.

But two important things happened that started a healing process that would lay the groundwork for rebuilding respect and trust: 1) he ended the affair and asked forgiveness of his wife and his family, and 2) his wife chose to stay with him, stand by him in public, and give him the opportunity to regain her trust as well as his own self-respect. She did not turn a blind eye or behave like some emotionally abused spouses who blame themselves and allow themselves to be cheated on over and over again. She upheld her own self-respect, gave him an ultimatum, and demanded certain changes in his lifestyle and behavior. Although her actions were important, his were the most important of all. He did not try to lie his way out of the situation. He asked forgiveness. He made the required changes and kept his word that he would not betray her trust again. And he faced his community, family, and neighbors with humility—not arrogance or self-righteousness. Everyone knew what had happened, and he knew that they knew. He wanted to regain their trust, as well. Over time, his marriage, his family, and his reputation began to heal. Though people don't <u>forget</u> these kinds of personal and public mistakes, one's attitude and change in character as well as behavior <u>can</u> rebuild trust and respect.

Certainly not everyone in such a situation would want to try to restore trust. But as this experience and others like it show, where people are willing, at least to some degree and in some situations, it is possible.

Another area that creates huge trust issues in personal relationships is money. As many marriage counselors affirm, money problems are a key cause of divorce. While many such problems are caused by lack of character (selfish or impulsive spending, attempts to control or restrict a partner's access to shared resources, or efforts to hide spending from a partner), many are also caused by lack of competence (lack of education or experience in money management). In addition, two people coming into a relationship are often scripted in different ways by family experience—for example, one may come from a background of spenders, while the other comes from a background of thrift.

One woman shared this story:

For years, my husband and I had problems managing our money. We would agree to spend our money in a certain way, then he would come home with some new thing we hadn't agreed on. It was very frustrating, and I eventually withdrew emotionally as a financial partner.

Over time, however, we both came to realize that this situation was negatively affecting the trust in our relationship, and we decided to change. He worked on being more responsible to act based on our agreements; I worked on expressing my opinions better and participating more fully in financial decisions. And together, we became involved in learning more about good financial habits, including budgeting and investing.

It's taken quite a while to shift old habits, but through it all, we've become amazingly close and more unified in our financial values, goals, and habits. In fact, I'd say that now, financial unity is one of our strengths. Doing something together that was this challenging has created even stronger bonds of trust in our entire relationship.

So often people caught up in low-trust situations feel like there's nothing they can do to create positive change. But examples like these and others go to show that, when people are willing—even in difficult situations in close, personal relationships—trust can be restored. And the very effort of restoring it can make it even stronger than before.

Self Trust

Often, the most difficult trust to restore is trust in ourselves. When we violate a promise we've made to ourselves, fail to follow through on a goal, or act in ways that go against our deepest values, our self trust can really take a dive. And when we have repeated infractions, we often beat ourselves up so thoroughly that we seriously wonder if we can ever have faith in ourselves again.

Some years ago, a friend of mine who had a good reputation, but wasn't a very good money manager, was forced to declare bankruptcy in his business. It was humiliating—even more so because everyone knew about it—and it severely undermined his self-confidence. He had to sell some personal possessions in order to keep his home, his wife had to start a home business, and he had to find another job.

Everyone thought that when this man declared bankruptcy that would be the end of his financial stress, and he could start all over again. But, as bad as he felt about his own situation, he felt even worse that he had put his creditors in the position where they were stuck with his debts. So he worked three or four jobs for several years—sometimes almost around the clock—to repay the debts he legally didn't have to pay. Finally he paid his last creditor and was free from the debts he had owed.

Several years later, the story came out (though not through him), and everyone was amazed at what he had done—especially since he'd had no legal obligation to pay those debts. His credibility with friends, neighbors, and family soared.

But more important to him was the credibility he had regained with himself. Though it had been extremely hard, he had behaved his way back to self trust, and he felt at peace.

Restoring self trust gives another dimension—a powerful dimension—to the Cores and Behaviors. Just think of how significantly the 13 Behaviors apply in your relationship with yourself:

Talk Straight means to tell it like it is—for good, as well as bad. Don't beat around the bush. Don't try to justify or rationalize what you've done, or tell yourself compelling stories. Instead, tell yourself what you should have done and what you need to do to improve. But *don't* tell yourself lies such as: I'm worthless. I've blown it, and I can never make things right. It's no use to even try. Tell yourself the truth: Even if it takes divine help, you *can* make things better if you want to and if you really try.

Demonstrate Respect for yourself. Don't beat yourself up over what you perceive as weaknesses or mistakes. Treat yourself with as much love as you would anyone else. Don't expect more of yourself than you would expect of any other human being in your situation.

Create Transparency in your own life. Be open and honest with yourself about your motives and decisions. Don't try to rationalize or justify. Don't try to hide weaknesses or faults; face them and deal with them directly. Be exactly what you are today—and work on being a little better tomorrow.

Right Wrongs you've done to yourself. Forgive yourself (which is often the most difficult forgiveness of all). Free yourself so that you can work on developing self trust and confidence again.

Show Loyalty to yourself. Don't talk negatively about yourself or put yourself down—in self-talk or in talking with others.

Deliver Results in your life in the things that you feel are important—whether anyone else considers them important or not. Set goals and make them happen.

Get Better. Set aside time in your life to constantly improve your capabilities. Enjoy the increase in self trust and confidence that comes from developing skills and using your unique talents and capacities, and also from rising to meet challenges that require you to develop new abilities or gain new knowledge.

Confront Reality. Don't live in denial or keep your head in the sand. Don't give in to pessimism and despair. Face what needs to be faced and move on with courage and hope.

Clarify Expectations. Be clear about what you expect of yourself. Don't let others talk you out of meeting your own expectations, and don't let the expectations of others govern your decisions and your life.

Practice Accountability. When you receive insight into something you feel you should do, write it down and hold yourself accountable to do it. Don't let the expectations of others take priority over your responsibility to follow your own inspiration.

Listen First to your own conscience, to your own inner voice. Don't let the opinions of others persuade you to violate the things you feel deep inside you should or should not do.

Keep Commitments to yourself. Make commitments to yourself carefully, and treat them with the same respect you feel you should treat commitments to others.

Extend Trust to yourself. Trust your instincts and your intuition. Trust your judgment. Trust your ability to receive guidance for your own life. Trust that when your own heart is right, the universe will provide and things will work together for your good.

As you do these things, you strengthen your 4 Cores. You increase Integrity, improve Intent, increase Capabilities, and improve Results. You become a person that *you*, as well as others, can trust.

IN SUMMARY . . .

Through my work, community service, and personal and family life over the past 20 years, I have seen enough to convince me that on every level—societal, market, organizational, relationship, and personal—people often have the ability to restore at least some measure of trust when they have lost it . . . *if* they're really serious about doing it. If they're not serious—or if they repeatedly abuse it after restoring it—the opportunity will likely be forfeited.

And in many cases, I know it is possible not only to restore trust but to actually enhance it. The difficult things that we go through with the important people in our lives can become fertile ground for the growth of enduring trust—trust that is actually stronger because it's been tested and proved through challenge.

In all cases, the 4 Cores and 13 Behaviors provide powerful restoration tools.

WHEN OTHERS HAVE LOST YOUR TRUST

Up to this point, we've talked about restoring trust when you're the one who's lost the trust of others. But what do you do when others have done something to lose your trust?

Just as you can't force anyone else to trust you when you've lost their trust, neither can anyone else force you to trust them when they have lost yours. For you to restore trust to someone who has broken it is a choice only you can make. But as you reflect on your options, I suggest you consider three guidelines that typically prove to be of great help.

Don't be too quick to judge. You know what it feels like when someone doesn't trust you. You probably also know what it feels like to be misunderstood, misinterpreted, misjudged, or not trusted through no fault of your own. So put the shoe on the other foot. Give others the benefit of the doubt. Don't automatically assume that a failure of competence is a failure of character. Many mistakes are not intentional; don't make them into something they're not.

Do be quick to forgive. I want to be very clear here that to forgive and to trust are two different things. For an abused spouse, for example, to keep "forgiving" over and over (meaning she keeps absolving and going back to a spouse who continues to abuse her) is *not* what I'm talking about. That is *not* Smart Trust.

What I *am* talking about is our ability to cleanse ourselves of feelings of anger, vindictiveness, blaming, accusing, or retribution toward anyone who has caused us offense, either intentionally or accidentally. I'm talking about refusing to take on the role of someone else's judge and jury, and about letting go of things that are out of our control—including other people's attitudes and behaviors and things that have happened in the past. I'm talking about freeing ourselves physically, mentally, spiritually, and emotionally from dependent responses to the mistakes, weaknesses, and bad choices of others.

A great example of forgiveness is Nelson Mandela. Following 27 years of imprisonment on Robben Island, he was released and became the president of South Africa. At his inaugural address, he personally invited his jailers to sit on the front row as an illustration of the forgiveness he felt was needed to heal his soul and his country.

Forgiveness is not always easy. In fact, for many of us, it requires divine intervention. But whether or not we choose to trust, we always need to forgive—both for our own sake and for the sake of others. In fact, until we forgive, we're really not free to exercise Smart Trust. We carry around emotional baggage that jades both our analysis and propensity to trust.

> *The weak can never forgive. Forgiveness is the attribute of the strong.*
>
> —MAHATMA GANDHI

Forgiveness is a principle of a better life. It's also part of our responsibility in righting wrongs. When we don't forgive, we violate this crucial behavior. Not only do we deprive ourselves of clear judgment, emotional freedom, and possible high-trust dividends, we may also get in the way of someone else's self-forgiveness and personal change.

Keep in mind that we garner strength to forgive those who have wronged us not by what *they* do, but by what *we* do. And we don't forgive to abdicate the "offender"; as Mandela modeled, we forgive to bring clarity and peace to ourselves.

> *He that cannot forgive others breaks the bridge over which he, too, must pass.*
>
> —LORD HERBERT, BRITISH PHILOSOPHER AND THEOLOGIAN

As global citizens, as part of the human race, and in our own best interests as well as the interests of others, we need to forgive. Then—in whatever direction we choose regarding trust—we are free to move ahead.

PRIORITIZE RESTORING TRUST

I have a close friend who shared this story:

Up to about age 14, our son was an "ideal" kid. He gladly participated in family activities, got good grades, had great friends—we thought we had it made. When he began to pull away a little, we assumed it was normal growing up and tried to roll with it. But when he began hanging out with a new set of friends and became more secretive about his activities, we knew we were in trouble.

So we decided to make our son our top priority. We spent more time with him. We cut back privileges, set family goals, talked to experts, and took him to experts. There were lectures, apologies, and promises made and broken. But the older he got, the more dangerous his choices became. We constantly felt frustrated and scared; but we determined to always make sure he knew that we were never going to give up on him and would never stop loving him—no matter what.

As things continued to go from bad to worse, we told him that we loved him too much to support him in the lifestyle he was choosing. He was welcome to live with us, but only on our terms. If he wanted to live differently, he'd have to live somewhere else.

So he moved out—and his lifestyle got even worse. As painful as it was, we tried to ignore it and to just keep living our values and reaffirm our love for him. We made sure he knew that he and his friends were always welcome in our home for a good Sunday dinner. We told them they would have to behave themselves while they were in our home, but they'd always be welcomed and loved and fed. Some Sundays, it was a pretty rough group that showed up, but no matter what they looked like, they always left full of food and love.

Gradually, our boy found himself. After working his way through some very difficult times, he had a complete change of heart and now has again that incredible spirit he had until he was 14. He told us that the one thread he hung on to over our five-year ordeal was that he knew we loved him and had his best interests at heart. He said he knew he could trust us—and now, thankfully, we know we can trust him, too.

Restoring trust in close relationships may be difficult and painful, and sometimes it may take years. But there are no higher dividends in life than those that come from prioritizing it and making it happen.

BROKEN TRUST: A BEGINNING

For many people, broken trust is a dead end. It's the end of a relationship, the end of an opportunity—sometimes even the end of self-confidence and the ability to ever trust again.

But it doesn't have to be. In fact, I contend that broken trust can actually become a significant beginning.

If you've broken trust with someone else, it's an opportunity to get your own act together, to improve your character and competence, to behave in ways that inspire trust. Hopefully this will influence the offended party to restore trust in you. But even if it doesn't, your effort may well affect others in positive ways, and it will definitely enable you to create more high-trust relationships in the future.

If someone has broken trust with you, it's an opportunity for you to grow in your ability to forgive, to learn how to extend Smart Trust, and to maximize whatever dividends are possible in the relationship.

In either situation, broken trust presents an opportunity for you to make huge leaps in building up your own self trust and personal credibility. As you go through the process of trying to restore trust you have lost with others, or forgiving and extending Smart Trust to those who have broken trust with you, you will grow in character and competence. You will gain confidence in your own discernment and ability to establish, grow, restore, and extend trust on every level of your life.

A PROPENSITY TO TRUST

I have found that by trusting people until they prove themselves unworthy of that trust, a lot more happens.
—JIM BURKE, FORMER CHAIRMAN AND CEO, JOHNSON & JOHNSON

Have you ever been in a situation where someone believed in you and trusted you when no one else did? How did it make you feel? What kind of difference did it make in your life?

I was in a situation like that shortly after I graduated from college. I was hired to work for Trammell Crow Company—at the time, the nation's largest real-estate developer and one of the original "100 Best Companies to Work For" in America. It was an unusual situation because typically a partner in a specific regional office would make the hire. However, in this case, I'd had a luncheon meeting with the managing partner of the company, and he had offered me a job as a leasing agent on the spot. He didn't know which office I'd work in, but was confident there would be a good fit somewhere.

I accepted the offer, and then visited some regional offices to interview with the partners there. But in office after office, none of the partners seemed very interested in me. While I had done well in school and had had some excellent work experience, I'd indicated on my résumé that my intent was to work for a couple of years and then go get my MBA. But the position I'd been hired to fill was the same position being offered to MBA graduates from the top schools. And they were being placed on a three-to-five-year fast-track path toward partnership. No one wanted to invest in training me only to have me work for two years and then leave. In addition, I had written on my résumé that my career objective was to go into management consulting and leadership development, which didn't impress these Trammell Crow partners, who were into real-estate development. So my résumé and career plans essentially created a huge disconnect with everyone. At the time, I was so naïve that I could barely see the problem, but I didn't feel that I could be untruthful about my intentions and simply say what people wanted to hear.

So for six weeks, I was in limbo, just working out of the corporate office but really doing nothing. After I had met with a dozen or so different partners, it became apparent that no one wanted to hire me, and I'm sure the managing director was wondering why he had. I was getting very discouraged. In fact, my confidence was at an all-time low.

Then I met with a new partner—John Walsh—who seemed excited to take a chance on me. He said, "I like this man. I believe in him. I want him on my team." He took me under his wing, and from the very first, he treated me exactly like he treated the MBAs and law school graduates he had also hired. I felt enormously grateful, motivated, and inspired. I did not want to let him down.

It was six months before I had any results. During that time, I often doubted myself. But John Walsh kept believing in me. Then, all of a sudden, things took off, and before my two years were up, I had become the top-producing leasing agent in the office and one of the top producers in the country.

John Walsh's faith in me paid off—not only for him in terms of company profits, but also for me in the way in which it shaped my leadership and my life. When I think of this man today, it is with great love and gratitude. Aside from my father, John Walsh has been the single biggest influence in my professional life (and also a profound influence in my personal life) because he believed in me and took a chance on me when no one else did. His extension of trust brought out the best in me.

> *I bring you the gift of these four words: I believe in you.*
>
> —BLAISE PASCAL, FRENCH PHYSICIST AND MATHEMATICIAN

INSPIRING TRUST

Somewhere along the way, most of us have had some kind of similar experience where someone believed in us and made an enormous difference in our lives. What's most exciting is the realization that *we can do the same for others!* We can believe in them. We can extend trust to them. We can help them rise to the challenge, discover their unseen potential, and make enormous contributions that benefit us all.

Just consider the difference made by people like Sam Walton, founder of Wal-Mart and Sam's Club. Dean Sanders, onetime executive vice president of operations, said that after Sam would go out on store visits, he would get back and call Dean and say, "Give this boy a store to manage. He's ready." When Dean would express concern about a particular person's level of experience, Sam would just say, "Give him one anyway. Let's see how he does."

> *Even an overdose of trust that, at times, involves the risk of being deceived or disappointed is wiser, in the long run, than taking for granted that most people are incompetent or insincere.*
>
> —WARREN BENNIS, AUTHOR OF *ON BECOMING A LEADER*

Consider the difference made by leaders of companies like Nordstrom, who trust their employees to use their good judgment, or Ritz-Carlton, where employees are financially authorized to resolve customer concerns, or BestBuy, where people can work wherever and whenever they like, as long as the job gets done.

Consider your own experience. How do you feel when someone tells you, "You can do this! You're credible. You have the character and competence to succeed. I believe in you; I trust you." Sometimes simply hearing those words creates all the inspiration needed for success.

Leaders who extend trust to us become our mentors, models, and heroes. We're overwhelmed with gratitude when we think about them and about the difference they have made in our lives. Companies that choose to extend trust to their employees become great places to work.

> *Our approach is based on the major findings of 20 years of research—that trust between managers and employees is the primary defining characteristic of the very best workplaces.*
>
> —GREAT PLACE TO WORK INSTITUTE

This same kind of leadership inspires trust at home. Just consider the difference it makes in the lives of children when parents tell them,

"I love you. I believe in you. I trust you," and help them develop character and competence by giving them meaningful stewardships—jobs with trust—to carry out. When people at our leadership programs share their feelings about the person who has impacted them most in their lives, it is most often a parent (or sometimes a teacher, a coach, or a mentor at work) who believed in them when no one else did.

As I've said before, the first job of a leader—at work or at home—is to inspire trust. It's to bring out the best in people by entrusting them with meaningful stewardships, and to create an environment in which high-trust interaction inspires creativity and possibility.

> It is better to trust and sometimes be disappointed than to be forever mistrusting and be right occasionally.
>
> —NEAL A. MAXWELL, EDUCATOR AND RELIGIOUS LEADER

MOST RESPOND WELL TO TRUST

Trust brings out the best in people and literally changes the dynamics of interaction. While it is true that a few abuse this trust, the vast, vast majority of people do not abuse it, but respond amazingly well to it. And when they do, they don't need external supervision, control, or the "carrot and stick" approach to motivation. They are inspired. They run with the trust they were extended. They want to live up to it. They want to give back.

Again, as Émile Durkheim has said, "When mores [cultural values] are sufficient, laws are unnecessary. When mores are insufficient, laws are unenforceable." I would amend that to say, "When *trust* is sufficient, laws are unnecessary. When trust is insufficient, laws are unenforceable." As my father has said, "Compelling trust is the highest form of human motivation."

No matter who we are, we have countless opportunities to extend and inspire trust in others. And in so doing, we make an amazing difference—not only in their individual lives, but also in the lives of all who are touched by what they do.

We also make a huge difference in our own lives. Trust is reciprocal—in other words, the more you trust others, the more you, yourself, are trusted in return. In the prework exercise where we give program participants picture cards of people they work with and ask them to sort them according to whether they trust them or not, we find that those who tend to not trust others are typically not trusted themselves. In the words of Lao Tzu, "No trust given, no trust received."

PROFOUND MOMENTS OF TRUST

The truth is that many meaningful events in business, history, literature, and life have hinged on profound moments of trust—on people who were willing to extend trust in amazing ways.

I think of a defining moment in the life of Alexander the Great, King of Macedon. King Darius III of Persia had offered 1,000 talents to anyone who would kill Alexander. Alexander had contracted pneumonia and was near death. The physicians were afraid to treat him because they thought he would not survive, and they were fearful that if he died they might be falsely accused of poisoning him and accepting Darius's bribe. But Philip, a friend and physician who had attended to Alexander since childhood, was willing to treat Alexander because he had confidence both in his treatment medicine and also in Alexander's friendship. As historian H. A. Guerber relates:

> *When the fever was at its worst, [Philip] said he hoped to save the king by means of a strong medicine which he was going to prepare.*
>
> *Just after Philip went out to brew this potion, Alexander received a letter which warned him to beware of his physician, as the man had been bribed by the Persian king, Darius III, to poison him.*
>
> *After reading the letter, Alexander slipped it under his pillow, and calmly waited for the return of his doctor. When Philip brought the cup containing the promised remedy, Alexander took it in one hand, and gave him the letter with the other. Then, while Philip was reading it, he drank every drop of the medicine.*
>
> *When the physician saw the accusation, he turned deadly pale, and looked up at his master, who smilingly handed back the empty cup. Alexander's great trust in his doctor was fully justified; for the medicine cured him, and he was soon able to go on. . . .*

I think of the Catholic bishop in Victor Hugo's epic *Les Misérables*, who not only forgave the thief Jean Valjean but affirmed his worth and extended trust to him, forever altering his life.

I think of the teacher Anne Sullivan, extending trust and confidence, with remarkable results, to a pupil who couldn't see, hear, or speak—Helen Keller.

I think of the entrepreneur Pierre Omidyar, founding a company on the basic premise that most people are good and can be trusted.

I think of a coach believing in the potential of an athlete.

I think of a friend staying true to someone in a difficult hour.

I think of a young child trusting a parent.

I *remember* a father extending trust to a seven-year-old boy.

CHOOSING TO TRUST

> Better trust all and be deceived,
> And weep that trust, and that deceiving,
> Than doubt one heart that, if believed
> Had blessed one's life with true believing.
>
> —FRANCES ANNE KEMBLE, BRITISH WRITER

We were born with a propensity to trust. As children, most of us were naïve, innocent, vulnerable, and gullible. Through life experience, many of us have become less trusting—sometimes with good reason.

But, whatever our situation, the reality is that we can choose to retain or restore our propensity to trust. The key is in our ability to forgive, and also in our ability to balance our propensity to trust with analysis, giving us the judgment to extend the Smart Trust that maximizes the dividends and minimizes the risk.

In my own life, I've been on both sides of the equation. I've been in situations where I was micromanaged, where trust was not extended. I know the powerful negative effect that had on my own feelings of engagement, commitment, excitement, and creativity, and on the release of my energy and talent. But I've also been in situations where trust was extended abundantly, and I know how that trust dramatically inspired and powerfully released the best inside me.

Occasionally I've been burned. I've trusted people who didn't come though. But for the most part, I've seen the incredible results when people have come through. I've seen them rise up to meet the expectation. I've seen them energized, excited, and engaged. I've seen them willingly give their hearts and minds as well as their hands and backs in doing their work. I've seen them overcome differences, transcend difficulties, and accomplish great things—*fast*—because someone had the wisdom to extend trust.

> *It is . . . happier to be sometimes cheated than not to trust.*
>
> SAMUEL SMILES, BRITISH AUTHOR AND BIOGRAPHER

There's no getting around the fact that in today's "flat," global economy, trust is essential to prosperity. In our personal and family relationships, trust is essential to satisfaction and joy.

And the truth is that we can establish it. We can grow it. We can extend it. We can restore it. We can become personally and organizationally credible. We can behave in ways that inspire trust. We can increase speed and lower cost in every dimension of our lives.

So why would we not want to do it? Why would we not want to live and lead in ways that inspire trust?

Perhaps Albert Schweitzer said it best:

In everybody's life, at some time, our inner fire goes out. It is then burst into flame by an encounter with another human being. We should all be thankful for those people who rekindle the inner spirit.

Extending trust to others rekindles the inner spirit—both theirs and ours. It touches and enlightens the innate propensity we all have to trust, and to be trusted. It brings happiness to relationships, results to work, and confidence to lives. Above all, it produces an extraordinary dividend in every dimension of our lives: the speed of trust.

ABOUT STEPHEN M. R. COVEY
& COVEYLINK WORLDWIDE

Stephen M. R. Covey is cofounder and CEO of CoveyLink Worldwide. A sought-after and compelling keynote speaker and advisor on trust, leadership, ethics, and high performance, he speaks to audiences around the world. He advocates that nothing is as fast as the speed of trust and that the ability to establish, grow, extend, and restore trust with all stakeholders is *the* critical leadership competency of the new global economy. He passionately delivers that message and is dedicated to enabling individuals and organizations to reap the dividends of high trust. Audiences and organizations alike resonate with his informed, practitioner approach to real-time issues that affect their immediate and long-term performance.

He is the former CEO of Covey Leadership Center, which, under his stewardship, became the largest leadership development company in the world. A Harvard MBA, he joined Covey Leadership Center as a client developer and later became national sales manager and then president and CEO.

Under Covey's direction, the company grew rapidly and profitably, achieving Inc. 500 status and recognition. As president and CEO, he nearly doubled revenues to over $110 million while increasing profits by 12 times. During that period, both customer and employee trust reached new highs and the company expanded throughout the world into over 40 countries. This greatly increased the value of the brand and company, which was valued at only $2.4 million when Covey was named CEO. Within three years, he grew shareholder value to $160 million in a merger he orchestrated with then Franklin Quest to form FranklinCovey.

Over the years, Covey has gained considerable respect and influence with executives and leaders of Fortune 500 companies, as well as with mid- and small-size private-sector and public-sector organizations he's consulted. Clients recognize his unique perspective on real-world organizational issues based on his practical experience as a CEO.

Covey currently serves on the board/advisory board of several entities, including the Human Performance Institute—the leader in energy management technology—where he serves as advisory board chairman.

Covey resides with his wife and children in the shadows of the Rocky Mountains.

Rebecca R. Merrill is a highly sought-after writer. In addition to her primary focus on home and family over the years, she is coauthor with Dr. Stephen R. Covey and Roger Merrill of the *New York Times* bestseller *First Things First*. She is coauthor with Roger Merrill of *Life Matters* and *Connections*. She also provided assistance to Dr. Covey on *The 7 Habits of Highly Effective People* and *The 7 Habits of Highly Effective Families*.

CoveyLink Worldwide is a boutique trust practice focused on measurably increasing the performance and influence of people and organizations worldwide by enabling them to lead in a way that inspires trust (thus increasing speed and lowering cost).

CoveyLink was cofounded by Stephen M. R. Covey and Greg Link, who together led the strategy that propelled Dr. Stephen R. Covey's *The 7 Habits of Highly Effective People* to one of the two most influential business books of the twentieth century, according to *CEO* magazine. Through their own direct experience as executive business leaders and advisors, and with over a decade of extensive research, they have become passionately convinced that trust is the root of all leadership influence and that the resulting speed is the ultimate competitive advantage in this "flat world" economy.

CoveyLink takes a very pragmatic approach to leadership and trust by focusing on practical, actionable skills and behaviors. They create high-trust, high-performance organizations by creating trusted, high-performance influencers—who in turn influence others. This ripple effect evidences itself in a measurable, sustainable model of organizational growth and momentum.

Enhancing your ability to establish, grow, extend, and restore trust with all stakeholders will significantly increase the opportunities and influence you have, whether as a leader, worker, business partner, customer, spouse, parent, or any of the myriad roles you play in life. Covey-Link provides various ways to access additional resources for both individuals and organizations to increase trust, including: open-enrollment *Leading at the Speed of Trust* workshops, on-site programs, train the trainer certification, webinars, individual and organizational assessments and measurement, application tools, advisory services, and custom consulting. Visit www.CoveyLink.com to learn more.

To find out who trusts you, go to www.WhoTrustsYou.com.

To find out if you qualify for a free 20-minute one-on-one discussion of your organization's specific situation by a senior CoveyLink consultant, go to: www. speedoftrust.com.

NOTES AND REFERENCES

NOTHING IS AS FAST AS THE SPEED OF TRUST

P. 3 **Edward Marshall quote:** Edward M. Marshall, *Building Trust at the Speed of Change* (NewYork: AMACOM, 2000), p. 3.

P. 4 **Naill Fitzgerald quote:** Naill Fitzgerald, *Address to the Advertising Association*, London, May 2001.

P. 5 **words of Jack Welch:** Jack Welch, *Winning* (New York: HarperCollins, 2005), p. 71.

P. 6 **Jim Burke quote:** Mukul Pandya and Robbie Shell, *Lasting Leadership: What You Can Learn from the Top 25 Business People of Our Times* (Upper Saddle River, NJ: Wharton School Publishing, 2005), pp. 45–46.

P. 11 **a 2005 Harris poll:** Harris Interactive, The Harris Poll #4, January 13, 2005.

P. 11 **British sociologist David Halpern:** David Halpern, "Trust in business and trust between citizens," Prime Minister's Strategy Unit, April 13, 2005; also, John Elliott and Lauren Quaintance, "Britain is getting less trusting," *The Sunday Times*, May 18, 2003; also David Halpern, *Social Capital* (Malden, MA: Polity Press, 2005).

P. 11 **only 51% of employees:** Watson Wyatt survey, "Work USA 2004/2005."

P. 11 **only 36% of employees:** Age Wave and The Concours Group, *New Employer/Employee Equation Survey*, New York, 2005 (conducted by Harris Interactive).

P. 11 **76% of employees:** KPMG, "Organizational Integrity Survey," 2000.

P. 12 **number one reason:** Gina Imperato, "How to Hire the Next Michael Jordan," *Fast Company*, December 1998, p. 212; also Marcus Buckingham and Curtis Coffman, *First, Break All the Rules: What the World's Greatest Managers Do Different* (New York: Simon & Schuster, 1999), p. 33.

P. 12 **one out of every two:** *Divorce* magazine and U.S. Census Bureau data.

P. 12 **Consider the percentage:** Donald McCabe survey, Rutgers University, 1992; also, Marianne M. Jennings, "Ethics: Why It Matters and How You Do It," *Journal of Government Financial Management*, Supplement Fall 2005.

P. 12 **76% of MBAs:** Marianne M. Jennings, *A Business Tale: A Story of Ethics, Choices, Success and a Very Large Rabbit* (New York: AMACOM, 2003), p. 87; also, Dawn Blalock, "Study Shows Many Execs Are Quick to Write Off Ethics," *Wall Street Journal*, March 26, 1996, C1, C22.

P. 12 **ethical dilemma exams:** Marc Ransford, "Convicts and MBA grads have similar ethics," Ball State University, 1999.

P. 13 **Robert Eckert quote:** Robert Eckert, commencement address to UCLA Anderson School of Management, June 18, 2004.

P. 14 **at $35 billion:** Candice S. Miller, "The Sarbanes-Oxley Act 4 Years Later: What Have We Learned," House Subcommittee on Regulatory Affairs, April 5, 2006 (from a memorandum submitted March 29, 2006).

P. 15　**Warren Buffett wrote:** Warren Buffett management letter, Berkshire-Hathaway Annual Report, 2004.

P. 15　**Rupert Murdoch quote:** "Business innovation: changing companies for a changing world,"*Principal Voices.* The Global CEO Study, "Expanding the Innovation Horizon," IBM, 2006

P. 15　*Executive EQ,* **the authors:** Robert K. Cooper and Ayman Sawaf, *Executive EQ: Emotional Intelligence in Leadership and Organizations* (New York: Berkley Publishing Group, 1996), p. 88.

P. 16　**Patricia Aburdene quote:** Patricia Aburdene, *Megatrends 2010: The Rise of Conscious Capitalism* (Charlottesville, VA: Hampton Roads Publishing Company, 2005), p. xiv.

P. 18　**John Whitney quote:** John Whitney, *The Trust Factor: Liberating Profits and Restoring Corporate Vitality* (New York: McGraw-Hill, 1994), front flap.

P. 19　**author Francis Fukuyama:** Francis Fukuyama, *Trust: The Social Virtues and the Creation of Prosperity* (New York: The Free Press, 1995), pp. 27–28.

P. 20　**Robert Shaw, has said:** Robert Bruce Shaw, *Trust in the Balance: Building Successful Organizations on Results, Integrity and Concern* (San Francisco: Jossey-Bass Publishers, 1997), p. xi.

P. 21　**as much as 40%:** Leslie P. Willcocks and Sara Cullen, "The Outsourcing Enterprise: The power of relationships," study by LogicaCMG and Warwick Business School, 2005.

P. 21　**A 2002 study:** Watson Wyatt, WorkUSA study, 2002.

P. 21　**study by Stanford professor:** Tony Bryk speech, "Trust Improves Schools," Stanford Educational Leadership Conference, November 5, 2004; also, Anthony S. Bryk and Barbara Schneider, *Trust in Schools: A Core Resource for Improvement* (New York: Russell Sage Foundation Publications, 2002).

P. 21　**Thomas Friedman quote:** Thomas L. Friedman, *The World Is Flat: A Brief History of the Twenty-First Century* (New York: Farrar, Straus and Giroux, 2005), p. 394.

YOU CAN DO SOMETHING ABOUT THIS!

P. 31　**Jack Welch:** Robert Slater, *Jack Welch and the GE Way* (New York: McGraw-Hill, 1999), pp. 37–38.

P. 31　**Jim Collins:** Jim Collins, *Good to Great: Why Some Companies Make the Leap . . . and Others Don't* (New York: HarperBusiness, 2001), p. 21. Also, Jim Collins and Jerry Porras, *Built to Last: Successful Habits of Visionary Companies* (New York: HarperBusiness, 1994), p. 80.

P. 31　**Warren Buffett:** Richard G. Hagstrom, *The Warren Buffett Way: Investment Strategies of the World's Greatest Investor* (New York: John Wiley, 2004), p. 102.

P. 31　**Ram Charan:** Ram Charan, *What the CEO Wants You to Know* (New York: Crown Business, 2001), p. 94.

P. 31　**Saj-Nicole Joni:** Saj-Nicole Joni, "The Geography of Trust," *Harvard Business Review,* March 2004.

P. 37　**Rich Jernstedt quote:** Golin/Harris press release, "Trajectory of Trust in American Business Shows Signs of Improvement If Brands Act Decisively," AME Info, April 27, 2003.

P. 37　**John Adams and Thomas Jefferson:** David McCullough, *John Adams* (New York: Simon & Schuster, 2001), pp. 312, 603, 604, 632, 640.

P. 40　**"Life to me is":** Margot Morrell, *Shackleton's Way: Leadership Lessons from the Greatest Antarctic Explorer* (New York: Penguin, 2001), p. 209.

P. 40　**Jim Burke quote:** Adrian Gostick and Dana Telford, *The Integrity Advantage: How Taking the High Road Creates a Competitive Advantage in Business* (Salt Lake City: Gibbs Smith, Publisher, 2003), p. 9.

THE 4 CORES OF CREDIBILITY

P. 43   **Anne Mulcahy quote:** PriceWaterhouseCoopers, *6th Annual Global CEO Survey: Leadership, Responsibility, and Growth in Uncertain Times, 2003.*

P. 44   **USA Today headline:** Greg Farrell, "Skilling set to testify today on own behalf: Verdict could hinge solely on his credibility on stand," *USA Today,* April 6, 2006, p. 1B.

P. 44   **the new headline read:** Greg Farrell, "Jurors: Ex-Enron execs not credible: Prosecution's witnesses backed each other up," *USA Today,* May 26, 2006, p. 1B.

P. 44   **"Given his track record":** Jesse Eisinger, "Buffett's Reputation May Be Tested," *Wall Street Journal,* March 31, 2005, p. 1C.

P. 44   **"Here's somebody who is":** Del Jones, "Buffett maintains respect of fellow CEOs," *USA Today,* March 30, 2005, p. 2B.

P. 44   **Jon Huntsman quote:** Jon M. Huntsman, *Winners Never Cheat: Everyday Values We Learned as Children (But May Have Forgotten)* (Upper Saddle River, NJ: Wharton School Publishing), p. 37.

P. 45   **only 8 percent actually keep them:** Ellen Tomson, "Skip the resolutions and make a commitment," Knight Ridder Newspapers, January 14, 2006.

P. 47   **story of Wally Thiim:** Greg Link interview with Wally Thiim, April 17, 2006.

P. 47   **Peter Drucker quote:** Peter Drucker, *Managing the Non-Profit Organization: Principles and Practices* (New York: HarperCollins, 1990), p. 9.

P. 48   **study by a leading:** "Updating the Meaning of Leadership," AchieveGlobal study, 1998.

P. 49   **Harvard Business School:** Harvard Business School, MBA Applicant Letter of Recommendation.

P. 49   **Gerard Arpey quote:** Eve Tahmincioglu, "Back from the Brink," *Workforce Management,* December 2004.

P 55   **Jon Huntsman quote:** Huntsman, *Winners Never Cheat,* p. 44.

P. 55   **Victor Fung quote:** PriceWaterhouseCoopers, *6th Annual Global CEO Survey: Leadership, Responsibility, and Growth in Uncertain Times, 2003.*

CORE 1—INTEGRITY: ARE YOU CONGRUENT?

P. 59   **Italia Masters Tournament:** Frank Deford, "Game, Set, Ma—: In losing a match, Roddick became a true sportsman," Sports Illustrated.com, May 11, 2005.

P. 60   **Hank Paulson quote:** Gostick and Telford, *The Integrity Advantage,* p. 73.

P. 61   **Patricia Aburdene quote:** Aburdene, *Megatrends 2010,* p. xiv.

P. 61   **As Chris Bauer:** Patrick J. Kiger, "Steal Big, Steal Little," Workforce Management Online, December 2005.

P. 63   **Desai responded:** Eknath Easwaran, *Gandhi the Man* (Petaluma, CA: Nilgiri Press, 1978), p. 112.

P. 63   **"All the good-to-great":** Collins, *Good to Great,* p. 22.

P. 64   **Jim Collins quote:** Ibid., pp. 12–13.

P. 68   **George Fischer quote:** Douglas Barry, *Wisdom for a Young CEO: Incredible Letters and Inspiring Advice from Today's Business Leaders* (Philadelphia: Running Press, 2004), p. 145 (this and other quotes are found in this excellent book of advice from CEOs).

P. 69   **A great example of integrity:** Huntsman, *Winners Never Cheat,* pp. 81–83.

P. 70   **Anne Mulcahy quote:** Douglas Barry, *Wisdom for a Young CEO,* p. 137.

P. 71   **Consider Anwar Sadat:** Anwar el-Sadat, *In Search of Identity: An Autobiography* (New York: HarperCollins, 1978).

P. 72   **Patricia Aburdene quote:** Aburdene, *Megatrends 2010,* p. xiv.

CORE 2—INTENT: WHAT'S YOUR AGENDA?

P. 76   **The World Economic Forum:** World Economic Forum trust survey, "Trust in Governments, Corporations and Global Institutions Continues to Decline," December 15, 2005.

P. 76   **surveys comparing trust levels:** MORI Social Research Institute, *Exploring Trust in Public Institutions, Report for the Audit Commission,* 2002.

P. 77   **a translator for CNN:** Canadian Broadcasting Association, "CNN in trouble with Iran over mistranslation," *CBC.CA Arts,* January 17, 2006.

P. 79   **Dennis LeStrange quote:** Bill Catlette and Richard Hadden, *Contented Cows Give Better Milk: The Plain Truth About Employee Relations and Your Bottom Line* (Germantown, TN: Saltillo Press, 2001), p. 108.

P. 80   **Jimmy Johnson quote:** Ibid., p. 88.

P. 80   **Jim Meehan quote:** Jim Meehan, *Reasons Have Hearts Too: Thoughts and Feelings Are Inseparable* (Allen, TX: Thomas More Publishing, 2000), p. 70.

P. 81   **Experience of Shea Homes:** Author interview with Buddy Satterfield, May 1, 2006.

P. 82   **Herb Kelleher quote:** Catlette and Hadden, *Contented Cows,* p. 87.

P. 82   **In 1997, three:** Andy Serwer, "Hot Starbucks to Go," *Fortune,* January 26, 2004; also, see the dedication page of Howard Schultz and Dori Jones Yang, *Pour Your Heart into It: How Starbucks Built a Company One Cup at a Time* (New York: Hyperion, 1997).

P. 82   **Only 29% of:** Age Wave and The Concours Group, *New Employer/Employee Equation Survey,* New York, 2005 (conducted by Harris Interactive).

P. 82   **Only 42% believe:** Towers Perrin HR Services, *The 2003 Towers Perrin Talent Report—WorkingToday: Understanding What Drives Employee Engagement,* 2003.

P. 83   **Sam Walton quote:** Charles Garfield, *Second to None: How Our Smartest Companies Put People First* (New York: Avon, 1992), p. 201.

P. 87   **Doug Conant, CEO:** Author interview with Doug Conant, April 21, 2006.

P. 88   **economist Paul Zane Pilzer:** Paul Zane Pilzer, *Unlimited Wealth: The Theory and Practice of Economic Alchemy* (New York: Crown, 1991).

P. 89   **on the Forbes 400:** "The 400 Richest Americans," *Forbes,* September 22, 2005.

P. 89   **Our whole goal:** Huntsman, *Winners Never Cheat,* p. 160.

P. 89   **Entrepreneur Ted Turner:** "Ted Turner donates $1 billion to 'U.N. causes,'" CNN.com, September 19, 1997.

P. 90   **I don't think of myself:** Marcia Nelson, *The Gospel According to Oprah* (Louisville, KY: Westminter, John Knox Press, 2005), p. x.

P. 90   **Laura Schlessinger quote:** Laura Schlessinger, *Bad Childhood—Good Life: How to Blossom and Thrive in Spite of an Unhappy Childhood* (New York: Harper-Collins, 2006), p. 15

CORE 3—CAPABILITIES: ARE YOU RELEVANT?

P. 92   **the Peter Principle:** Laurence J. Peter and Raymond Hull, *The Peter Principle* (New York: Bantam Books, 1970), p. 7.

P. 95   **parable of the talents:** Matthew 25, the Bible.

P. 96   **I was blessed:** Eugene O'Kelly, *Chasing Daylight: How My Forthcoming Death Transformed My Life* (New York: McGraw-Hill, 2006), pp. 1–2.

P. 97   **Steve Jobs has said:** Guy Kawasaki, *The Art of the Start* (New York: Portfolio, 2004), p. 101.

P. 98   **"You can have":** Dan Goodgame, "The Game of Risk: How the Best Golfer in the World Got Even Better," *Time,* August 14, 2000.

P. 98 **"I'd like to play":** Jaime Diaz, "The Truth About Tiger: Why the Most Dominant Player in History Decided He Had to Change His Swing," *Golf Digest*, January 2005.

P. 98 **"What is most remarkable":** Goodgame, "The Game of Risk."

P. 98 **"curse of competence":** Jim Collins interview with Fast Company Real Times, Phoenix, October 2000.

P. 99 **Anne Mulcahy quote:** Barry, *Wisdom for a Young CEO*, p. 114.

P. 99 **information now doubles:** James Gelatt, "Scanning for Megatrends in the Nonprofit World," *Contributions Magazine*, September/October 2000.

P. 99 **told by Marion D. Hanks:** Marion D. Hanks, "Good Teachers Matter," *Ensign*, July 1971.

P. 101 **Every few months:** Pamela Kruger and Katharine Mieszkowski, "Stop the Fight," *Fast Company*, September 1998, p. 93.

P. 101 **[John Mackey] doesn't:** Charles Fishman, "The Anarchist's Cookbook," *Fast Company*, July 2004, p. 70.

P. 101 **called Chainsaw Al:** David Plotz, "Al Dunlap: The chainsaw capitalist," *Slate*, August 31, 1997; also Albert J. Dunlap with Bob Andelman, *Mean Business: How I Save Bad Companies and Make Good Companies Great* (New York: Fireside, 1997), p. 125.

P. 102 **the Gallup organization:** Marcus Buckingham and Donald O. Clifton, *Now Discover Your Strengths*. (New York: The Free Press, 2001), p. 6.

P. 102 **Jim Collins talks:** Collins, *Good to Great*, p. 13.

P. 103 **General Eric Shinseki quote:** Tom Peters, *Re-imagine!: Business Excellence in a Disruptive Age* (London: Dorling Kindersley Ltd., 2003), p. 3.

P. 103 **According to a 2003 article:** Andrew Park, "What You Don't Know About Dell," *BusinessWeek*, November 3, 2003.

P. 104 **by *Fortune* magazine:** "America's Most Admired Companies," *Fortune*, March 7, 2005.

P. 106 **Harvey Golub quote:** Barry, *Wisdom for a Young CEO*, p. 121.

P. 106 **at the end of the day:** Author interview with Jack Trout, December 2, 2005.

P. 107 **Christopher Galvin quote:** Barry, *Wisdom for a Young CEO*, p. 67.

CORE 4—RESULTS: WHAT'S YOUR TRACK RECORD?

P. 109 **Craig Weatherup quote:** Shaw, *Trust in the Balance*, p. 73.

P. 111 **Jack Welch quote:** Welch, *Winning*, pp. 20–21.

P. 113 **"We thought that":** Jill Rosenfeld, "Here's an Idea!" *Fast Company*, April 2000, p. 97.

P. 113 **Reputation Quotient survey:** Ronald Alsop, "Ranking Corporate Reputations," *Wall Street Journal*, December 6, 2005.

P. 113 **Continental significantly improved:** Continental Airlines, Annual Reports, 2002–5.

P. 117 **David Sokol, CEO:** Susan Pulliam and Karen Richardson, "Warren Buffett, Unplugged," *Wall Street Journal*, November 12, 2005.

P. 119 **Walkman was born:** "From a Small Piece of Wood," Sony History, sony.net.

P. 119 **following standard operating:** Tom Peters, *Thriving on Chaos: Handbook for a Management Revolution* (New York: Knopf, 1987), p. 307.

P. 120 **"Johnson outlined his company's":** Tamara Kaplan, "The Tylenol Crisis: How Effective Public Relations Saved Johnson & Johnson," Pennsylvania State University, 1998.

P. 122 **study by Dr. Robert Rosenthal:** Wikipedia.org.

p. 122   **Rosabeth Moss Kanter has observed:** Rosabeth Moss Kanter, *Confidence* (New York: Crown Business, 2004), pp. 7, 29.

THE 13 BEHAVIORS

P. 128   **sang (somewhat disparagingly) to "Freddy":** Alan Jay Lerner, *My Fair Lady*, Sony, 1964.

P. 129   **Hank Paulson quote:** Gostick and Telford, *The Integrity Advantage*, p. 94.

P. 130   **I love the story:** Credited to Dr. George Crane, source unknown.

BEHAVIOR #1: TALK STRAIGHT

P. 137   **Dell Inc.'s Code:** Dell.com.

P. 137   **For example, he writes:** Warren Buffett, Berkshire Hathaway Annual Reports, 2004, 2005.

P. 139   **only 40 percent:** Mercer Human Resource Consulting, *2005 What's Working Survey*, New York, 2005.

P. 139   **"The Emperor's New Clothes":** Mette Norgaard, *The Ugly Duckling Goes to Work: Wisdom for the Workplace from the Classic Tales of Hans Christian Andersen* (New York: AMACOM, 2004), p. 21.

BEHAVIOR #2: DEMONSTRATE RESPECT

P. 144   **"There's a common thread":** James Blanchard speech at the Beta Gamma Sigma International Honoree Luncheon, April 22, 2005, as reported by the Beta Gamma Sigma International Society and available at betagammasigma.org.

P. 145   **the "Waiter Rule":** Del Jones, "CEOs vouch for Waiter Rule: Watch How People Treat Staff," *USA Today*, April 14, 2006, p. 1B.

P. 146   **came to the last question:** Adapted from *The Motivational Manager.*

P. 146   **three pillars of trust:** Great Place to Work Institute, Inc., greatplacetowork.com.

P. 146   **Sirota Survey Intelligence:** News in Brief, "The Longer Employees Work at a Company, the Less Happy They Are, Study Finds," Workforce Management.com, February 10, 2005; also, David Sirota, Louis A. Mischkind, and Michael Irwin Meltzer, *The Enthusiastic Employee: How Companies Profit by Giving Workers What They Want* (Upper Saddle River, NJ: Wharton School Publishing, 2005).

P. 149   **only 29 percent:** Age Wave and The Concours Group, *New Employer/Employee Equation Survey*, 2005.

P. 149   **only 42 percent:** Towers Perrin, *The 2003 Towers Perrin Talent Report.*

P. 149   **was Tom Peek:** Greg Link interview with Tom Peek, March 11, 2006.

BEHAVIOR #3: CREATE TRANSPARENCY

P. 152   **negotiating $1.8 billion:** Eve Tahmincioglu, "Back from the Brink," *Workforce Management*, December 2004.

P. 152   **According to *BusinessWeek*:** Wendy Zellner, "What Was Don Carty Thinking?," *BusinessWeek* online, April 24, 2003.

P. 153   **"Some people think":** Richard Wachman, "The man who keeps American in the air," *The Observer*, January 29, 2006.

P. 153   **Jean-Cyril Spinetta quote:** Sally Bibb and Jeremy Kourdi, *Trust Matters: For Organisational and Personal Success* (New York: Palgrave Macmillan, 2004), p. 29.

P. 153   **"The only way to build":** Tahmincioglu, *Workforce Management.*

P. 154   **PriceWaterhouseCoopers:** Samuel A. DiPiazza Jr. and Robert G. Eccles, *Building Public Trust: The Future of Corporate Reporting* (New York: John Wiley & Sons, 2002), p. 3.

P. 155 **process knowledge is expected:** Phillip Evans and Bob Wolf, "How Toyota and Linux Keep Collaboration Simple," *Harvard Business School Working Knowledge*, August 1, 2005.

P. 155 **Rollin King quote:** Catlette and Hadden, *Contented Cows Give Better Milk*, p. 99.

BEHAVIOR #4: RIGHT WRONGS

P. 160 **James Frey's book:** Carol Memmott, "Winfrey grills 'Pieces' author, apologizes for backing book," *USA Today*, January 27, 2006, p. 1E.

P. 160 **"Chrysler let executives":** Gostick and Telford, *The Integrity Advantage*, p. 37.

P. 161 **In his letter, Wead said:** Greg Link interview with Doug Wead, June 27, 2006 (letter used with Mead's approval); also see Doug Wead, "I'm Sorry, Mr. President," *USA Today*, March 14, 2005, p. 18A.

P. 162 **Jon Huntsman quote:** Huntsman, *Winners Never Cheat*, p. 55.

P. 162 **wide receiver Terrell Owens:** Bob Brookover, "Owens apologizes, but Eagles won't let him come back," *Daily Herald*, November 9, 2005, p. 1C.

P. 163 **get sued less:** Berkeley Rice, "Why Some Doctors Get Sued More Than Others," *Medical Economics*, July 11, 2003. Also, Lindsey Tanner, "Doctors Advised: An Apology a Day Keeps the Lawyer Away," Associated Press, November 12, 2004.

BEHAVIOR #5: SHOW LOYALTY

P. 166 **"It's all very logical":** John Marchica, *The Accountable Organization: Reclaiming Integrity, Restoring Trust* (Palo Alto: Davies-Black Publishing, 2004), p. 167.

P. 166 **"the window and the mirror":** Collins, *Good to Great*, pp. 33–35.

P. 167 **Jack Welch quote:** Welch, *Winning*, p. 71.

P. 167 **author Dottie Gandy:** Dottie Gandy, *30 Days to a Happy Employee: How a Simple Program of Acknowledgment Can Build Trust and Loyalty at Work* (New York: Fireside, 2001), p. 27.

P. 169 **article in *USA Today:*** Richard Willing, "Friends say Alito 'down to earth' despite success," *USA Today*, November 2, 2005, p. 5A.

BEHAVIOR #6: DELIVER RESULTS

P. 172 **Dave Ulrich quote:** Frances Hesselbein, Marshall Goldsmith, and Richard Beckhard, eds., *The Leader of the Future: New Visions, Strategies and Practices for the Next Era* (San Francisco: Jossey-Bass, 1996), pp. 212–13.

P. 174 **Jack Welch quote:** Welch, *Winning*, p. 323.

P. 174 **Peter Lowe quote:** James Watson, "Building the trust in today's industry," *Computing*, October 7, 2004.

P. 175 **"My perspective on trying":** Ibid.

P. 175 **J. P. Rangaswami quote:** Ibid.

BEHAVIOR #7: GET BETTER

P. 179 **as fast, constant learners:** Mukul Pandya and Robbie Shell, *Lasting Leadership: What You Can Learn from the Top 25 Business People of Our Times* (Upper Saddle River, NJ: Wharton School Publishing, 2005), p. xx.

P. 180 **As *Fast Company:*** Ian Wylie, "Calling for a Renewable Future," *Fast Company*, May 2003, p. 46.

P. 180 **Jeffrey Imelt quote:** Erick Schonfeld, "GE sees the light by learning to manage innovation: Jeffrey Immelt is remaking America's flagship industrial corporation into a technology and marketing powerhouse," *Business 2.0*, July 1, 2004.

P. 182   **A promising junior executive:** Warren Bennis and Burt Nanus, *Leaders: Strategies for Taking Charge* (New York: HarperCollins, 1985), p. 70.

BEHAVIOR #8: CONFRONT REALITY

P. 185   **Max DePree quote:** Max DePree, *Leadership Is an Art* (New York: Bantam Doubleday, 1989), p. 11.

P. 185   **author Kathleen Ryan:** Kathleen D. Ryan and Daniel K. Oestreich, *Driving Fear out of the Workplace: How to Overcome the Invisible Barriers to Quality, Productivity and Innovation* (San Francisco: Jossey-Bass Publishers, 1991), pp. 77–90.

P. 186   **"You must never confuse":** Collins, *Good to Great*, p. 85.

P. 186   **"the Stockdale Paradox":** Collins, *Good to Great*, p. 86.

P. 186   **in *Fortune* magazine:** Betsy Morris, "The Accidental CEO," *Fortune*, June 23, 2003.

P. 186   **"Whatever you think":** Ibid.

P. 187   **stock dropped 26 percent:** Ibid.

P. 188   **John Case suggests:** John Case, *Open-Book Management: The Coming Business Revolution* (New York: HarperBusiness, 1995), pp. 175–180.

P. 188   **"If folks are not truly":** Melanie Trottman, "Airline CEO's Novel Strategy: No Bankruptcy," *Wall Street Journal*, April 17, 2006, B1.

P. 188   **Jon Huntsman quote:** Huntsman, *Winners Never Cheat*, p. 62.

P. 189   **only 39 percent:** Mercer Human Resource Consulting, *2005 What's Working Survey*, New York, 2005.

P. 189   **"In confronting the brutal facts":** Collins, *Good to Great*, p. 81.

BEHAVIOR #9: CLARIFY EXPECTATIONS

P. 194   **by 20 to 40 percent:** LogicaCMG and Warwick Business School outsourcing study.

P. 195   **Dan Jorndt quote:** Collins, *Good to Great*, p. 32.

P. 196   **study by the AMA/HRI:** American Management Association/Human Resource Institute, *AMA/HRI Business Ethics Survey 2005*, New York, 2006.

BEHAVIOR #10: PRACTICE ACCOUNTABILITY

P. 200   **2002 Golin/Harris:** Golin/Harris survey, "Trust in American Business," 2002.

P. 200   **"culture of accountability":** DiPiazza and Eccles, *Building Public Trust*, p. 4.

P. 201   **window and the mirror:** Collins, *Good to Great*, pp. 33–35.

P. 202   **"For my entire career":** Scott Waddle with Ken Abraham, *The Right Thing* (Brentwood, TN: Integrity Publishers, 2002), pp. 200–201.

P. 202   **headline in *USA Today*:** Andrea Stone, "Ex-FEMA chief blames locals," *USA Today*, September 28, 2005, p. A1.

P. 203   **CNN.com's headline:** Ted Barrett, "Brown puts blame on Louisiana officials," CNN.com, September 28, 2005.

P. 204   **J. Willard Marriott quote:** J. Willard Marriott, "Money, Talent and the Devil by the Tail," *Management Review*, January 1985.

P. 205   **Mulcahy reported in *Fortune*:** Betsy Morris, "The Accidental CEO," *Fortune*, June 23, 2003.

BEHAVIOR #11: LISTEN FIRST

P. 210   **Peter Drucker lists eight:** Peter Drucker, "What Makes an Effective Executive," *Harvard Business Review*, June 2004.

P. 210   **Charles Cawley quote:** Barry, *Wisdom for a Young CEO*, p. 52.

P. 210   **Mike Garrett became:** Author interviews with Mike Garrett, December 12, 2003, and May 1, 2006.

P. 211   **Jack M. Greenberg quote:** Barry, *Wisdom for a Young*, p. 56.

P. 212   **Gary Chapman quote:** Gary Chapman, *The Five Love Languages: How to Express Heartfelt Commitment to Your Mate* (Chicago: Northfield Publishing, 1992), p. 15.

P. 212   **As Heinrich Pierer:** Barry, *Wisdom for a Young CEO*, p. 76 (miniature edition).

P. 212   **55 percent body language:** Albert Mehrabian, *Silent Messages: Implicit Communication of Emotions and Attitudes* (Belmont, CA: Wadsworth, 1981); also, Wikipedia.org.

BEHAVIOR #12: KEEP COMMITMENTS

P. 215   **Reuben Mark quote:** Barry, *Wisdom for a Young CEO*, p. 158.

P. 216   **Hank Paulson quote:** Gostick and Telford, *The Integrity Advantage*, p. 95.

P. 216   **Dennis Ross quote:** Michael Benoliel with Linda Cashdan, *Done Deal: Insights from Interviews with the World's Best Negotiators* (Avon, MA: Platinum Press, 2005), p. 112.

P. 217   **2005 study on business ethics:** AMA/HRI Business Ethics Survey 2005.

P. 217   **number one trust breaker:** World Economic Forum, "Voice of the People" Survey, 2002, conducted by Gallup International and Environics International.

P. 218   **"Enron by the Sea":** John Ritter, "San Diego now 'Enron by the Sea,'" *USA Today*, October 25, 2004, p. A3.

P. 218   **Greek words *chronos* and *kairos*:** Stephen R. Covey, Roger Merrill, and Rebecca Merrill, *First Things First: To Live, to Love, to Learn, to Leave a Legacy* (New York: Simon & Schuster, 1994), p. 27.

BEHAVIOR #13: EXTEND TRUST

P. 223   **"I decided that we":** Patricia Sellers, "Procter & Gamble," *Fortune*, February 21, 2005, p. 98.

P. 225   **$2,000 without approval:** Author interview with Horst Schulze, April 26, 2006.

P. 225   **the retailer Nordstrom:** Nordstrom employee handbook.

P. 226   **Vice President Vince Stabile:** Eve Tahmincioglu, "Keeping Spirits Aloft at JetBlue," Workforce Management Online, December 2004.

P. 226   **60 Minutes program:** Leslie Stahle, "Working 24/7," *60 Minutes*, April 2, 2006.

P. 226   **Gordon Forward quote:** Gordon Forward interview with Fred Luthans, "Conversation with Gordon Forward," *Organizational Dynamics*, Vol. 20, No. 1, p. 63–72.

P. 228   **Robert Galvin Jr. quote:** Joseph F. McKenna, "Bob Galvin Predicts Life After Perfection," *Industry Week*, January 21, 1991, pp. 12–15.

THE THIRD WAVE—ORGANIZATIONAL TRUST
THE PRINCIPLE OF ALIGNMENT

P. 236   **Peter Drucker quote:** Peter Drucker, "Managing Oneself," *Harvard Business Review*, March-April 1999.

P. 239   **John O. Whitney quote:** Whitney, *The Trust Factor*, p. 14.

P. 239   **Kouzes and Posner quote:** James M. Kouzes and Barry Z. Posner, *The Leadership Challenge* (San Francisco: Jossey-Bass, 2003), p. 247.

P. 241   **CEO David Neeleman:** James Wynbrandt, *Flying High: How JetBlue Founder and CEO David Neeleman Beats the Competition . . . Even in the World's Most Turbulent Industry* (Hoboken, NJ: John Wiley & Sons, 2004), pp. 207–208. Also, Greg Link interview with Jenny Dirvin, JetBlue corporate comminications, June 27, 2006.

P. 241   **Henk Broeders quote:** Robert Galford and Anne Seibold Drapeau, *The Trusted Leader: Bringing Out the Best in Your People and Your Company* (New York: The Free Press, 2002), p. 242.

P. 242   **"placed great faith":** David Packard, *The HP Way: How Bill Hewlett and I Built Our Company* (New York: HarperBusiness, 1995), p. 135; also, Peter Burrows, "Hewlett & Packard: Architects of the Info Age," BusinessWeek Online, March 29, 2004.

P. 242   **front of the card reads:** Nordstrom, employee handbook.

P. 243   **According to David Sirota:** David Sirota, et al., *The Enthusiastic Employee*, p. 121.

P. 248   **John Kotter quote:** *Fast Company*, May 2005.

P. 249   **David Packard quote:** Packard, *The HP Way*, p. 135.

P. 250   **30 to 50 percent:** Gary A. Gack, "Core Set of Effectiveness Metrics for Software and IT," iSixSigma.com.

P. 251   **U.S. at $1.1 trillion:** W. Mark Crain, "The Impact of Regulatory Costs on Small Firms," Office of Advocacy of the U.S. Small Business Administration, September 2005.

P. 251   **4 to 6 percent of revenues:** European Movement in Serbia, "German EU Presidency to Fight Red Tape, says Merkel," EMinS.org, January 26, 2006.

P. 251   **$399 billion:** Medical News Today, "USA wastes more on health care bureaucracy than it would cost to provide health care to all of the uninsured," medicalnewstoday.com, May 28, 2004.

P. 251   **the "enemy within":** Lawrence B. Macregor Serven, *The End of Office Politics as Usual: A Complete Strategy for Creating a More Productive and Profitable Organization* (New York: AMACOM, 2002), pp. 1–10, 36–44.

P. 252   **$250 to $300 billion:** Gallup Management Journal, "Be Nice: It's Good for Business," gmj.gallup.com, August 12, 2004.

P. 252   **28 percent of U.S.:** Gallup Management Journal, "Gallup Study Finds That Many Employees Doubt the Ethics of Corporate Leaders," gmj.gallup.com, October 10, 2002.

P. 252   **96 percent of engaged employees:** Ibid.

P. 252   **as Gallup's research suggests:** Buckingham and Coffman, *First, Break All the Rules*, p. 33.

P. 252   **it costs companies:** Cathy Healy, "A Business Perspective on Workplace Flexibility: When Work Works, an Employer Strategy for the 21st Century," Families and Work Institute.

P. 252   **Kent Murdoch quote:** Gostick and Telford, *The Integrity Advantage*, p. 36.

P. 253   **Colleen Barrett says:** Marchica, *The Accountable Organization*, pp. 166–67.

P. 253   **as much as 500 percent!:** GartnerG2 survey, "GartnerG2 says Retail Financial Services Companies Must Make Customer Retention No. 1 CRM Priority," August 8, 2002.

P. 253   **In a 2004 study:** Association of Certified Fraud Examiners, "2004 Report to the Nation on Occupational Fraud and Abuse."

P. 254   **Watson Wyatt 2002 study:** Watson Wyatt, *WorkUSA study*, 2002.

P. 255   **2005 study:** Great Place to Work Institute and Russell Investment Group study of *Fortune*'s "100 Best Companies to Work For," March 15, 2005.

P. 255 **"Employees treasure the freedom:** Geoff Colvin, "The 100 Best Companies to Work For 2006," *Fortune,* January 11, 2006.

P. 255 **CEO John Brennan:** Fred Reichheld, *Loyalty Rules: How Today's Leaders Build Lasting Relationships* (Boston: Harvard Business School Press, 2001), p. 29.

P. 255 **most innovative company:** Jena McGregor, "The World's Most Innovative Companies," *BusinessWeek,* April 24, 2006, pp. 63–76.

P. 256 **John Marchica quote:** Marchica, *The Accountable Organization,* p. 155.

P. 256 **Dr. Michael Hammer:** Robert Malone, "Collaboration as Opportunity," Forbes.com, January 31, 2006.

P. 256 **"We found that contracts":** LogicaCMG/Warwick Business School study.

P. 257 *Strategy+Business* **magazine readers:** Art Kleiner, "Our 10 Most Enduring Ideas," *strategy+business,* December 12, 2005.

P. 257 **In a 2006 study:** FranklinCovey/Coca-Cola Retail Research Council study, 2006.

P. 257 **High trust companies elicit:** Reichheld, *Loyalty Rules;* and Frederick F. Reichheld, *The Loyalty Effect: The Hidden Force Behind Growth, Profits, and Lasting Value* (Boston: Harvard Business School Press, 1996).

P. 257 **Dr. Larry Ponemon:** Privacy Trust Survey for Online Banking, Watchfire Inc. and the Ponemon Institute, 2005.

P. 257 **Jim Burke quote:** James Burke, *Harvard Business School Working Knowledge,* October 27, 2003.

THE FOURTH WAVE—MARKET TRUST
THE PRINCIPLE OF REPUTATION

P. 263 **"building trust worldwide":** Al Golin, *Trust or Consequences: Build Trust Today or Lose Your Market Tomorrow* (New York: AMACOM, 2004), p. vii.

P. 263 **Robert Eckert quote:** Eckert commencement speech to UCLA, 2004.

P. 263 **Charles Giordano quote:** Larry Ponemon, "Opinion: When done right, targeted marketing can help build trust," *Computerworld,* February 3, 2005.

P. 265 **"I respect him":** Del Jones, "Buffett maintains respect of fellow CEOs," *USA Today,* March 30, 2005, p. B2.

P. 265 **Most Admired Companies:** Anne Fisher, "Most Admired Companies," *Fortune,* March 6, 2006, pp. 65–124, see Fortune.com website for global companies.

P. 266 **Golin/Harris Poll:** Golin/Harris study, "Trust in American Business," 2003.

P. 266 **Edelman Trust Barometer:** Edelman, Annual Edelman Trust Barometer, 2006, www.edelman.com.

P. 266 **Hank Paulson quote:** Gostick and Telford, *The Integrity Advantage,* p. 54.

P. 267 **U.S. brands were discounted:** Edelman, Annual Edelman Trust Barometer, 2006.

P. 268 **Reputation Quotient (RQ) 2005:** Alsop, "Ranking Corporate Reputations" *Wall Street Journal,* December 6, 2005.

P. 268 **135 million people:** Kevin Maney, "10 years ago, eBay changed the world, sort of by accident," *USA Today,* March 22, 2005.

P. 268 **Ellen Ryan Mardiks quote:** Golin/Harris press release, AME Info, April 27, 2003.

P. 269 **"Would you recommend":** adapted from Frederick Reichheld, *The Ultimate Question: Driving Good Profits and True Growth* (Boston: Harvard Business School Press, 2006), p. 28.

P. 270 **"I believe we should":** William Weldon, address to PhRMA, *Pharma Marketing News,* April 2005.

P. 270 **"system is utterly transparent":** Robert D. Hof, "The eBay Economy," BusinessWeek Online, August 25, 2003.

P. 271   **Superquinn's CEO, Feargal Quinn:** Polly LaBarre, "Leader—Feargal Quinn," *Fast Company*, November 2001, p. 88.

P. 271   **Roberto Goizueta quote:** Robert Goizueta, Network News, a Publication of the Coca-Cola Company, April 1997.

THE FIFTH WAVE—SOCIETAL TRUST
THE PRINCIPLE OF CONTRIBUTION

P. 272   **late April of 1992:** Golin, *Trust or Consequences*, pp. 15–16; also, Richard Martin, "Thugs maul LA restaurants," *Nation's Restaurant News*, May 11, 1992.

P. 274   **Thomas Friedman quote:** Friedman, *The World Is Flat*, p. 394.

P. 275   **"Persons of the Year":** Nancy Gibbs, "The Good Samaritans," *Time*, December 26, 2005.

P. 275   **Bill Gates announced:** Larry Dignan and Mary Jo Foley, "Gates to Step Aside, Focus on Philanthropy," eWeek.com, June 15, 2006.

P. 275   **Warren Buffett announced:** Elliot Blair Smith, "Buffett pledges $37.1B to charity," *USA Today*, June 26, 2006, p. 1A.

P. 275   **Oprah Winfrey created:** Oprahsangelnetwork.org.

P. 276   **in excess of $200 million:** Newmansown.com.

P. 276   **Best Corporate Citizens:** David Raths, "100 Best Corporate Citizens for 2006," *Business Ethics Magazine*, Spring 2006.

P. 276   **"Social Capitalist" awards:** Cheryl Dahle, "Filling the Void," *Fast Company*, January 2006.

P. 277   **Deborah Dunn quote:** Christine Canabou, "Fast Talk: Hail, global citizens!," *Fast Company*, January 2004.

P. 277   **Grameen Bank in Bangladesh:** "UN Declares 2005 the International Year of Microcredit," Globalization101.org, August 22, 2005.

P. 277   **can trust complete strangers:** "eBay's Founder Starts Giving," *Fortune*, November 28, 2005, p. 49.

P. 278   **Alan Greenspan quote:** Testimony of Alan Greenspan before the Committee on Banking, Housing, and Urban Affairs, U.S. Senate, July 16, 2002.

P. 278   **Paul Dolan, CEO:** Paul Dolan, *True to Our Roots: Fomenting a Business Revolution* (Princetown, NJ: Bloomberg Press, 2003), p. 62; also, John Elkington, *Cannibals with Forks: The Triple Bottom Line of the 21st Century Business* (Stony Creek, CT: New Society Publishers, 1988).

P. 279   **"The evolution of capitalism":** James Surowiecki, "A Virtuous Cycle," *Forbes*, December 23, 2002.

P. 279   **Patricia Aburdene:** Patricia Aburdene, *Megatrends 2010: The Rise of Conscious Capitalism* (Charlottesville, VA: Hampton Roads Publishing Company, 2005), p. 36.

P. 279   **six of the seven:** Ibid.

P. 279   **Tachi Kiuchi quote:** Canabou, *Fast Company*, January 2004.

P. 280   **branded as socially irresponsible:** Mercer Investment Consulting Survey, "Survey: Majority of Investment Managers Link Corporate Responsibility to Asset Performance," GreenBiz.com, March 17, 2006.

P. 280   **"Only a small proportion":** Carol Hymowitz, "Asked to Be Charitable, More CEOs Seek to Aid Their Business as Well," *Wall Street Journal*, February 22, 2005, p. B1.

P. 280   **Shelley Lazarus quote:** Ibid.

P. 282   **Jorma Ollila quote:** Nokia, "Corporate Responsibility Report," 2004, p. 4.

EXTENDING "SMART TRUST"

P. 288   **Stephen Carter has observed:** Stephen L. Carter, *Civility: Manners, Morals, and the Etiquette of Democracy* (New York: HarperCollins Publishers, 1998), p. 62.

P. 298   **Doug Conant quote:** Doug Conant, interview with author, April 21, 2006.

RESTORING TRUST WHEN IT HAS BEEN LOST

P. 300   **"The truth is":** Stever Robbins, "Truth and Trust: They Go Together," *Harvard Business School Working Knowledge*, April 25, 2005.

P. 304   **Watson Wyatt study:** Watson Wyatt, WorkUSA 2002 and Work USA 2004/2005.

P. 304   **drawing nearly 25 percent:** David Heenan, *Flight Capital: The Alarming Exodus of America's Best and Brightest* (Palo Alto, CA: Davies-Black Publishing, 2005), pp. 25–56.

P. 305   **"Good friends of ours":** Kristen Anderson and Ron Zemke, *Tales of Knock Your Socks Off Service: Inspiring Stories of Outstanding Customer Service* (New York: AMACOM, 1998), pp. 27–28.

P. 306   **Chairman Phil Knight:** Nike Report Review Committee, *Corporate Responsibility Report*, nikebiz.com, 2004, p. 2.

P. 306   **listed as #13:** Raths, *Business Ethics*, Spring 2006.

P. 306   **"We want to build trust":** Nike Report Review Committee, *Corporate Responsibility Report*, nikebiz.com, 2004, p. 9.

P. 313   **Following 27 years:** Nelson Mandela, *Long Walk to Freedom: The Autobiography of Nelson Mandela* (Boston: Back Bay Books, 1995).

A PROPENSITY TO TRUST

P. 316   **Jim Burke quote:** "Management Review," *American Management Association*, October 1, 1996, Vol. 85, No. 10.

P. 316   **"100 Best Companies":** Robert Levering and Milton Moskowitz, *The 100 Best Companies to Work for in America* (Reading, MA: Addison-Wesley, 1983).

P. 318   **"Give this boy a store":** Sam Walton with John Huey, *Made in America: My Story* (New York: Doubleday, 1992) p. 142.

P. 318   **Great Place to Work Institute quote:** Great Place to Work Institute, greatplacetowork.com.

P. 320   **H. A. Guerber relates:** H. A. Guerber, *The Story of the Greeks* (New York: American Book Company, 1896), pp. 240–41.

INDEX